TWO PAYCHECKS

SAGE FOCUS EDITIONS

TWO PAYCHECKS
Life in Dual-Earner Families

edited by
JOAN ALDOUS

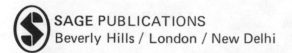 SAGE PUBLICATIONS
Beverly Hills / London / New Delhi

Portions of this book are reproduced from a special issue of the *Journal of Family Issues,* June 1981.

For information address:

SAGE Publications, Inc.
275 South Beverly Drive
Beverly Hills, California 90212

SAGE Publications India Pvt. Ltd.
C-236 Defence Colony
New Delhi 110 024, India

SAGE Publications Ltd
28 Banner Street
London EC1Y 8QE, England

Printed in the United States of America

Library of Congress Cataloging in Publication Data

Main entry under title:

Two paychecks.

(Sage focus editions ; 56)
"Portions of this book are reproduced from a special issue of the Journal of family issues, June 1981"—T.p. verso.
Includes bibliographies.
Contents: Overview: From dual-earner to dual-career families and back again / Joan Aldous. Dual-earner families, their economic and demographic characteristics / Howard Hayghe. Dual-career families, vanguard of the future or residue of the past? / Janet G. Hunt and Larry L. Hunt — [etc.]
1. Married people—Employment—United States—Addresses, essays, lectures. I. Aldous, Joan.
HQ536.T85   1982   306.8'7   82-10538
ISBN 0-8039-1882-8
ISBN 0-8039-1883-6 (pbk.)

FIRST PRINTING

Contents

Acknowledgments

Two Paychecks: Life in Dual-Earner Families is the outgrowth of a special issue I edited on the subject for the *Journal of Family Issues,* which appeared in June 1981. Graham Spanier, the regular editor of the *Journal,* made the issue possible through his policy of encouraging guest editors to prepare issues devoted to particular problems. He was understanding of the usual problems attending such enterprises, including too many pages, missed deadlines, and first too few and then too many high-quality articles. I am grateful.

The reviewers for the special issue provided wise counsel concerning which articles to publish from those available. They included Elizabeth Almquist, Jessie Bernard, Wendy Carlton, Mariam K. Chamberlain, Marianne Ferber, Rodney Ganey, Harriet Gross, Sharon Houseknecht, Joan Huber, David Klein, Gary Lee, David Lewis, Robert Lewis, Helena Lopata, Kristin Moore, Jeylan Mortimer, Gerhard Neubeck, Joseph Pleck, Helen Raschke, John Scanzoni, Joseph Scott, Myra Strober, and Jacqueline Wiseman.

Adele Updike added her competent assistance in straightening out notes and taking care of other matters that loom too large to be termed minutiae. My thanks, also, to the authors whose perceptiveness gave the book its raison d'être.

—Joan Aldous
Notre Dame, Indiana

PART I

Overview

This section provides basic information concerning the past and present of dual-earner families, with some speculation as to the character of a future society in which both men and women are free to follow occupational careers. Aldous begins the book with a brief summary of the recent history of these families, provides a rationale for the use of the term "dual-earner," and indicates how the various articles that follow add to our understanding of the phenomenon. Hayghe supplies a current picture of two-earner families and their systematic variation. He concludes with a brief discussion of the elderly and child-care issues, which loom large in any consideration of two-earner families. These matters, along with the unequal division of labor in such families (a question addressed by Aldous), provide the basis for Hunt and Hunt's concern about dual-career families. They develop a typology of the families that will be found when women's earnings outside the home become widely accepted as well as widely practiced. Unlike earlier researchers, they do not see dual-career families as providing models for other two-earner families. For them, "dual careers" and "families" are contradictory terms, due to work organizations' failure to adjust to such families' needs. Families with earning wives in the past were usually viewed with alarm; Hunt and Hunt's article represents a present-day critique of one such family variant.

1

From Dual-Earner to Dual-Career Families and Back Again

JOAN ALDOUS

The increase in studies devoted to dual-earner or, more commonly, dual-career families suggests that there is something relatively new about the phenomenon of wives joining their husbands as breadwinners. Such an interpretation of the labor force participation data, however, can be misleading. There has been an increase in the proportion such families constitute of all families. As Hayghe points out in his chapter describing two-earner families, by 1980 they constituted over half (52%) of all married couples. Families in which husbands alone brought home a paycheck and wives were presumably full-time homemakers had shrunk in number to less than a third (31%). Twelve years earlier, 45% of married couples, still a high proportion, were of this type, with an equal proportion having the husband-only breadwinner structure. The remaining couples were without earners, or the husband was not an earner. Thus, the big change in recent decades is in the proportion of traditional economic arrangement families, not in the proportion of dual-earner families.

It is true that earlier U.S. Census figures present a picture of wives devoted to domestic concerns. In 1890, the first year for which there was "usable labor force information," just over 4%

of married women were counted in the labor force (Smuts, 1959: 3). Forty years later, census enumerators were still reporting that less than 15% of married women were employed outside the home (Smuts, 1959: 32).

However, too much can be made of these recent developments, so that the very real contribution wives of earlier eras made to the family purse can be overlooked. Wives in low-income, immigrant, black, and farm families particularly earned money. As far as farming is concerned, ninety years ago almost half of all U.S. women lived on farms.[1] Wives' sales of butter and eggs, produce from their gardens, and homemade products made them family earners, and so workers in the restricted economic sense of persons whose activities are exchanged for money.

The end of slavery did not free black wives to narrow their concerns to domesticity. Discrimination and poverty have always forced a sizable proportion of them to work for wages. Studies of Atlanta, Georgia, Nashville, Tennessee, and Cambridge, Massachusetts in 1896, for example, showed the proportion of employed black wives to range from 44% to 65%. Immigrant wives also were wage earners, although in smaller proportion. In Chicago, in the same year, some 15% of wives of Italian immigrants were working outside the home, and in the same period one-fifth of married women, the "great majority" of whom were immigrants, worked in the textile mills of Fall River and Lowell, Massachusetts (Smuts, 1959: 57).

It was easy for census enumerators to overlook wives' breadwinning roles, because until the end of the last century they usually did not leave home to earn their money. The so-called Mom-and-Pop stores in which wives as well as husbands waited on customers and kept the business going were common sights in quiet neighborhoods and on busy thoroughfares. Often, these stores were located in their owners' homes. This proximity eliminated the family/earning place separation that hampers men's and women's participation in both worlds today. Wives could also serve as seamstresses and laundresses for other families using their residences as workplaces, and did.

They, along with other family members, put together cigars, artificial flowers, collars and cuffs, and other piecework products that companies depended upon such workers to produce.

Wives also opened their homes to outsiders and provided board and room for a price. Until World War II, keeping boarders was a common means among native-born and immigrant families for householders to supplement the family income. Modell and Harevan (1973: 469) estimate that, for at least half a century, from 15% to 20% of urban households contained lodgers or boarders at any one time. Among working-class households, the proportion was higher. A 1907 New York City study showed one-half of such households to contain boarders (Smuts, 1959: 14). Thus wives, as the persons largely responsible for maintaining the rooms and supplying the meals for which the lodgers/boarders were paying, were the earners of these funds.

Like all the other women described above, these wives received pay for their work. But to label them as members of dual-worker families, while correct, would not distinguish this group from the total number of families in which women perform productive effort without specific monetary pay. Thus, this book deals with dual-earner families. This term, as Piotrkowski (1980) pointed out, avoids the value trap of limiting the term "work" to effort that is reimbursed. "Dual earner" also has the advantage of being broad enough to include two-job couples as well as two-career couples. The latter group is limited to families in which both spouses have occupations requiring special training, and the occupations entail a regular sequence of related jobs in a hierarchy of prestige through which persons move (Wilensky, 1961: 523).

That these earlier dual-earner families have sometimes been overlooked in the recent flurry of interest in the topic can be seen as another manifestation of the general ahistorical stance of the social scientists, aside from the historians, doing a major share of the research on the subject. Another reason, however, may have to do with the largely working-class character of these earlier families. In recent years, dual-career couples have received much scholarly attention. They were the topic of Rapoports' (1969) ground-breaking study, and the subject is personally congenial to researchers dealing with such arrangements in their own private lives. As Glick (1975: 18) points out, professional women, in the 1960s and 1970s, made up a large proportion of those who have attempted to combine marital and occupational careers. They are therefore especially attuned to investigations of how their peers are managing this relatively novel kind of family type (compare Tavris and Offir, 1977: 227).

This "narcissistic" element that may have focused scholars' attention on dual-career families is suggested by the higher proportion of writers on the subject who are women, or women and men with a common last name (supposedly dual-career couples), than is usual in other areas of investigation. Glass et al. (1980), in their bibliography with abstracts of the dual-career literature, found 79% (142) of 180 entries specifically devoted to the topic to be authored or coauthored by women. This included 17% (31) by couples having the same last name.[2] To provide a comparison to these proportions, a random selection of 178 articles published from 1971 to 1980 in the *Journal of Marriage and the Family*, a journal which covers a broad range of subject matter concerning families, produced the following results. Of the 160 articles where gender of the authors was ascertainable, 45% (72) had a woman as sole author or coauthor, and couples wrote 1% (2) of the articles. When one turns to a bibliographic source for an entire discipline, the higher proportion of women writers in the dual-career literature is even more evident. In the *Sociological Abstracts* for the years 1971-1980, 30 pages selected at random showed 28% (42) of 147 articles authored or coauthored by women, with one article written by a couple.[3]

Another reason dual-career families may have attracted attention is because women in such families generally are attached to the labor force, in terms of full-time commitment, in a fashion similar to men. When professional women do not follow other aspects of the career patterns male professionals have established, this has been a topic of investigation. Yet it is well to remember that married women's attachment to the labor force, unlike their participation, is still exceptional. Although a majority of married couples are dual-earners, the proportion falls by about one-half if one limits dual-earner families to those where wives are employed all year, full-time. Only about one-half of earning wives are full-time earners (Masnick and Bane, 1980: 86). Women, by and large, continue to follow their traditional priorities of fitting their employment schedules to their family responsibilities, rather than the reverse, as men do (Degler, 1980: 436). And in Sweden, where it is national policy for men and women to be equally involved in family and work place, women continue to be more caught up in family matters (Haas, 1981). The earlier dual-career studies permit us to take a broader and harder look at the whole phenomenon of dual-earner families, in part because of their very documentation of the continuing importance of family roles, even among professional women. These findings make it apparent that male patterns of labor force attachment and job or career sequences provide an inappropriate standard for women. If such is the case, one of the primary issues concerning dual-earner families becomes how the work situation outside the home can be accommodated to women's family commitments.

The present collection of studies makes three general contributions to broaden and to specify the literature on two-paycheck families. First, the interface of work and two-earner families is delineated in chapters by Pleck and Staines, by Marsh, by Sharda and Nangle, and by Piotrkowski and Crits-Christoph. Specific working conditions husbands and wives experience on the job and their effects on families are discussed, along with the influence marital relationships have on occupational success. Thus, the interdependence of the economy and families, instead of the more customary but misleading one-way causation model of effects going only from the occupation to the family, appears. Moreover, these articles deal with two-earner families rather than being restricted to professional and managerial couples.

Second, marital and parent-child relations in dual-earner families are explored in depth in the chapters by Simpson and England, by Poloma, Pendleton, and Garland, by Model, and by Carlson. Since it is still uncommon for dual-earner couples to share household responsibilities (Pleck, forthcoming), the reports of Model and Carlson on the participation of husband-fathers in child care and housework, its causes and consequences, represent a welcome specification of many policy recommendations. In addition, building upon previous research, Simpson and England, and Poloma and her associates examine how particular theoretical perspectives can explain what goes on in two-earner families.

Third, a general stocktaking of the two-earner family field appears in the chapters by Rapoport and Rapoport and by Hunt and Hunt. The former authors, on the basis of their survey of the literature, set a series of research priorities for the field in the 1980s and give their rationale. Hunt and Hunt challenge the usual positive view of dual-career families, (see Rapoport and Rapoport, 1978, for exceptions) and develop a typology of families based on their varying commitments to paid employment or family life.

The chapters appearing in Part I place the two-earner phenomenon in context. Hayghe, on the basis of U.S. Census data, discusses the ways such families differ from others. As one would suspect, they tend to be younger, better educated, and more affluent, and it is wives' paychecks that make for this economic well-being. Husbands in such couples as a rule earn less than husbands who are the only breadwinners. Hayghe's data provide some grounding for the concern expressed by gerontologists that employed wives will lack time and energy to devote to the elderly (Brody, 1981). Two-earner families are smaller than traditional families, but not because of fewer children under 18 years of age. Instead, it is elderly relatives and adult children who are more often absent. This finding suggests that adult children not yet ready to form their own households or at loose ends due to failed marriages or straitened finances, along with elderly kin unable physically or financially to maintain a separate residence, may be less able to find homes with busy dual earners.

Hunt and Hunt, in a somber piece devoted to dual-career couples, see the above situation as inevitable, due to the unwillingness of work organizations to accommodate to the needs of families. Occupational careers, they argue, may be open to women and men alike, but this greater personal freedom will be at the expense of families. Given the lack of structural change in economic organizations, careerists cannot achieve in the workplace and also fulfill the values of caring, cooperation, and self-sacrifice traditionally embodied in the family institution. The polarization of traditional families with children and the increasingly child-free dual-career couples will prevent the two groups working together for needed legislation to provide support substitutes. Consequently, Hunt and Hunt predict that the helpless, whether the young, the old, the unemployed, or the handicapped, will suffer from lack of attention. In the course of their argument, they create a three-fold typology of couples. It includes *traditionalists*, who are committed to the homemaker/breadwinner division; *prioritizers*, who have discarded conventional gender-role prescriptions; and *integrators*, couples who play marital and parent roles, as well as job roles, and who work together in some occupational pursuit.

The argument is controversial but worthy of attention. The authors appear somewhat optimistic in their assumption that women have equal access to occupational careers or to their rewards (Lloyd and Niemi, 1979), and integrator couples may fall prey to malaise due to direct competition. (See Oppenheimer's 1977 discussion of the assumptions underlying Talcott Parsons's argument concerning this competition.) Moreover, the previous historical summary indicates that the breadwinner/homemaker division of labor has been "traditional" only for a limited period of time, and not for all families, even in that period.

Recent U.S. Census data, however, do support Hunt and Hunt's posited higher proportions of childlessness and smaller families among the career-oriented. Considerably higher proportions of women in professional, managerial, and administrative occupations are planning to remain without children than are women in other occupational groups. To take just one example, 19% of the women in the former group, as compared with 13.6% of sales and clerical workers, expect to have no children (U.S. Bureau of the Census, 1982). College-educated women, who presumably would more often be in dual-career marriages, also have different fertility timing schedules. They postpone children until after their careers are well launched and have the highest fertility rates for women 30 years of age and over. Among such women, high school graduates have 27 childbirths per 1000 women; women with four years of college, 61 per 1000; and women with five or more years of college, 46 per 1000. It is doubtful, however, that this later-years fertility upsurge will raise the childbirth levels of the college-educated to that of high school graduates (O'Connell and Rogers, forthcoming).

Despite the support these data provide for the linkage between two-career couples and few or no children, they cannot provide us with information for the next step in the argument, namely, that the variety of family lifestyles entails less commitment to family values and the welfare of the weak. A contrary prediction would be that having fewer children and having those by choice will enhance their preciousness to parents and so parental concern for their welfare. Fears of a falling birthrate, particularly among the more highly educated, could even encourage governmental action in the way of child welfare legislation.[4]

Part II, on the interdependence of occupational characteristics and family life, begins with Pleck and Staines's painstaking analysis of how job schedules can affect conflict between work and families. They examine as possible conflict sources the number of hours employed, the days employed, and whether the worker is on a standard work shift. Their results point up, again, the critical importance of child-present stages for women in understanding dual-earner family relations, an issue Hunt and Hunt and Poloma, Pendleton, and Garland also discuss. Pleck and Staines found that conflict for earning wives increased in a "crossover" effect when their husbands were employed on weekends. Such a work schedule reduces the amount of time husbands can devote to child care and housework. In contrast, women's weekend employment has little effect on the amount of time they give to such activities, nor does it increase their husbands'. Home and child care continue to remain female responsibilities, even when wives join husbands in earning.

Marsh, too, investigates the association between husbands' and wife's working hours outside the home. The more hours one spouse works, he reports, controlling for possible con-founding variables, the more hours the other works. Only among salaried, white husbands, black wives on salaries, and white wives who were union members did their spouses' hours of employment seem to substitute for their own. Lesser need for income in the salaried men's families and the supplementary nature of the wives' earnings to family incomes among the women may account for the exceptions.

Piotrkowski and Crits-Christoph examine how other aspects of jobs, such as their intrinsic gratifications, security, and resulting moods, are associated with marital satisfaction, family relations, and home mood in women. Among women in both low-status and high-status occupations, there appears to be more interpenetration of job characteristics and family relationships than marital satisfaction. The authors speculate that there is spillover between husbands' jobs and marital satisfaction, while wives' jobs are associated with family relations, particularly those of wives with children, a result consistent with the finding of Pleck and Staines discussed above. Such an interpretation fits with the primacy of wives' child-care roles and their greater dependency on spouses'

earnings and marriage itself as a status source. Husbands'
reactions to their wives' employment would constitute the
intervening variable in influencing wives' marital satisfaction.

A longitudinal study of how marriage differentially affects
occupational attainment in dual-earner couples constitutes
Sharda and Nangle's investigation of the relation between
families and the wage-work setting. The different perspective
of family effects on job factors is strengthened by the authors'
abilities to establish some temporal order in the relationship.
They find, not surprisingly, that the male mobility model does
not predict wives' job achievements. Postmarital education
gains do not have the occupational payoffs for wives that they
do for husbands. The primacy of husbands' jobs and wives'
family roles appear influential in the finding. But if husbands'
attainments put a damper on wives' attainments, the data also
show a negative relation between wives' occupational status at
marriage and their husbands' subsequent occupational attainments. The authors use their findings to argue the necessity for
examining not just the interdependence of occupational and
family roles, but also the interdependence of the spouses' role
performances in these areas.

The studies included in Part III deal in one way or another
with the issue of the domestic interaction of family members
when both spouses are earners, since families, rather than work
organizations, have done the major portion of the adjustment
to the situation. Simpson and England look at the sensitive
issue of how marital solidarity fares when both spouses are
employed. They theorize that the symmetry of spouses' family
and breadwinner roles in such families should be associated
with greater marital solidarity. This role homophily theory is
consistent with Piotrkowski and Crits-Christoph's argument
that job satisfaction can have a positive effect on family
relationships. The Simpson and England theory does seem to
account for their data better than the bargaining or sex-role
differentiation theories, theories also found wanting with
respect to marital satisfaction by other scholars (Jorgensen,
1979; Aldous et al., 1979).

Poloma, Pendleton, and Garland, in their rare longitudinal study of dual-career couples, specify the Simpson and England theory by indicating how family life-cycle stages, when children are present, present strains on women committed to family and professional roles. Again, women's central commitment to family roles is highlighted. Model's research further indicates this by showing that wives continue to perform the major share of the household tasks even when sharing earner roles with their husbands. Family life-cycle stage does make some difference as Poloma, Pendleton, and Garland found, with wives more active when children are present. Only in the few cases when wives' earnings approach those of their husbands do the latter tend to help more.

The previous three chapters focus on marital relations, but Carlson contributes to our scanty knowledge of parent-child relations when fathers are active in household tasks. As she predicts, preschoolers are less stereotyped in their views of fathers' roles when this is the family situation. Moreover, contrary to stereotypes prevalent among the general public, she finds that paternal power in household decision making is not related to son's masculinity. An even more unexpected result is the absence of statistical differences in masculinity scores as measured by the IT scale between those rare boys whose fathers shared caregiving tasks with their mothers and boys in homes with the traditional division of household labor. This result is the more surprising, since correlation analysis shows a negative relation between paternal household participation scores and sons' IT scale scores. These findings beg for further painstaking research, such as Carlson's, using larger, more representative samples, as she notes, and in which current changes in gender-role conceptualizations of masculinity and femininity would be incorporated.

The last section of the book complements the first. Where the first section presented an overview of dual-earner families as they were and are with less emphasis on future trends, the last chapter by Rapoport and Rapoport presents a set of priorities for future research. There, the authors go beyond the dual-career tradition they did so much to establish and deal with the broader dual-earner topic in the context of work and the family. The broad context in which they place dual-earner families is reflected in the multilevel organizational perspective of their priorities. Some, like greater gender equality, relate to governmental and corporate policies at the highest level. Creating support systems for dual-earner families is a priority concerning the transactions between families and workplaces. Finally, the priority of studying dual-earner couples over the family life cycle has much to do with what goes on in family units.

The studies included in this volume deal with the Rapoport and Rapoport priorities, as they note, and also meet some of the criticisms leveled at the dual-career literature (Poloma, 1980). Studies like those by Pleck and Staines, Marsh, Model, and Simpson and England are based on findings from larger, more representative samples than has generally been the case in earlier work. Fathers, mothers, and their preschool children were all studied in Carlson's research, and there are two longitudinal studies, one by Poloma, Pendleton, and Garland, and another by Sharda and Nangle. Finally, there is some attempt at theorizing, as in the chapters by Simpson and England and Hunt and Hunt.

The studies also pique our curiosity and make us want to know more. The disproportionate share of household tasks wives perform is an example. Although represented in the present collection and widely reported in the literature, the topic needs to be conceptualized in the broader prespective that recognition of women's commitment to family roles allows. In an excellent integration of the literature, Pleck (1981) shows that according to existing surveys, a majority of wives, regardless of earning status, prefer to perform household tasks—an area which can provide their family power base. However, more is involved than considerations of couple power politics.

A factor that may help to account for the general lack of change in domestic arrangements when women are employed outside the home is the view of mothers held by feminists and traditionalists alike—that mothers are all-powerful with respect to their children's futures (Chodorow and Contratta, 1981). Women, particularly those whose earning is through choice, can bear a considerable amount of guilt about being away from their children. If so, women would be loath to part with child-care responsibilities. Because wives bring in less money, they may also agree with their husbands that they should compensate by maintaining the usual wife-centered division of labor. Yet wives' working is related to the efficacy of their spouses' breadwinning ability. Family income has a negative effect on women's working outside the home just as their wage rates have a positive effect. In the period between 1968 and 1978, however, women's labor market participation went up despite a slowdown in the increase in their real earnings. Why? Because there was an even greater slowdown in husbands' total incomes coupled with higher rates of marital instability (O'Neill, 1980). Thus, women's wage employment is associated with husbands' inability to earn sufficient income. This inability is not reflected in husbands' taking on household tasks, even though their wives' inability to escape such tasks may be related to the gender-associated lower incomes they earn.

But demographic shifts can assist young employed women to negotiate the household division of labor before marriage or in the prechild period of the family life cycle. The so-called marriage squeeze is reversing itself (see Glick, 1977, for the marriage squeeze argument). Males born in the latter part of the boom and now of marrying age, if they follow the traditional pattern of marrying younger women, are competing for the smaller female birth cohorts born in the postboom period. The shortage of potential wives, therefore, could increase women's power with respect to domestic tasks if they choose to bargain, and younger cohorts of wives more accustomed to working outside the home may be prepared to insist on more help.

If, however, most women, like women in earlier historical epochs, continue to find their greatest satisfaction in domestic roles, they will not press for great changes in household arrangements even at the expense of greater equality in the economy (Degler, 1980). Rossi (1980: 30-31) contends that the expectation of outside employment with attendant preparations for it may lessen for younger wives the strain currently appearing among middle-aged women. Thus, our task as researchers is to continue to examine dual-earner families' household division of labor, but in the light of women's and men's family role commitments, as well as their expected labor force attachment patterns and earnings. The power, preference, and precedent factors affecting the household division of labor in dual-earner families need to be taken into account, for if Rossi is right, the lesser female attachment to the labor force may be spreading to males. Women's labor force patterns then would become the model for men in an intriguing reversal of form.

I have taken some space to discuss the troublesome issue of the household division of labor in dual-earner families to demonstrate that what we have learned about them permits a better definition of basic issues. Since dual-earner families can no longer be ignored, neither can the factors associated with their functioning. High divorce rates and high labor force participation rates mean that many women and men will be in transit with respect to entering and leaving both families and workplaces. The dualness of couples and their earning behaviors are set in bold relief. The chapters that follow address our concern for greater knowledge of such families, while they indicate how much more we need to discover.

NOTES

1. In the earlier years of the Republic, an overwhelming majority of families were rural. Wives as well as husbands were involved in farm work. Smelser (1959) provides additional evidence of the role of wives in breadwinning. See his analysis of how industrialization in the nineteenth century led to the decline of whole families working as earning units in the cotton industry of Lancashire, England.

2. The proportion of the 168 articles that have a dual-earner in addition to a dual-career focus and authored or coauthored by women in the Glass et al. (1980)

bibliography is smaller. It is 68% (114), with 4% (7) having authors with the same last name. This smaller proportion, given the limitations of the present rough surveys, would be expected if social scientist women are particularly interested in dual-career families.

3. My thanks go to Linda Luhn, who carried out the surveys upon which these figures are based.

4. Aldous and Dumon (1980: 272-273) supply the example of Sweden, a low-birthrate country, which is spending a disproportionate amount of money on children.

REFERENCES

Aldous, J. and W. Dumon
    1980   "European and United States perspectives on family policy: a summing up."
            pp. 253-275 in J. Aldous and W. Dumon (eds.) The Politics and Programs
            of Family Policy. Notre Dame, IN: Univ. of Notre Dame Press.
Aldous, J., M. W. Osmond, and M. W. Hicks
    1979   "Men's work and men's families," pp. 227-256 in W. R. Burr et al. (eds.)
            Contemporary Theories about the Family, Volume I. New York: Macmillan.
Brody, E. M.
    1981   "'Women in the middle' and family help to older people." The Gerontolo-
            gist 21, 5: 471-480.
Chodorow, N. and S. Contratta
    1981   "The fantasy of the perfect mother," in B. Thorne (ed.) Rethinking the Fam-
            ily: Some Feminist Views. New York: Longman.
Degler, C. N.
    1980   At Odds: Women and the Family in America from the Revolution to the
            Present. New York: Oxford Univ. Press.
Glass, C. R., D. B. Arnkoff, M. Coogan, C. D. Gaddy, M. McCabe, and S. Meeks
    1980   "Bibliography on dual-career couples." Unpublished manuscript, Catholic
            University of America.
Glick, P. C.
    1977   "Updating the life cycle of the family." J. of Marriage and the Family 39,
            1: 5-14.
    1975   "A demographer looks at American families." J. of Marriage and the Fam-
            ily 37, 1: 15-28.
Hass, L.
    1981   "Domestic role-sharing in Sweden." J. of Marriage and the Family 43, 4:
            957-968.
Jorgensen, S. R.
    1979   "Socioeconomic rewards and perceived marital quality: a reexamination."
            J. of Marriage and the Family 41, 4: 825-835.
Lloyd, C. B. and B. T. Niemi
    1979   The Economics of Sex Differentials. New York: Columbia Univ. Press.
Masnick, G. and M. J. Bane
    1980   The Nation's Families: 1960-1990. Cambridge, MA: Joint Center for Urban
            Studies of M.I.T. and Harvard University.

Modell, J. and T. K. Hareven
   1973   "Urbanization and the malleable household: an examination of boarding and lodging in American families." J. of Marriage and the Family 35, 3: 466-479.
O'Connell, M. and C. C. Rogers
   forthcoming   "Differential fertility in the United States: 1976-1980." Family Planning Perspectives.
O'Neill, J. A.
   1980   A Time Series Analysis of Women's Labor Force Participation. Washington, DC: The Urban Institute.
Oppenheimer, V.
   1977   "The sociology of women's economic role in the family." Amer. Soc. Rev. 42, 3: 387-406.
Piotrkowsky, C. S.
   1980   Personal communication.
Pleck, J. H.
   forthcoming   "Husbands' paid work and family roles: current research issues," in H. Z. Lopata (ed.) Research on the Interweave of Social Roles: Women and Men, Volume 3. Greenwich, CT: Jai.
Poloma, M. M.
   1980   "Book review." J. of Marriage and the Family 42, 2: 212-214.
Rapoport, R. and R. N. Rapoport
   1978   "Dual-career families: progress and prospects." Marriage and Family Rev. 1, 5: 1-12.
   1969   "The dual-career family: a variant pattern and social change." Human Relations 22, 1: 3-30.
Rossi, A.
   1980   "Life-span theories and women's lives." Signs 6 (Autumn): 4-32.
Smelser, N. J.
   1959   Social Change in the Industrial Revolution. Chicago: Univ. of Chicago Press.
Smuts, R. W.
   1959   Women and Work in America. New York: Columbia Univ. Press.
Tavris, C. and C. Offir
   1977   The Longest War: Sex Differences in Perspectives. New York: Harcourt Brace Jovanovich.
U.S. Bureau of the Census
   1982   "Fertility of American women: June, 1981 (advance report)." Current Population Reports, Population Characteristics Series P-20, No. 369, March 1982.
Wilensky, H. L.
   1961   "Orderly careers and social participation: the impact of work history on social integration in the middle mass." Amer. Soc. Rev. 26, 4: 521-539.

2

Dual-Earner Families

Their Economic and
Demographic Characteristics

HOWARD HAYGHE

Over the past decade, the dual-earner family—the family in which both the husband and wife work—has come to occupy the prominent position once held by the traditional family, in which the husband was the breadwinner and the wife the homemaker. There have been other changes relating to family structure, such as the increase in single-parent families. However, none of these changes has been, or is likely to be in the near future, as significant as the growing prominence of dual-earner families.

This chapter looks at some of the economic and demographic characteristics of dual-earner families and is intended to provide a broad base of information to help researchers, policymakers, and other interested persons gain a better understanding of this increasingly prevalent family type.[1] As used here, the term "dual-earner family" refers to married couples when *both* husband and wife were earners at some time during a calendar year. A "traditional-earner family" is one in which the husband but not the wife was an earner. In both kinds, other members may also be earners and there may or may not be children under age 18.

Any count of dual-earner or traditional families based on the foregoing definition includes some families in which the husband or wife may work only a small part of the year. It should be emphasized, however, that this is not the case in most dual-earner families. For example, in 1978, the majority of spouses in dual-earner families worked at least forty weeks, as shown below:

	Husbands in Dual-Earner Families	Wives in Dual-Earner Families	Husbands in Traditional Families
Total who worked	100%	100%	100%
Worked 40 weeks or more	90	67	88
Full-time	88	51	84
Part-time	2	16	4
Worked fewer than 40 weeks	10	33	12
Full-time	8	17	9
Part-time	2	16	3

TRENDS

The industrial revolution of the nineteenth century created certain paid jobs that women—and sometimes children—filled. But decennial census figures show that in the closing years of the nineteenth century and the early years of the twentieth century, the overwhelming majority of wives did not work for pay (Hill, 1928: 76):[2]

Year	Percentage of Wives Gainfully Employed
1890 (est.)	4.6
1900	5.6
1910	10.7
1920	9.0

The social dictum, "the wife's place is in the home," continued to be observed for many subsequent years. As a result, relatively little attention was paid to dual-earner families until the late 1960s, when it became widely known that wives' labor force participation rates were increasing dramatically.

In 1968, the number and proportion of dual-earner families about equaled those of traditional-earner families. Out of a total of 43.8 million married couples in 1968, 19.7 million (45%) were dual-earner and 19.8 million (also 45%) were traditional-carner families. (In the remaining married-couple families, there were either no earners at all or the earners did not include the husband.)

Over the next twelve years, the number of dual-earner families increased by about 5.8 million (or nearly 30%), while the number of traditional-earner families declined by about 4.8 million. Thus, by 1980, dual-earner families accounted for 52% of all married couples, while just 31% were of the traditional-earner type.

The growth in the number of dual-earner families between 1968 and 1980 resulted directly from the increase in wives' labor force participation. During this period, the number of married women in the labor force rose by more than 600,000 a year, on average, as many factors affected the supply and demand for women workers. On the supply side, the postwar baby-boom generation entered the labor force in huge numbers. Moreover, young women were delaying marriage and postponing their first child. For this reason they were far more likely than wives in previous decades to have established strong labor force ties that they could maintain following marriage and childbirth. Also, American society has become more accepting of the working wife and mother and of the notion that responsible long-term care can be provided on a daily basis by someone other than the mother or father. Finally, increasing numbers of women were continuing their education beyond high school, thus acquiring skills useful to a broader range of jobs.

On the demand side, the United States' economy was continuing its trend toward service-producing industries (such

TABLE 1

Occupations of Husbands and Wives, March of Selected
Years, 1960-1981 (in percentages)

Occupations	Husbands				Wives			
	1960	1968	1978	1981	1960	1968	1978	1981
Total	100.0	100.0	100.0	100.0	100.0	100.0	100.0	100.0
Professional-technical	11.6	14.4	16.1	17.1	13.0	15.1	17.0	18.3
Managerial	15.8	16.1	17.2	17.9	5.0	4.9	6.9	7.8
Sales	5.8	5.6	6.3	6.1	8.4	7.1	7.0	6.5
Clerical	6.4	6.3	5.5	5.5	28.3	32.2	34.9	35.3
Craft	20.9	21.8	22.8	22.8	1.0	1.2	1.8	1.9
Operative	19.7	19.8	17.2	16.0	18.6	17.5	12.5	11.0
Nonfarm labor	5.9	5.0	4.9	4.3	.3	.4	.9	1.0
Private household service	*	*	*	*	6.2	4.2	1.9	1.9
Other service	5.5	5.5	6.2	6.6	15.9	15.1	15.7	15.1
Farm	8.2	5.5	3.8	3.7	3.3	2.2	1.3	1.2

*Less than 0.05 percent.
NOTE: Due to rounding, sums of individual items may not equal totals.

as banking, real estate, government, and health care) in which most of the kinds of jobs where women predominate are to be found. Moreover, technological innovations in computer science, electronics, and chemistry were being introduced into households and industries, simplifying many chores, creating new kinds of jobs, and altering the nature of many old jobs.

These developments, especially the shift toward service-producing industries, affected not only the number of wives in the labor force, but also the kinds of jobs that were available to them and their husbands as they entered the job market. For example, the proportion of employed wives working in clerical as well as professional-technical and managerial jobs rose, while the proportion who were operatives fell between 1968 and 1981 (Table 1). Among husbands, where the occupational distribution was more diverse, similar increases in the percentage who were professional-technical and managerial workers also took place. Over the longer term (1960 to 1981), these changes are even more striking.

Despite the changing occupational distribution of husbands and wives, the proportion of husbands in professional-technical or managerial jobs whose wives worked in the same general occupational group was nearly the same in 1981 as in 1968. Instead, the most significant changes in the occupations of spouses in dual-earner families have come about because of increases in the proportion of wives in clerical occupations. For instance, in 1968, 35% of the wives of craft workers were in clerical occupations, as were 21% of the wives of laborers and 27% of operatives' wives. By 1981, these proportions were 40%, 33%, and 33%, respectively.

DEMOGRAPHIC CHARACTERISTICS

The demographic characteristics of dual-earner families are considerably different from those of traditional families. Many of these differences, including the ages of the spouses and their children, the formal education of husband and wife, and their race or Hispanic origin, are highlighted in the following discussion. (For some of these subjects, 1978 data are the latest available.)

AGE

Dual-earner families are considerably younger than traditional-earner families. In 1978, for example, husbands and wives in dual-earner families were about 7 years younger (on average) than were their counterparts in traditional-earner families. Median ages for dual-earner husbands and wives were 39 and 36 years, respectively, compared with 46 and 43 years for spouses in traditional families. That there is such a wide age gap between the two types of families is not very surprising, because the preponderance of the labor force gains for wives between 1968 and 1978 occurred among those under 35. Over the ten-year period, wives 20 to 34 years old accounted for nearly two-thirds of the six million increase in the number of married women in the labor force—a trend that continues.

FAMILY SIZE AND PRESENCE OF CHILDREN

Traditional families tend to be somewhat larger than dual-earner families. About half the traditional-earner families contained at least four persons, compared with 44% of dual-earner families. Evidently, traditional families are somewhat more likely to include adult offspring or elderly relatives than dual-earner families; the proportion of both types of families that contain children under 18 is approximately the same.

EDUCATION

Dual-earner couples generally have more education than their traditional-earner counterparts. As shown below, the percentage of husbands and wives with thirteen years or more of schooling (some college) was greater for dual-earner spouses than for those in traditional families:

	0-11 Years	12 Years Only	13 Years or More
Husbands in:			
Dual-earner families	22	37	41
Traditional families	29	36	35
Wives in:			
Dual-earner families	18	48	33
Traditional families	30	47	24

Nearly six out of ten husbands in dual-earner families with thirteen years or more of formal education had graduated from college, about the same proportion as for their counterparts in traditional families. For wives, five out of ten in dual-earner families had that much schooling, as did four out of ten in traditional-earner families.

RACE AND HISPANIC ORIGIN

The incidence of dual-earner families was higher among blacks than among either whites or Hispanics. In 1980, 55% of black married couples were dual-earner families, compared with about 50% of either whites or Hispanics. However, Hispanic couples were more likely to be of the traditional-earner type (39%) than were whites or blacks (30% and 24%, respectively).

The fact that Hispanic families are more likely to be in the traditional-earner category stems at least in part from their cultural heritage. Hispanic Americans, although they are of several distinct national backgrounds (principally Mexican, Puerto Rican, and Cuban) with different histories and traditions, are linked by a common Spanish colonial heritage. Also, typical of Latin cultures in Europe as well as other parts of the world, women's labor force participation rates are relatively low (Newman, 1968: 3, 5).

Black wives, on the other hand, historically have had higher labor force participation rates than other wives, so that dual-earner families have been substantially more common among blacks. However, it should be noted that the labor force participation rate of white wives has been rising faster than for blacks in recent years.

Because the Hispanic population is, on average, younger than the white or black populations, Hispanic spouses in both dual- and traditional-earner families were younger than their white or black counterparts, and Hispanic families of both types were more likely to have children under 18.

Hispanic spouses in dual-earner families lagged well behind their black and white counterparts in terms of years of school completed. Nearly half the Hispanic husbands and 44% of the wives had not completed high school, compared with 36% and 29%, respectively, for blacks and 21% and 17%, respectively, for white husbands and wives in dual-earner families. Even higher proportions of Hispanic husbands and wives in traditional families had not completed high school (Table 2).

TABLE 2
Selected Characteristics of White, Black, and Hispanic
Dual-Earner and Traditional-Earner Families, 1978

Characteristic	White	Black	Hispanic
	Median Age of Spouses (in years)		
Dual-earner			
Husbands	39.2	38.6	35.9
Wives	36.3	36.0	33.1
Traditional-earner			
Husbands	46.1	45.6	38.4
Wives	42.8	41.4	35.0
	Years of School Completed (in percentages)		
Dual-earner			
Husbands, total	100.0	100.0	100.0
0-11 years	20.5	36.1	47.7
12 years only	37.5	37.2	28.7
13 years or more	42.0	26.7	23.6
Wives, total	100.0	100.0	100.0
0-11 years	16.8	28.7	43.5
12 years only	49.3	40.6	38.8
13 years or more	33.9	30.7	17.7
Traditional-earner			
Husbands, total	100.0	100.0	100.0
0-11 years	27.6	51.5	58.7
12 years only	36.4	32.2	24.9
13 years or more	36.0	16.3	16.4
Wives, total	100.0	100.0	100.0
0-11 years	28.5	48.2	62.5
12 years only	47.1	37.5	27.9
13 years or more	24.4	14.3	9.6
	Presence of Children under Age 18		
Percent with children			
Dual-earner	56.7	67.5	71.9
Traditional-earner	60.1	60.3	76.9

INCOME

As might be expected, dual-earner families have considerably higher annual money incomes than do traditional-earner families. Annual money income includes income from the earnings of all family members as well as from other sources, such as investments and pensions. In 1980, median dual-earner family income was over $27,700, 24% higher than the median for traditional-earner families (Table 3). Looking at the difference another way, close to one-third of all dual-earner couples had incomes in 1980 that placed them in the upper fifth of the family income distribution, while only 5% were in the lowest quintile. In contrast, 13% of families whose earnings patterns were traditional were in the lowest quintile, and less than one-fourth were in the highest.

Although husbands in dual-earner families earn more, on average, than their wives, their earnings lag behind those of husbands in traditional families. In 1978, for example, median annual earnings of husbands in dual-earner families were $14,900, compared with $16,000 for husbands in traditional families. However, this difference was more than offset by wives' earnings, which averaged around $5,700 and accounted for 26% of family income in 1978. When the wife worked year-round and full-time, her earnings and contribution to family income were even greater: $9400 and 37%, respectively, in 1978.

The trends in family income during the 1970s were affected not only by two economic downturns—one in 1970 and another in 1974-1975—but also by relatively high levels of inflation. The recessionary periods had an adverse impact not only on the growth in the number of dual-earner families, but also, especially when combined with inflation, on their income.

During the recessions, no significant growth was recorded in the number of dual-earner families, because of the effects of the downturns on the trends of working husbands and wives. Over the decade as a whole, the proportion of husbands who worked at some time during the year declined—by half a percentage point or so per year, on average—while the proportion of wives who worked increased. However, during the slowdowns, the proportion of working husbands continued to fall, while the proportion of wives who worked during the year remained fairly constant. As a result, the number of families in which both spouses were earners changed very little.

Moreover, during economic downturns, family members may experience unemployment or be forced to work fewer

TABLE 3

Median Family Income by Type of Family and Relationship of Earners in Married-Couple Families, Selected Years, 1968-1980 (in current and constant 1967 dollars)

Characteristic	Year						
	1968	1970	1972	1974	1976	1978	1980
Current Dollars							
Married-couple families, total	$ 9,140	$10,520	$11,900	$13,850	$16,350	$19,410	$23,260
Dual-earner	10,630	12,150	13,880	16,580	19,080	22,730	27,740
Traditional-earner	8,700	10,010	11,490	13,480	15,480	18,990	22,400
Husband only earner	8,060	9,150	10,590	12,360	14,430	17,450	20,470
Husband nonearner	6,040	6,870	7,980	9,630	11,020	13,140	15,490
No earners	3,130	3,610	4,440	5,520	6,570	7,850	10,190
Constant Dollars							
Married-couple families, total	$ 8,770	$ 9,050	$ 9,500	$ 9,380	$ 9,590	$ 9,940	$ 9,420
Dual-earner	10,200	10,450	11,080	11,230	11,190	11,640	11,230
Traditional-earner	8,350	8,610	9,170	9,130	9,080	9,720	9,070
Husband only earner	7,730	7,870	8,450	8,370	8,460	8,940	8,290
Husband nonearner	5,800	5,910	6,370	6,520	6,460	6,730	6,270
No earners	3,000	3,100	3,540	3,740	3,850	4,020	4,120

hours than usual. As a result, family income may not grow as rapidly as in better times. This, when combined with inflation, can have a serious impact on families' purchasing power. For example, during the 1974-1975 recession, prices rose by around 20% (as measured by the Consumer Price Index) and the real income of dual-earner and traditional-earner families declined by 4% and 6%, respectively. As can be seen from Table 3, this experience was repeated in the 1980 downturn.

How do dual-earner families spend their income? Typically, they spend relatively more of their income than traditional families on goods and services related to the work needs of the wife (Strober, 1977). While spending about the same (relative to income) on durable items, such as washing machines and refrigerators, dual-earner families tend to purchase more convenience items and services that reduce the time the wife must devote to such tasks as food preparation, laundry, and child care. Moreover, expenditures on transportation tend to be larger. Partly as a result of the relatively higher expenses related to the nondurable items, and partly because a working wife helps provide an economic cushion, dual-earner families tend to save less than their traditional counterparts.

POVERTY

There were relatively few dual-earner families whose income fell below the government's poverty threshold.[3] In 1980, only about 540,000, or 2.1%, of dual-earner families had incomes at or below the poverty level. Among traditional-earner families, the proportion in poverty was 7.2%, or 1.1 million families. Blacks, who made up only 7% of dual-earner families, accounted for 18% of those in poverty.

Working couples below the poverty threshold were younger and less well educated than those with incomes above the poverty line. For example, in 1978, the median age for the husband in poor dual-earner families was about 35 years and that of wives, 31 years, compared with 40 and 37 years, respectively, for spouses not in poverty. Moreover, husbands and wives in poverty averaged about twelve years of schooling, compared with 12.8 and 12.7 years for dual-earner spouses not in poverty. In addition, those in poverty were more likely to have children than were nonpoverty families.

These characteristics—relative youth, less education, and the presence of children—do not in and of themselves lead to poverty, although they are certainly contributing factors. What is significant, though, is the fact that the spouses in dual-earner families in poverty work less than their counterparts in families with incomes above the poverty level. In 1978, only 62% of the husbands and 22% of the wives in poor dual-earner families worked full-time for forty weeks or more, compared with 88% and 51%, respectively, for the spouses in nonpoor families.

THE FUTURE

This chapter has provided an overview of dual-earner families largely in the context of their labor force behavior and income. However, the ramifications of the dual-earner phenomenon extend far beyond the labor market.

Several examples of the current and future impact of dual-earner families on American society come easily to mind. For instance, child care is certainly a major problem for dual-earner parents. In March 1981, 53% of all children under 18 in married-couple families and 45% of those under 6 had working mothers. At the beginning of the 1970s, the proportions were 38% and 28%, respectively. Currently, the major caretakers of children are public schools and nuclear families, supplemented by a wide variety of other means, formal as well as informal. The use of so many different child-care methods, sometimes in combination, stems from many sources, including limited availability of institutional settings for day care, parents' financial considerations, and parents' desire to control their children's upbringing to the greatest extent possible (Bane et al., 1979). Assuming that the proportion of children in dual-earner families will continue to grow as the number of such families increases, the demand for child care will impose an ever-increasing strain on current resources. However, it remains unclear how this demand will be met: whether the necessary funding and facilities will be provided by the government, whether they will be supplied by the private sector, or some combination of both.

Similar observations may be made with respect to care of the elderly—parent care—which can pose major difficulties for some dual-earner families. As the nation's population ages, the dimensions of this problem may increase.

Many other areas of present concern, such as accommodating work schedules to family needs and equity in taxation and pension benefits, are also likely to become more pressing as the number of dual-earner couples increases. It is of the utmost importance that current research in these areas be continued and augmented if practical steps are to be taken to deal with the problems and concerns of this growing family type.

NOTES

1. Unless otherwise indicated, data in this article are based on information collected by the 1969 through 1981 March supplements to the Current Population Survey (CPS) and relate to the calendar year preceding the March collection date. The CPS is conducted for the Bureau of Labor Statistics by the Bureau of the Census, which also tabulated most of the data. Additional information for this report on dual-earner families in calendar year 1978 was tabulated from the March 1979 CPS microtape by the Data Services Group of the Office of Current Employment Analysis, Bureau of Labor Statistics.

Estimates based on a sample, such as those used in this chapter, may vary considerably from results obtained by a complete count, especially in cases where the estimated numbers are small. Therefore, differences between small numbers or the percentages based on them may not be statistically significant. For more information on the interpretation of such differences, see *Marital and Family Characteristics of Workers, March 1979*, Special Labor Force Report 219 (Bureau of Labor Statistics, 1979).

2. The term "gainfully employed" is not strictly comparable to "employed" as used in labor force concepts since 1940. For a detailed account of the differences between the gainful worker concept and the current labor force concept of employment, see

Alba M. Edwards, *Comparative Occupation Statistics for the United States, 1870 to 1940* (U.S. Department of Commerce, Bureau of the Census, 1943). Also see *Historical Statistics of the United States—Colonial Times to 1957* (U.S. Department of Commerce, Bureau of the Census, 1960), p. 68.

3. See Table 17, p. 27, in "Money Income and Poverty Status of Families and Persons in the United States: 1978" (Advance Report), Current Population Reports, Series P-60, No. 120 (U.S. Department of Commerce, Bureau of the Census) for poverty-level cutoffs by size and type of family.

REFERENCES

Bane, M. J., L. Lein, L. O'Donnell, C. A. Stueve, and B. Wells
    1979   "Child care arrangements of working parents." Monthly Labor Rev. (October): 50-56.
Hill, J. A.
    1928   "Women in gainful occupations, 1870 to 1920." U.S. Bureau of the Census Monograph IX. Washington, DC: Government Printing Office.
Newman, M. J.
    1978   "A profile of Hispanics in the U.S. work force." Monthly Labor Rev. (December): 3-14.
Strober, M. H.
    1977   "Wives' labor force behavior and family consumption patterns." Amer. Econ. Rev. (February): 410-417.

3

Dual-Career Families

Vanguard of the Future or
Residue of the Past?*

JANET G. HUNT
LARRY L. HUNT

Research interest in dual-career families stems not from their numbers—they are still a statistically minor lifestyle variant—but from their presumed embodiment of key features of a family form that will be more common in the future (Bird, 1979; Epstein, 1971; Pepitone-Rockwell, 1980; Rapoport and Rapoport, 1969, 1971, 1976, 1980). Dual-careerists are seen as in the vanguard of societal movement toward fuller employment of women, greater sex equality, and more "symmetrical" (Young and Willmott, 1973) families. The educational attainment and high work involvement of these couples is assumed to be especially generative of effective coping strategies and institutional change. As "lifestyle pioneers" (Bird, 1979; Rapo-

*A portion of this chapter appears in our article entitled, "The Dualities of Careers and Families: New Integrations or New Publications?" Social Problems, Vol. 29, No. 5, June 1982, pp. 499-510, and is reprinted here by permission of the Society for the Study of Social Problems. In that essay we focus on the possible psychic and economic costs of a growing polarization of career- and family-centered lifestyles, and the need for a national family policy to reduce those costs. This chapter explores more generally the dimensions of lifestyle variation that may accompany the institutional separation of careers and families, and the social and political fragmentation this may produce.

port and Rapoport, 1971, 1976), these couples are forging the way not only for a growing number of dual-career families but for the more typical dual-earning families of the future as well, to whom many adaptive aspects of the more elite dual-career lifestyle will filter down.

An alternative perspective is offered in this chapter. We contend that dual-career families have not represented a major departure from conventional sex-role patterns of the past. Moreover, they are not of strategic significance for understanding the lifestyle implications of women's increasing labor force participation and pressures toward sex equity, especially the "new integrations of work and family" (Rapoport and Rapoport, 1976) that may evolve. Rather, dual careers will remain a minor family form among a wider range of lifestyles, which increasingly will tend to be organized around specific life priorities.

SOME COMMONALITIES BETWEEN
DUAL CAREERS AND THE
TWO-PERSON CAREER

Social analysts have highlighted the distinctive features of dual-career families by playing on the contrast between dual careers and "two-person careers" (see, for example, Bird, 1979; Hunt and Hunt, 1977; Pepitone-Rockwell, 1980). The two-person career is a uniquely American phenomenon in which the talents and energies of highly educated women have been channeled into the performance of an auxiliary role relative to their husbands' career success rather than used as a vehicle for women's personal mobility (Papanek, 1973). This arrangement fit a concept of the "companionate" or "egalitarian" marriage that emphasized the wife's emotional support role rather than her household labor, but did not question the breadwinner/homemaker role division between spouses. In the dual-career family, the wife is able to invest in her own career development, implying movement toward a principle of equity based on role "symmetry" between spouses (Young and Willmott, 1973). The assumption is that as women take on careers, men engage in more domestic work, generating a more balanced sharing of breadwinning and homemaking responsibilities between spouses.

In focusing on the differentiation of the dual-career from the two-person-career pattern, some important contextual and structural similarities between the two forms have been ignored. The same circumstances that facilitated the development of the two-person career, we submit, made dual careers a viable form of lifestyle deviation during a particular period. In the 1980s, the historical moment for both of these family types may be passing.

The dual-career families that are described in the published research literature were products of a time that predates the supportive cultural atmosphere that stimulated their study. Most of the data were collected in the 1960s or early 1970s from couples who grew up and embarked on their lifestyles in the aftermath of World War II. This was a period when feminist voices were unusually quiet and familism was the dominant cultural ethos—embodied in what has been referred to as "the feminine mystique" (Friedan, 1963) and "the cult of domesticity" (Filine, 1974). It was a time when women's place in the home was idealized, and employed women, especially employed mothers, were portrayed unsympathetically. The myth of expanding affluence prevailed, minimizing perception of social inequality and many women's need for paid jobs (Skolnick, 1978).

In this context, high-income families could make use of the captive labor of women denied sufficient alternative employment opportunities as cheap domestic help. This facilitated the pattern of the "idle wife," whose relative freedom from housebinding domestic chores permitted an active public life of social and volunteer activities. The idleness of these wives, however, was more apparent than real. Their activity was a form of "status production work" for their families (Papanek, 1979). They displayed their husbands' success, managed the couple's strategic social connections, and ran the household, despite their exemption from much of the physical labor. They performed, that is, the supportive role in the most successful of two-person careers.

Cheap domestic service was also important for dual careers. Major studies report that the use of household help, often live-in help, has been considered essential by the dual-career couples of the past (Holmstrom, 1972; Rapoport and Rapoport, 1971, 1976). With this additional resource, the highly educated women in these families could substitute at least a "career of limited ambition" (White, 1979) for the nonpaid public role of the idlè wife. In both instances, one class of women escaped some of the constraints of sex stratification through utilization of the labor of the class of women most severely limited by it. Moreover, both the idle wife and the dual-career wife extricated themselves in a manner that avoided modification of the male role. Researchers agree that there has been little departure among dual-career couples from the conventional domestic division of labor (Garland, 1972; Holmstrom, 1972; Paloma, 1972; Rapoport and Rapoport, 1971, 1976). The career wife instead has managed to perform two roles (Myrdal and Klein, 1956) through the skillful allo-cation of her own time and energies and effective utilization of the labor of other women.

The survival strategies of career women benefited also from the particularistic treatment accorded career women in a familistic era. Familism legitimated restricted employment and professional opportunities for women—saying that women do not need or want jobs because of their primary identification with the family. But the other side of the coin was that the token women who were sponsored into professional and business roles were expected to have career paths that differed from men's—career paths that were slowly paced, often interrupted, and "neither upward-moving nor 'success-oriented' but [which recognized] their commitment to family responsi-bilities" (White, 1979: 365). It was not a universalistic world of sex-blind policies; it was a world that largely excluded women but had special rules for those allowed to enter. This permitted the lives of dual-career men to be essentially similar to those of other career men, while the lives of dual-career wives were juggling acts that provided a measure of career involvement as long as it did not inconvenience the family.

By today's standards, the lack of symmetry in the marriages of those first-studied dual-career couples seems odd. But the sense of reasonableness and fairness is always relative to available points of reference. Compared to women around them, dual-career women were privileged to have careers at all. And their husbands could compare themselves to other men and feel they were doing their full share by "letting" their wives pursue careers and making the smallest of concessions to the arrangement (Miller, 1972). Domestic tension was probably reduced further by the need to maintain a low profile and project as much normality as possible to minimize "environmental sanctions" (Rapoport and Rapoport, 1971, 1976). That is, while sex-role asymmetries may generate some internal strain, they contributed to the management of tension with the social environment. Additionally, to scrutinize themselves too closely and question seriously the imbalances would be to risk alienating their most important source of support—each other (Johnson and Johnson, 1980).

Dual careerists, then, could survive most comfortably in the early decades following World War II by retaining a high degree of structural similarity to other high-status families. This included having children. It is the presence of children that made it possible to construe male success-striving as "breadwinning" and to justify women's noninvolvement in their own careers in the name of "homemaking"—a role division that is a requisite to the availability of women for two-person careers. Children were also essential for the legitimation of dual careers. Children, more so than anything else, established normality and minimized the salience and visibility of the wife's career involvement. Moreover, the pressure to conform and the couple's own probable inability to articulate clearly an alternative to parenting undoubtedly reduced the experience of conflict over the decision to parent and the competing demands of career and motherhood roles.

In sum, as long as dual careers were deviant, conformity to conventional sex roles was necessary for dual-career couples in most areas of their lives. This ensured asymmetries in these marriages but minimized marital tension over them. It also ensured that these couples would tend to have children but reduce the conflicts of employed mothers. With increasing cultural emphasis on sex equality, the viability of the old dual-career pattern is breaking down. The women who used to be available as household help are looking increasingly to other forms of employment. The old particularistic treatment of career women has given way to greater universalism—and the requirement that women's career development and involvement more closely approximate men's. Moreover, the environmental pressures on dual-career couples are shifting. While Rapoport and Rapoport (1976) emphasize the reduction in strains that has resulted from growing social acceptance of dual careers, this new, more positive social atmosphere in some ways expects more of dual careerists. The burden now on dual-career couples is not to maximize their conventionality but to live up to the ideal of symmetry. Also, the wives, especially, may now find more support for role change outside the marriage than within it (that is, from women's support groups rather than from husbands). All of this means that the potential for marital tension over perceived inequities has increased considerably in recent years, and there is less tolerance for the compromises of the past. The question is, will the changes generate more, and more equitable, dual-career families, or will the dual-career family actually have a diminishing place among the lifestyles of the future?

THE DISINTEGRATION OF
CAREERS AND FAMILIES

The dual-career family literature assumes that the future will be one of fewer two-person careers and more dual-career families (Pepitone-Rockwell, 1980). In response to women's greater labor force participation and men's greater involvement in domestic life, American society will evolve toward what Alice Rossi (1969) has termed the "hybrid model of sex equality." This model envisions a new breed of men and women and new social institutions that synthesize elements of men's and women's roles, values, and perspectives. This means work and political institutions that reflect values beyond rationality and efficiency—that are socially responsible, flexible, and responsive to families' obligations and the circumstances of their members. It means families that support all of their members—that no longer "greedily" consume the services of wives to promote the success and actualization of husbands and children (Coser, 1974).

The first flaw in this reasoning is the assumption that the institutions that foster careerism will become more responsive to the needs of families. Accommodating families would be self-defeating for institutions whose primary goals are power and profit, as long as sufficient numbers of people—of either gender—are willing to adapt to the requirements of careers. Careerism is an elite track to which many are called but few are chosen. Those chosen are marked by a high level of work involvement and commitment to organizational goals and relative exemption from family constraints and responsibilities (Hochschild, 1976; Slater, 1970). As women become more qualified and motivated to enter the career race, the competition will increase, and the pace for survivors will accelerate. The tension between the requirements of career success and the needs of families will not be resolved by a lessening of the demands of the business and professional worlds but by the choices men and women will be forced to make between lifestyles compatible with those demands and styles more consistent with family values.

The second flaw in the hybrid model is the assumption that career-oriented men and women will continue to have families. Sex-role change means not simply different, more symmetrical, families, but also fewer families. The principle of sex equality, says Judith Lorber (1980), calls into question more than a particular division of labor and rewards between the sexes. It challenges the structural mechanisms that have maintained the institution of the family. Heterosexual union and procreation have been ensured in the past by the functional interdependence of men and women. Women were dependent on men, who provided for them economically; women, in return, performed essential services for men and reared the children produced by their union. As women gain independence from marriage through their own employment and men derive fewer automatic and/or indispensable services from wives, we can expect heterosexual unions to be less permanent, sexuality to be less tied to procreation, and women to be less available to rear children. Sex equality, that is to say, implies a diminishing place of the family in society.

The breakdown of institutional captivity in families and the normative changes that are accompanying it will free men and women in the future to pursue careers instead of families. In the new social climate of sex equity, the normalizing function of marrying and mothering has become less essential. Independence is seen as a more positive attribute in women, and childless has become child-free. Moreover, the potential for overextension of women trying to combine careers and families is increasing, as the career race tightens, women are forced to pace their careers more similarly to men's, and household help becomes less available. One does not have to posit total disinterest in families to anticipate that with the old stigmas removed, more highly career-committed women will, either eagerly or reluctantly, avoid stress and risk to their careers by bypassing motherhood. As for men, they too have less need today to justify their career behavior by having families, and the prospect of having to assume more domestic responsibilities and give their wives' careers equal billing may diminish the attractiveness and feasibility of dual-career families from their standpoint as well. For the highly success-oriented of both sexes, that is to say, families will be less necessary, less helpful, and more of a liability than in the past. The reality of this changing attitude toward parenting on the part of career-committed young adults is evidenced in recent studies of childlessness (Burgwyn, 1981; Veevers, 1980).

On the other hand, there remains cause for many Americans to continue to marry and have children, despite women's paid work roles and growing demands for equal sharing of housework and child care. Commitment to family values, notwithstanding a growing tolerance and even idealization of the alternatives, still runs deep in our culture—witness the great upsurge of familism in this country as we enter the 1980s. This reflects not only residual traditionalism but certain realities of modern life as well. For most Americans, neither paid work nor any other links to the public world are sufficient to provide a sense of efficacy, purpose, accomplishment, and security. For many Americans, including many of the highly educated, there is nothing compelling enough to draw them away from family life. This is not to say that these people lack need or interest in employment and even a measure of self-fulfillment through their paid work roles. Rather, it is to say that for these people, all-consuming careers are either unavailable or undesirable, and family remains the primary source of life satisfaction (Bane, 1976; Skolnick, 1978). Where this is the case, women undoubtedly will continue to compromise their careers as they have in the past, and men will be forced more and more to do so as well. There is every indication that men have been slow to respond to pressures to assume more domestic responsibilities (Bird, 1979; Hofferth and Moore, 1979; Vanek, 1980). But women appear to be in the labor force to stay, and it probably is inevitable that in time men's roles will have to adjust to this reality. Men, therefore, will be less free in the future to invest themselves in careers without interference, and they, too, will have to make career sacrifices, if they are to have families.

Thus, while the gender ascription of career and family roles is diminishing, the roles themselves remain resistant to synthesis. Women now can become "sociological men"—persons who develop primarily their public work lives and enjoy the social power and independence that it provides—and men can become "sociological women"—persons who invest themselves primarily in their families and forfeit power and personal destiny control. But we do not appear to be developing roles and institutions that transcend these two types. The likely result is not more dual-career families, in which a second career role is added to the conventional career and family package, but growing institutional separation of careers and families. For some, this will mean new integrations of work and family and greater role symmetry, but the innovators in this development will tend not to be careerists but those who have forsaken careers for forms of work involvement more conducive to sharing family responsibilities.

WORK AND FAMILY IN THE LIFESTYLES OF THE FUTURE

The dual-career family literature exaggerates the importance of this family form in the process of social change and provides an overly coherent view of the new life patterns that eventuate. We can anticipate that work and family will continue to be major lifestyle foci and that the combination of the two will remain a goal of many. But the variations, strains, and deprivations produced will be far greater than the dual-career literature foretells. In this final section, we want to speculate briefly on three dimensions of differentiation and the possible tensions associated with them.

THE CLASH OF TWO CULTURES

The feminism of the 1960s and 1970s has altered irrevocably the consciousness of many Americans. These people can no longer organize any aspect of their lives on the basis of unquestioned assumptions about gender. For them, marriage is no longer inevitable; it is no longer founded on women's economic dependence and a specific division of labor between spouses. Marriage is a new partnership in which men and women negotiate commitments, responsibilities, and concessions to each other's work lives. While the degree of equity and/or symmetry achieved is variable and debatable, the taken-for-granted quality of the old marriage bargain based on stereotyped gender roles is gone, and marriage has become a more flexible and also more fragile institution (Skolnick, 1978).

Coexisting with the new gender culture is a more conventional gender culture that has hardly been penetrated by feminism and women's changing roles. "Yes, there's been enormous change in 10 or 15 years," observes Ellen Goodman (1982) in a recent syndicated column. "But today it is less a matter of two stages, one replacing the other, than of two cultures, existing side by side." Those who share the more conventional world view continue to find gender the most obvious basis for role assignment and assumption. They experience marriage and family as a natural and/or moral destiny, breadwinning as a core male identity, and homemaking as the heart of female identity. While the breadwinner/homemaker sex-role division is actually a feature of modern rather than traditional societies, the contemporary conventional culture fuses this role allocation with its version of traditionalism.

Where they can afford it, traditionalists will adopt a single-breadwinner lifestyle, with wives remaining out of the labor force indefinitely to devote themselves full-time to domestic duties, mothering, volunteer activities, and facilitation of husbands' careers. More and more, however, traditionalists will begin to yield to the need or lure of two incomes. This will require compromise but not abandonment of gender-based role definitions. Wives' employment will be treated as secondary, their incomes as supplemental. Their employment will not tend to make maximal use of their abilities or credentials, as their first responsibility will remain to serve their families and accommodate their husbands. The husbands in these two-paycheck marriages may help with domestic chores and care for children while wives are away at work, but they will not substantially alter their own work lives or personal goals to assume domestic responsibilities. Traditional men may have careers or they may have jobs. The wives, regardless of educational attainment, will rarely have careers but will often have jobs. Dual-employed traditionalists will experience the problems associated with this new pattern in camouflaged form and will resist the redefinition necessary to treat those problems as legitimate objects of social policy.

The men and women who adhere to these two gender cultures live in separate Americas. In some ways the distance may minimize tension. But the traditionalists are becoming increasingly politicized, as evidenced by the recent proliferation of right-wing political pressure groups and the clash between this political element and more liberal factions on issues ranging from abortion to publicly funded child care. At least one major voice from the women's movement is calling for rapprochement of the two groups and a more positive united effort to support women and families (Friedan, 1981). It is probably more realistic, however, to expect the cleavage to continue and even widen. This may have a paralyzing effect on the development of national policy to deal with the needs of working parents for shorter and more flexible hours, parental leaves, and child care; for problems associated with family instability; and for the special circumstances of single parents and low-income families.

THE POLITICS OF PRIORITIES

While the most obvious implication of the new gender culture is reallocation of breadwinning and homemaking responsibilities, the more subtle implication is increased variation in the way in which and the degree to which occupational and family roles are combined. It is no longer obligatory to do it all, and to try will tend to create overload. In a society that has no policy for relieving that overload, the right to choose becomes the imperative to choose. At a minimum, it forces young people to select the order in which they will pursue life goals and the order in which they will compromise or forego them. For some the choices will be easy and welcomed. For others they will be made with ambivalence and a sense of loss, if one life goal must be sacrificed to another. Out of this process will emerge lifestyles that reflect distinctive priorities. Those who give priority to careers (or other highly individuated pursuits) or adult relationships (marriage or informal alignments) will increasingly postpone and/or avoid parenthood. Those for whom families with children represent the highest priority will limit work involvement and withdraw from the fast-paced, adult-centered social worlds of the child-free (nonparents and absentee parents).

The differentiation of lifestyles defined by central life priorities will create distinct interest groups that will begin to compete for resources and contend over public policy. Their expenses will be different; their needs for benefits and services will be different; their consumptive patterns will be different. Under these conditions, those with families, particularly, will be vulnerable. Their added workload and financial obligations will be treated as lifestyle choices freely made and for which they are individually responsible. While their earning power will be limited by family commitments, they will be expected to absorb personally most of the growing costs of families and/or trade important benefits, such as retirement pensions, for child care or family health insurance. Their standard of living, compared to that of those without children, will decline, regardless of educational attainment and the other variables that in the past have been predictive of living standards.

Thus, at a time when both the actual and "opportunity" costs of children are increasing (Bird, 1979; Jones, 1980), those costs are also becoming more concentrated. As more people exercise their option to remain child-free and withhold support for the use of public funds to pay for "other people's children," fewer people will begin to absorb a higher portion of the costs of families. Most nations in the developed world have anticipated the practical needs and special financial burdens of families, as women enter the labor force and men and women are emancipated from the inevitability of families. In recognition of the general societal need for children and stake in their development, and in the name of making parenthood as well as nonparenthood an affordable and viable option, most countries subsidize families (with such measures as family allowances and health insurance) and support families (with measures including child care and maternal or parental leaves) to a degree still barely conceivable to Americans (see Kamerman and Kahn, 1978, for a review of family policies in fourteen countries). In contrast, Adams and Winston (1980: 8) observe that "with few exceptions, American policymakers view these necessary tradeoffs as private decisions, outside the realm of governmental concern or action. They do not see government as having any particular obligation to reduce or redistribute the costs."

Neglect of the needs of families, legitimized by the freedom-of-choice rhetoric of the family-free, will discourage many from having children and penalize those who do. This could spawn a host of social problems, as children more often grow up in financially strained and overloaded households, as their numbers diminish and the population ages, and as declining fertility becomes especially marked among the highly educated and affluent.

THE ISOLATION OF THE INTEGRATORS

A consequence of women's employment and growing sex equality, we have argued, is institutional separation of careers and families and greater difficulty combining work roles and parenting without overload and economic deprivation. This generalization presumes that spouses have separate work lives outside the home. A significant exception is the case where spouses work together, as colleagues in the same field (for example, two psychotherapists share a practice), as a team that combines different skills or roles (such as a physician and a journalist who pool their talents to write popular medicine books), or as owners and operators of their own business. The degree of integration of work, marriage, and family roles for such persons is considerably greater than for other dual careerists or dual earners. Even more so than in the instance of the two-person career, these spouses are implicated together in a worklife, and there is no sharp segregation of work and family roles. To the degree that worklife spills over into homelife or is based at home or in the couple's own work establishment, parental as well as spousal roles may overlap considerably with work roles. This overlap means that what requires separate time in the more typical dual-earning arrangement occurs more simultaneously. This reduces the experience of overload and conflict over life priorities.

The structural strength of the coworking family form is its internal integration, which is higher than both the conventional breadwinner/homemaker family and the usual dual-earning family. Work and family roles reinforce rather than compete with each other, and commitment to one enhances rather than diminishes commitment to the other. On the other hand, the extent of integration of the nuclear family with nonfamilial institutions actually may be lower for coworker couples than for others. Spouses who work together will not be assimilated easily into the networks of individual workers or the couples formed by these workers and their nonemployed or separately employed spouses. Because of the colleagueship or partnership built into the marriage, coworking couples may experience less need for the usual work relationships. As genuine colleagues or partners with their husbands (instead of providers of domestic services, second persons in two-person careers, or secondary earners), coworking wives may have less time and inclination to organize extensive social lives with neighbors, work associates, or kin, or become involved in conventional female networks or activities. This lower level of integration of the coworking couple into nonfamilial networks may leave them ill-prepared to deal with stressors, such as prolonged illness or financial loss, that require resources beyond the nuclear unit. For these couples, nuclear family integration may be achieved at the price of nuclear family isolation, in a society that provides few formal structural supports for families. When

Bird (1979) comments that spouses who work together have more at stake in a marriage, she is referring to the interdependence of marriage and worklife. We would add that the stakes also may be high because bridges to extrafamilial resources are weak.

CONCLUSIONS

The reorganization of work and family in the lifestyles of Americans coming of age in the 1980s and 1990s will be extensive. We have identified several variants, each of which will be associated with distinctive life experiences and political outlooks. Some of the young, as well as the old, will continue to be *traditionalists* who do not fundamentally question conventional sex-role destinies, even in dual-earning marriages, and will resist structural adaptations to sex-role change. On the other hand, those who reject gender scripts and embrace the new rhetoric of lifestyle choice will tend to become *prioritizers*. Some will organize lives around adult-centered priorities, and others will fashion lives more compatible with family priorities. The differentiation of the interests and perspectives of these two groups from each other, as well as from the traditionalists, will prevent consensus on family policy issues. Yet another variant will be the *integrators*, couples who work together. These coworking couples will tend to become relatively self-sufficient islands, cut off from the work and family role definitions and dilemmas experienced by most others.

Some celebrate the growing heterogeneity of lifestyles as a sign of significant gains in individual rights and personal freedom (Bird, 1979; Skolnick, 1978). These are meaningful values, however, only where material needs are met, gross inequities in standard of living are eliminated, and support systems for the young, old, unemployed, handicapped, alone, abandoned, and otherwise needful are strong. The United States has been slow among nations to develop national policy in any of these areas. The retreat of the Reagan administration from the limited redistributive, national insurance and the "safety net" programs enacted since World War II reveals the precariousness of our national commitment. The absence of commitment is at least in part a consequence of the fragmenting and polarizing effects of lifestyle variation. Margaret Mead (1975: 310) warns that

> a society that cuts off older people from meaningful contact with children, a society that segregates any group of men and women in such a way that they are prevented from having or caring for children, is greatly endangered. . . . It is only through precise, attentive knowledge of particular children that we can become—as we must—informed advocates for the needs of all children and passionate defenders of the right of the unconceived to be well born.

Mead's warning about the generations, it would seem, applies to the segregation by lifestyle of any major social categories. Given the growing separation of the social worlds of Americans, we must wonder where are going to be found the core experiences and common values on which guardianship of the general welfare can rest.

REFERENCES

Adams, C. T. and K. T. Winston
  1980   Mothers at Work: Public Policies in the United States, Sweden, and China. New York: Longman.
Bane, M. J.
  1976   Here to Stay: American Families in the Twentieth Century. New York: Basic Books.
Bird, C.
  1979   The Two-Paycheck Marriage. New York: Rawson, Wade.
Burgwyn, D.
  1981   Marriage Without Children: Men and Women Tell What It Is Like to Be Childless by Choice or Chance. New York: Harper & Row.
Coser, L. A.
  1974   Greedy Institutions. New York: Free Press.

Epstein, C. F.
   1971   "Law partners and marital partners: strains and solutions in the dual career family enterprise." Human Relations 24: 549-563.
Filine, P. G.
   1974   Him/Her/Self: Sex Roles in Modern America. New York: New American Library.
Friedan, B.
   1981   The Second Stage. New York: Summitt Books.
   1963   The Feminine Mystique. New York: Dell.
Garland, T. N.
   1972   "The better half: the male in the dual profession family," pp. 199-215 in Constantina Safilios-Rothschild (ed.) Toward a Sociology of Women. Lexington: Xerox College Publishing.
Goodman, E.
   1982   "Suffering feminist fatigue." Washington Post (March 27): A19.
Hochschild, A. R.
   1976   "Inside the clockwork of male careers," pp. 251-266 in Jerome H. Skolnick and Elliott Currie (eds.) Crisis in American Institutions. Boston: Little, Brown.
Hofferth, S. L. and K. A. Moore
   1979   "Women's employment and marriage," pp. 99-125 in Ralph E. Smith (ed.) The Subtle Revolution. Washington, DC: Urban Institute.
Holmstrom, L. L.
   1972   The Two-Career Family. Cambridge: Schenkman.
Hunt, J. G. and L. L. Hunt
   1977   "Dilemmas and contradictions of status: the case of the dual-career family." Social Problems 24: 407-416.
Johnson, C. L. and F. A. Johnson
   1980   "Parenthood, marriage, and careers: situational constraints and role strain," pp. 143-161 in Fran Pepitone-Rockwell (ed.), Dual-Career Couples. Beverly Hills, CA: Sage.
Jones, L. Y.
   1980   Great Expectations: America and the Baby Boom Generation. New York: Ballantine.
Kamerman, S. B. and A. J. Kahn (eds.)
   1978   Family Policy: Government and Families in Fourteen Countries. New York: Columbia Univ. Press.
Lorber, J.
   1980   "Beyond equality of the sexes: the question of children," pp. 522-533 in J. Henslin (ed.) Marriage and Family in a Changing Society. New York: Free Press.
Mead, M.
   1975   Blackberry Winter. New York: Pocket Books.
Miller, S. M.
   1972   "The making of a confused, middle-aged husband," pp. 245-253 in C. Safilios-Rothschild (ed.) Toward a Sociology of Women. Lexington: Xerox College Publishing.

Myrdal, A. and V. Klein
  1956 Women's Two Roles. London: Routledge & Kegan Paul.
Paloma, M. M.
  1972 "Role conflict and the married professional woman," pp. 187-198 in C. Safi-
         lios-Rothschild (ed.) Toward a Sociology of Women. Lexington: Xerox
         College Publishing.
Papanek, H.
  1979 "Family status production: the 'work' and 'non-work' of women." Signs
         4: 775-781.
  1973 "Men, women, and work: reflections on the two-person career," pp. 90-110
         in J. Huber (ed.) Changing Women in a Changing Society. Chicago: Chi-
         cago Univ. Press.
Pepitone-Rockwell, F. (ed.)
  1980 Dual-Career Couples. Beverly Hills, CA: Sage.
Rapoport, R. and R. Rapoport
  1980 "Three generations of dual-career family research," pp. 23-48 in F. Pepi-
         tone-Rockwell (ed.) Dual-Career Couples. Beverly Hills, CA: Sage.
  1976 Dual-Career Families Re-Examined: New Integrations of Work and Fam-
         ily. London: Martin Robertson.
  1971 Dual-Career Families. London: Penguin.
  1969 "The dual-career family: a variant pattern and social change." Human Rela-
         tions 22: 2-30.
Rossi, A.
  1969 "Sex equality: the beginnings of ideology." The Humanist 29: 3-6, 16.
Skolnick, A.
  1978 The Intimate Environment. Boston: Little, Brown.
Slater, P.
  1970 The Pursuit of Loneliness. Boston: Beacon Press.
Vanek, J. J.
  1980 "Household work, wage work, and sexual equality," pp. 275-291 in S. F.
         Berk (ed.) Women and Household Labor. Beverly Hills, CA: Sage.
Veevers, J. E.
  1980 Childless by Choice. Toronto: Butterworths.
White, M. S.
  1979 "Women in the professions: psychological and social barriers to women in
         science," pp. 359-370 in J. Freeman (ed.) Women: A Feminist Perspective.
         Palo Alto: Mayfield.
Young, M. and P. Willmott
  1973 Thy Symmetrical Family. New York: Penguin.

PART II

The Interdependence of Occupations and Families

This section is concerned with the interface of conditions on the job and in families. The studies by Pleck and Staines and by Marsh deal with hours spent on the job and how one spouse's time schedule affects the other's. Pleck and Staines also include in their analysis the shifts spouses work, whether it is the standard "eight to five" or another variant, and whether the job demands weekend effort instead of only weekdays. They find that women's child-care roles make them particularly vulnerable to their husbands' nonconventional job days. The importance of women's child-care roles show up again in Sharda and Nangle's discussion of how family factors affect status attainment in the occupation. In their welcome reversal of the usual procedure of viewing family behavior as dependent on the job, they find women's postmarriage educational gains—though they have less payoff in terms of job status compared with men's postmarital educational gains—are dependent on women's delaying childbirth. Piotrkowski and Crits-Christoph's research also shows the importance of maternal roles in job-related matters. In their sample, family relations, presumably including relations with children but not marital satisfaction, was associated with women's job satisfaction, job status, and job security. Thus, the long arm of the job seems to inconvenience women as wives less than women as mothers.

4

Work Schedules and Work-Family Conflict in Two-Earner Couples

JOSEPH H. PLECK
GRAHAM L. STAINES

Wives' employment and the emerging majority of two-earner families are receiving increased social attention. The impact of job schedules on various dimensions of family life, including levels of work-family conflict, is also of great contemporary interest (Bohen and Viveros-Long, 1981; Pleck et al., 1978, 1980; O'Brien, 1980). In investigating the new issues raised by work schedules and work-family conflict in two-earner families, recent research has adopted two complementary approaches. The first approach concerns the effects of spouses' employment status, while the second addresses the effects of spouses' job schedules within the subgroup of couples in which both husband and wife are employed.

Specifically, the first, "between-groups" approach inquires systematically into the effects of having an employed spouse on an individual's own job schedule, work-family conflict, and the relationship between the two. The questions raised by the first approach are unarguably important. One's spouse being employed does complicate one's own problem of integrating work and family roles, whatever other positive effects it has. It might do so by influencing one's own job schedule. Having an employed spouse might also directly exacerbate certain types of work-family conflict in the individual or make a particular characteristic of one's own schedule cause more stress than it otherwise would (that is, spouses' employment might act as a moderator variable). Such hypothetical processes can be tested in research designs that compare couples in which both partners are employed with couples in which one spouse, either husband or wife, is not employed.

The second, "within-group" approach explores the effects of variations in the job schedules of employed spouses on the individual's own job schedule, work-family conflict, and the relationship between the two. Without doubt, the effects of spouses' exact job schedules hold considerable importance. A difficult work schedule on the part of the husband or wife in a two-earner family may alter the other partner's work schedule. In addition, it may affect the family by increasing the work-family conflict of the spouse who has the difficult schedule, as well as the conflict of the spouse with the "normal" schedule (via a "crossover" affect). While the first research approach compares the dual-earner and single-earner couples, the second approach utilizes research designs that examine variations among couples in which the two spouses are employed. Both between-groups and within-group comparisons are useful, although obviously they yield different information.

This chapter pursues these two basic approaches in reviewing research on work schedules and work-family conflict in dual-earner families.[1] It focuses on three major dimensions of work schedules: pattern of days worked each week, pattern of hours worked each day (that is, shift), and number of hours worked each week. It distinguishes among several types of work-family conflict but emphasizes scheduling problems in particular. The chapter reviews available evidence on six specific relationships, three associated with the between-groups approach and three with the within-group approach.

The following discussion considers the effects of *spouses'* employment status and job schedules. Wherever possible, the chapter examines sex similarities and differences in the pattern of findings. In reality, most research on the correlates of spouses' employment status actually concerns only wives' employment status. Little previous research has focused specifically on the effects of one spouse's job schedule on the partner; but most research on other aspects of job schedules has involved males' job schedules. In spite of the skewed nature of past research, we hold that it is most useful to formulate the research issues in this area as concerning spouses' employment and, within this context, to note similarities and differences between effects for husbands and wives.

POTENTIAL EFFECTS OF
SPOUSES' EMPLOYMENT STATUS

Speculations vary as to the impact of spouses' employment status on either of the schedule variables concerning the pattern of time: pattern of days worked and pattern of hours worked. One possibility is that having an employed spouse encourages a worker to seek simpler and more conventional patterns of days and hours. On number of hours worked each week, however, it is highly plausible that individuals would work fewer hours if their spouses were employed. The spouse brings in income, which reduces the need for the individual to earn income. The effect of husbands' employment on wives may exceed the effect of wives' employment on husbands, since husbands' employment produces higher income on the average.

It is reasonable to expect that spouses' employment increases an individual's work-family conflict, particularly concerning scheduling. In principle, work-family schedule conflict can take one of two forms: (1) *job-family* scheduling conflict— incompatibilities between an individual's own job and family schedules; or (2) *job-job* schedule conflicts—conflicts directly between or indirectly generated by the two spouses' job schedules. The distinction between these two types of schedule conflict is apparent in intensive studies of two-earner families

(Lein et al., 1974; Hood and Golden, 1979). An alternate formulation of this distinction is one between within-individual schedule conflict and between-spouse schedule conflict. Husbands' and wives' job and family schedules are, of course, inextricably interrelated, so that it is difficult to draw an entirely firm boundary between conflicts within and between individuals, or between conflicts primarily involving job schedules versus job *and* family schedules. Nonetheless, the distinction between job-family and job-job conflict is heuristic.

In light of this distinction, the experience of employed spouses in two-earner families differs from that in one-earner families, in that the two-earner spouse can encounter both job-family and job-job schedule conflict, while the one-earner spouse can exhibit only the first. In short, the important aspects of work schedules and their effects on families differ somewhat between two- and one-earner families. The difference is that couples with both spouses employed are uniquely vulnerable to job-job schedule conflict.

We speculate that, compared to husbands, wives experience more of the second subtype of work-family schedule conflict. Regardless of possible differences between the sexes on the first subtype of scheduling conflict (job-family), employed wives may be much higher on job-job conflict, since wives may accept more responsibility than husbands do for coordinating family members' schedules or for disrupting their own schedules to resolve others' schedule problems. In support of this hypothesis, among workers reporting moderate or severe levels of total work-family conflict in the 1977 Quality of Employment Survey, nearly twice as many employed wives as employed husbands reported experiencing work-family schedule conflict—38.7% vs. 22.4%. In further support, nearly 50% of both two-earner husbands and wives in this survey with children 12 or under said they use a family-care, home-care, or group-care arrangement (not including elementary school) for their children during the parents' working hours. About 22.8% of two-earner mothers with a formal child-care arrangement said it causes them to be late for work, to miss work, or to experience other work schedule problems. However, only 2.1% of two-earner fathers did (Pleck et al., 1978). Women's possible higher level of job-job conflict may be part of a more general pattern of women's greater acceptance of responsibility for accommodating to other family members' schedules.

Job-job schedule conflict may have a deeper implication for two-earner couples. It has been observed that, controlling for other factors, wives' employment has a small but significant statistical association with increased likelihood of divorce or other marital disruption. The usual interpretation (Ross and Sawhill, 1975) of this effect is that wives' earnings increase the viability of wives' alternatives to marriage, thus facilitating marital disruption. (It also increases family standard of living, which inhibits marital disruption, but this countervailing effect appears to be smaller.) In addition to these already established effects, wives' employment may have an additional association to marital disruption because wives' employment creates opportunities for job-job schedule conflict that do not exist in the one-earner couple. This additional conflict causes stress in the two-earner couple when it occurs.

It seems likely that having an employed spouse should intensify the relationship between one's own schedule and level of work-family conflict. For example, having a nondaytime-shift job may elevate an individual's work-family conflict more if his or her spouse is employed than if the spouse is not.

POTENTIAL EFFECTS OF
SPOUSES' JOB SCHEDULES

Spouses' job schedules can have one of three possible relationships with each other. They may be similar, unrelated, or complementary. Spouses may arrange their schedules so as to have a high degree of overlap in order to maximize their off-work time together. Alternatively, spouses may try to arrange to have nonoverlapping schedules so that their child-care responsibilities are covered as much as possible by one or the other parent rather than by others (Lein et al., 1974).

While the individual's own job schedule presumably has the stronger effect on his or her work-family conflict, the spouse's schedule may also have an influence. In particular, we expect that a nonstandard work schedule held by the spouse will be associated with elevated work-family conflict in the individual. We expect that this might be particularly true for the effects of husbands' nonstandard schedules on wives.

Also worth investigating are the effects of spouses' job schedules on the association between own job schedule and work-family conflict. This pattern of effects is a rather abstract and difficult one, but it is nonetheless conceptually important. Put concretely, does the negative effect of a nonstandard schedule (such as nondaytime-shift work) on an individual's work-family conflict become intensified (or diminished) if the spouse also works a nonstandard schedule? Spouses' job schedules are considered here as a variable moderating (or conditioning) the effect of job schedule on the individual. The conditioning effect of the husband's schedule on the degree to which a wife's schedule causes conflict for the wife may be greater than the obverse moderating effect of the wife's schedule on the extent to which the husband's schedule causes conflict for him.

REVIEW OF RESEARCH ON EFFECTS OF SPOUSES' EMPLOYMENT STATUS

This section reviews available empirical evidence on the effects of spouses' employment status on three different factors: work schedules, reports of conflict between work and family life, and the relationship between the two. While the present review includes a number of different studies, it gives special emphasis to analyses of one dataset, the 1977 Quality of Employment Survey. This survey involved structured personal interviews with a nationally representative sample of 1515 workers, a worker being defined as anyone 16 years or older currently employed for remuneration twenty hours or more per week. Quinn and Staines (1979) have provided an overview of the survey's findings. Two other empirical reports on the survey have focused on topics concerning work and family life for the subsample of workers who live with a spouse or with a child under 18 (Pleck et al., 1978, 1980; Staines and Pleck, 1982). Some of the analyses reported here come from these earlier reports; others were performed especially for this chapter.

The present review of empirical evidence concerning spouses' employment status draws on both bivariate and multivariate analyses in the available studies. Bivariate relationships, of course, provide only a preliminary indication of the effects of spouses' employment status, since they fail to control on other (possibly spurious) factors. Multivariate analyses come much closer to identifying the effects uniquely attributable to spouses' employment status. On many of the ensuing empirical issues, unfortunately, existing studies have provided only bivariate information; researchers have not yet conducted the requisite multivariate tests.

The effects of spouses' employment status are composed of two influences: the effects of wives' employment status on husbands and the effects of husbands' employment status on wives. Most of the existing information pertains to the effects of wives' employment status on husbands. Much of the explanation for this asymmetry begins with the fact that the proportion of employed husbands whose wives work is roughly equal to the proportion whose wives do not work. The two groups are thus readily compared. By contrast, most employed wives have employed husbands. Those whose husbands do not work constitute a relatively small group and one that is notably heterogeneous, since it really consists of four subgroups (employed wives whose husbands are retired, disabled, unemployed, or students). In fact, a report based on the 1977 Quality of Employment Survey (Staines and Pleck,

1982) offers one of the few analyses of the effects of husbands' employment status on wives' work schedules and work-family conflict; even this analysis is hampered by the small size of its sample of employed wives whose husbands do not work.

EFFECTS ON WORK SCHEDULES

Does having an employed spouse affect the type of work schedule one has in one's main job? To answer this question, one must first decide how to conceptualize schedules. Staines and Pleck (1982) concluded that three dimensions capture the most important distinctions among work schedules on main jobs: pattern of days worked each week, pattern of hours worked each day (shift), and number of hours worked each week.

Pattern of Days Worked Each Week. Staines and Pleck divided patterns of days worked each week into three categories: (1) a standard pattern in which workers adhere to a fixed (or nonvariable) pattern of days that excludes weekend work (that is, nonvariable weekdays); (2) a nonstandard pattern in which workers work the same days each week but in which at least one of those days is a Saturday or Sunday (that is, nonvariable weekend days); and (3) another nonstandard pattern, according to which workers do not work the same days each week (that is, variable days).

Table 1 presents bivariate data from the 1977 Quality of Employment Survey on the effect of wives' employment status on husbands' patterns of days worked. It establishes that employed husbands whose wives work are significantly more likely than those married to housewives to work the conventional pattern of nonvariable weekdays and less likely to work one of the two nonconventional patterns of days (nonvariable weekend days or variable days). To be specific, 65.2% of working husbands with working wives work a regular pattern of weekdays, compared to 55.9% of employed husbands married to housewives.

TABLE 1
Employed Husbands' Pattern of Days Worked by Wives'
Employment Status[a]

Husbands' Pattern of Days	Wives' Employment Status[b]		All Employed Husbands
	Wife Employed	Wife Nonemployed	
Nonvariable weekdays	178 65.2%	267 55.9%	445 59.3%
Nonvariable weekend days	64 23.4	139 29.1	203 27.0
Variable days	31 11.4	72 15.1	103 13.7
All patterns[c]	273 36.4	478 63.6	751 100

a. The table includes unweighted data, since weighted data produce very similar percentages and unweighted data permit tests of statistical significance: $\chi^2 = 6.31$, 2 d.f., p $<$ .05.
b. Although all employed husbands in the table work at least twenty hours per week, a wife's employment status is determined by whether she does *any* work for pay (for example, an employed husband whose wife works five hours per week appears in the category of wife employed).
c. Percentage sum to 100 across this row; all other percentages are column percentages.

Table 2 presents comparable bivariate data from the same 1977 survey on the effects of husbands' employment status on wives' patterns of days worked. The data suggest a trend in the opposite direction. Employed wives whose husbands work are less likely than employed wives married to nonemployed husbands to work a regular pattern of weekdays. Again, the difference amounts to around 10 percentage points (65.5% versus 75.6%, respectively), but this time the difference does not reach statistical significance. It remains unclear whether this difference would persist and attain significance with a larger sample of employed wives married to nonemployed husbands. In short, the bivariate data indicate that wives' employment may have the effect of encouraging husbands to keep to a regular pattern of weekdays, but they do not establish

TABLE 2
Employed Wives' Pattern of Days Worked by Husbands'
Employment Status[a]

| Wives' Pattern of Days | Husbands' Employment Status[b] | | All Employed Wives |
	Husband Employed	Husband Nonemployed	
Nonvariable weekdays	148	31	179
	65.5%	75.6%	67.0%
Nonvariable weekend days	48	4	52
	21.2	9.8	19.5
Variable days	30	6	36
	13.3	14.6	13.5
All patterns[c]	226	41	267
	84.6	15.4	100

a. The table includes unweighted data, since weighted data produce very similar percentages and unweighted data permit tests of statistical significance: $\chi^2 = 2.95$, 2 d.f., n.s.
b. Although all employed wives in the table work at least twenty hours per week, a husband's employment status is determined by whether he does *any* work for pay (for example, an employed wife whose husband works five hours per week appears in the category of husband employed).
c. Percentages sum to 100 across this row; all other percentages are column percentages.

a significant effect of husbands' employment status on wives' patterns of days worked.

Pattern of Hours Worked. Staines and Pleck (1982) likewise divided the pattern of hours worked each day into five categories of shift, one standard and four nonstandard: (1) the day (or standard) shift, in which the worker begins work each day between 3:30 a.m. and 11:59 a.m.; (2) the afternoon shift, beginning each day between noon and 7:59 p.m.; (3) the night shift, beginning each day between 8 p.m. and 3:29 a.m.; (4) rotating shifts; and (5) other irregular patterns of hours (variable hours).

Again based on the 1977 Quality of Employment Survey, Table 3 summarizes the bivariate data on the effects of wives' employment status on husbands' patterns of hours, and Table 4

TABLE 3
Employed Husbands' Shift by Wives' Employment Status[a]

| Husbands' Shift | Wives' Employment Status[b] | | All Employed Husbands |
	Wife Employed	Wife Nonemployed	
Day	199	329	528
	73.7%	69.7%	71.2%
Afternoon	17	22	39
	6.3	4.7	5.3
Night	8	16	24
	3.0	3.4	3.2
Rotating	11	29	40
	4.1	6.1	5.4
Other	35	76	111
	13.0	16.1	15.0
All shifts[c]	270	472	742
	36.4	63.6	100

a. The table includes unweighted data, since weighted data produce very similar percentages and unweighted data permit tests of statistical significance: $\chi^2 = 3.88$, 4 d.f., n.s.

b. Although all employed husbands in the table work at least twenty hours per week, a wife's employment status is determined by whether she does *any* work for pay (for example, an employed husband whose wife works five hours per week appears in the category of wife employed).

c. Percentages sum to 100 across this row; all other percentages are column percentages.

does the same for the effect of husbands' employment status on wives' patterns of hours. To a certain degree, the data in Tables 3 and 4 parallel those in Tables 1 and 2. Employed husbands whose wives work tend to report conventional patterns of hours (that is, day shifts) more frequently than do employed husbands whose wives do not work, and employed wives whose husbands work tend to have conventional daily schedules less frequently than employed wives whose husbands do not work. The differences are small, however, and fail to achieve statistical significance for either sex. The bivariate data, in sum, do not provide convincing evidence of the effect of spouses' employment status on patterns of hours worked.

TABLE 4
Employed Wives' Shift by Husbands' Employment Status[a]

| Wifes' Shift | Husbands' Employment Status[b] | | All Employed Wives |
	Husband Employed	Husband Nonemployed	
Day	168	32	200
	75.0%	78.0%	75.5%
Afternoon	15	1	16
	6.7	2.4	6.0
Night	7	0	7
	3.1	0	2.6
Rotating	7	4	11
	3.1	9.8	4.2
Other	27	4	31
	12.1	9.8	11.7
All shifts[c]	224	41	265
	84.5	15.5	100

a. The table includes unweighted data, since weighted data produce very similar percentages and unweighted data permit tests of statistical significance: $\chi^2 = 6.26$, 4 d.f., n.s.
b. Although all employed wives in the table work at least twenty hours per week, a husband's employment status is determined by whether he does *any* work for pay (for example, an employed wife whose husband works five hours per week appears in the category of husband employed).
c. Percentages sum to 100 across this row; all other percentages are column percentages.

Number of Hours Worked. The third dimension of work schedules concerns number of hours worked each week. Table 5 displays the bivariate evidence from the 1977 Quality of Employment Survey on the effects of spouses' employment status for both sexes. Employed husbands with working wives work about two hours a week less than employed husbands with nonemployed wives. The difference between the two groups proves statistically significant. Employed wives with employed husbands work one and a half hours longer than employed wives with nonemployed husbands, but the difference does not attain significance.[2]

TABLE 5
Mean Number of Hours Worked per Week by Spouses'
Employment Status[a]

| | Mean Number of Hours Worked per Week | | Significance of Difference Between Columns |
	Spouse Employed[b]	Spouse Nonemployed[b]	
Employed husbands	45.9	48.0	$p < .05$
Employed wives	39.3	37.8	n.s.

a. The table includes unweighted data, since weighted data produce very similar mean scores and unweighted data permit tests of statistical significance.
b. Although all employed husbands and employed wives in the table work at least twenty hours per week, a spouse's employment status is determined by whether the spouse does *any* work for pay (for example, a worker whose spouse works five hours per week appears in the category of spouse employed).

Several other studies have also addressed the issue of the effect of wives' employment status on husbands' number of hours worked. Mooney (1981a, 1981b) reported a multivariate analysis in which wives' regular employment over a five-year period was associated with a substantial (9%) and significant reduction in husbands' average work hours. A similar study by Dickinson (1974) obtained a significant but somewhat lower figure (4%). The bulk of the bivariate and multivariate evidence thus suggests that, among employed husbands, wives' employment is associated with a decrement in the number of hours worked each week.

EFFECTS ON WORK-FAMILY CONFLICT

Does having an employed spouse affect the level of interference between one's work and one's family life? The 1977 Quality of Employment Survey included several measures of work-family conflict. To obtain a measure of *total conflict*, interviewers asked all workers living with a family member: "How much do your job and your family life interfere with each other? A lot, somewhat, not too much, or not at all?" Respondents answering "a lot" or "somewhat" were then asked: "In what ways do they interfere with each other?" The two most frequent responses to the latter question were *hours conflict* (that is, complaints about excessive work hours interfering with family life), and *schedule conflict* (complaints about some form of scheduling problem involving work and family activities).

Bivariate comparisons reported by Pleck et al. (1978: Table 1, p. 45) explored the effects of spouses' employment status on work-family conflict but included no tests of statistical significance. Wives' employment status appeared to have little effect on total conflict. Among employed husbands of employed wives, 31.5% reported severe ("a lot") or moderate ("somewhat") levels of total conflict; the corresponding figure for employed husbands of housewives was 36.3%. A larger percentage difference emerged for the effect of husbands' employment on wives: 38.1% of employed wives of employed husbands reported severe or moderate total conflict, compared to 25.6% for employed wives of nonemployed husbands. The small number of women in the last category, however, renders the latter difference unreliable.

Pleck et al. (1978: Table 2, p. 46) also presented bivariate data on the effects of wives' employment status on husbands' hours conflict and schedule conflict. Wives' employment, they found, had little effect on either measure of conflict. Among workers reporting at least moderate levels of total conflict, the proportions mentioning hours conflict were 62.8% for employed husbands whose wives work and 55.8% for employed husbands married to housewives; the corresponding figures on schedule conflict were 22.4% and 18.6%, respectively. Pleck et al. did not present parallel bivariate data on the effects of husbands' employment status on wives' hours conflict and schedule conflict because the number of employed women married to nonemployed husbands and reporting at least moderate levels of total conflict was too small to sustain meaningful comparisons.

Using multiple regression, however, Staines and Pleck (1982: Table 3.3) conducted a multivariate analysis of the effects of spouses' employment status on the three measures of work-family conflict. Controlling on family life-cycle stage and other demographic factors and work schedule characteristics, the investigators determined that wives' employment status had no substantial or significant effect on any of the measures of work-family conflict (total conflict, hours conflict, or schedule conflict). On the other hand, although husbands' employment status had no substantial effect on either total conflict or hours conflict, husbands' employment was associated with an elevated regression coefficient for schedule conflict. With other factors controlled, that is, employed wives whose husbands work appeared to register higher schedule conflict than employed wives whose husbands remain outside the labor force. The particular strategy for significance testing used by Staines and Pleck, nonetheless, did not include a test of significance for this (or any other) effect of husbands' employment status.

Bohen and Viveros-Long (1981: Table 13) presented comparisons of work-family "role strain" between husbands of employed and nonemployed wives, in various subgroups and using various measures; no differences emerged. To recapitulate, the evidence indicates that under multivariate control, wives' employment status has no effect on any measure of husbands' work-family conflict but that husbands' employment may contribute to wives' level of schedule conflict.

EFFECTS ON THE RELATIONSHIP BETWEEN WORK SCHEDULE AND WORK-FAMILY CONFLICT

Little research has explored whether spouses' employment status affects the relationship between work schedules and work-family conflict. Pleck et al. (1978: Table 3, p. 48) reported some relevant trivariate analyses. They computed correlations between certain measures of work schedules (day shift, afternoon shift, night shift, rotating shift, number of hours worked) and total conflict for two groups of employed husbands: those married to employed wives and those married to housewives. Staines and Pleck (1982: Appendix B) used moderator regression to test for selected effects of spouses' employment status on the relationship between work schedules and work-family conflict. Their analysis tested specifically for the effect of wives' employment status yet found no significant moderator effects of wives' employment status on the relationship between any of the measures of work schedules (pattern of days, shift, number of hours) and any of the measures of work-family conflict (total conflict, hours conflict, schedule conflict).

Staines and Pleck's analysis also presented data relevant to the effect of husbands' employment status on the relationship between work schedules and work-family conflict among employed wives but did not test these interactions for significance. Staines and Pleck's findings revealed a tendency for both rotating shift and irregular patterns of hours to elevate total conflict among employed wives married to employed husbands but to reduce such conflict among employed wives whose husbands do not work. As noted, the foregoing effects of husbands' employment status were not tested for statistical significance. Suffice to say that existing research fails to substantiate wives' employment status as a moderator of the relationship between husbands' work schedules and work-family conflict, and is inconclusive regarding the moderator effects of husbands' employment status on the corresponding relationship between work schedules and work-family conflict among employed wives.

Overall, the data from relevant studies indicate that wives' employment may have the effect of inducing husbands to take on less stressful work schedules (working a regular pattern of weekdays and/or working shorter hours each week) but does not seem to affect husbands' work-family conflict or the relationship between their work schedules and their work-family conflict. Existing data, however, do not permit a credible assessment of the corresponding effects of husbands' employment status.

REVIEW OF RESEARCH ON EFFECTS OF SPOUSES' JOB SCHEDULES

This section reviews evidence on the effects of spouses' job schedules on job schedules, work-family conflict, and the relationship between the two. It draws heavily on findings in the 1977 Quality of Employment Survey, which included a sample of 500 husbands and wives currently in two-earner couples (but not married to each other). The review includes both bivariate and multivariate analyses.

EFFECTS ON WORK SCHEDULE

Analyses within the two-earner sample from the 1977 Quality of Employment Survey address the effects of one partner's job schedule on the other partner's schedule for all three major dimensions of work schedules.

Pattern of Days Worked. Husbands' and wives' patterns of days worked are positively associated; they have more similar patterns than would be expected by chance (Table 6). A husband or wife who works a regular weekday schedule is more likely to have a spouse with the same kind of schedule; a husband or wife with a schedule involving weekend work on a regular basis is more likely to have a spouse with the same; and likewise for working a variable schedule.

TABLE 6
Wives' Pattern of Days Worked by Husbands' Pattern
of Days Worked[a]

| Wives' Pattern of Days | Husbands' Pattern of Days | | | |
	Nonvariable Weekdays	Nonvariable Weekend Days	Variable Days	All Patterns
Nonvariable weekdays	225	74	37	336
	71.0%	60.7%	60.7%	67.2%
Nonvariable weekend days	42	28	8	78
	13.2	23.0	13.1	15.6
Variable days	50	20	16	86
	15.8	16.4	26.2	17.2
All patterns[b]	317	122	61	500
	63.5	24.4	12.2	

a. Difference between husbands' and wives' distributions (comparison of row and column marginals): χ^2 = 14.48, 2 d.f., p < .001; association between husbands' and wives' patterns of days worked: χ^2 = 10.75, 4 d.f., p < .05.
b. Percentages sum to 100 across this row; all other percentages are column percentages.

Pattern of Hours Worked. Husbands' and wives' shifts show no statistically significant relationship to each other (Table 7). That is, a husband working on one particular shift schedule (say, early day shift) is neither more nor less likely to have a wife working on some other shift. If husbands and wives attempt to select job shifts in accommodation to each other, it must be either that they have relatively little freedom to do so or that one spouse may accommodate to a schedule held by the other in a variety of different ways.

Number of Hours Worked. There is a nonsignificant association between husbands' and wives' number of hours worked (Table 8).[3] That is, contrary to one school of thought, a husband working long hours does not appear to generate enough income to permit his wife to work shorter hours.

TABLE 7
Wives' Shift by Husbands' Shift[a]

| Wives' Shift | Husbands' Shift | | | | |
	Early Day Shift	Late Day Shift	Nonday Shift	Variable	All Shifts
Early day shift (3:30-7:59 a.m. starting time)	58 28.3%	32 20.3%	7 18.9%	22 23.4%	119 24.2%
Late day shift (8:00-11:59 a.m. starting time)	89 43.4	88 55.7	17 45.9	39 42.4	233 47.4
Nonday shift	25 12.2	11 6.7	5 13.5	8 8.7	47 9.6
Variable	35 17.1	27 17.1	8 27.6	23 25.0	93 18.9
All shifts[b]	205 41.7	158 32.1	37 7.5	92 18.7	492 100

a. Difference between husbands' and wives' distributions (comparison of row and column marginals): $\chi^2 = 38.46$, 3 d.f., $p < .001$; association between husbands' and wives' shifts: $\chi^2 = 11.82$, 9 d.f., n.s.
b. Percentages sum to 100 across this row; all other percentages are column percentages.

In related research, Marsh (1981) found no consistent relationship between each spouse's hours of work in the 1976 Panel Study of Income Dynamics sample. The two were positively related for a number of subgroups but negatively related in three other categories (white salaried husbands, black salaried wives, and white union wives). Thus, the preponderance of research suggests a clear-cut relationship between spouses' job schedules for only one of the three major dimensions of schedules, namely, a positive relationship for pattern of days worked. Significant associations do not emerge consistently for the other two dimensions, shift and number of hours worked. In the latter case, however, results for aggregated samples may conceal both positive and negative relationships within particular subgroups.

TABLE 8
Wives' Number of Hours Worked by Husbands' Number
of Hours Worked[a]

Wives' Number of Hours Worked	Husbands' Number of Hours Worked			All Categories
	<40	40	>40	
<40	44	72	118	234
	59.5%	46.2%	43.7%	46.8%
40	22	56	92	170
	29.7	35.9	34.1	34.0
>40	8	28	60	96
	10.8	17.9	22.2	19.2
All categories[b]	74	156	270	500
	14.8	31.2	54.0	

a. Difference between husbands' and wives' distributions (comparison of row and column marginals): $\chi^2 = 16.66$, 2 d.f., $p < .001$; association between husbands' and wives' hours/week: $\chi^2 = 5.96$, 4 d.f., n.s.
b. Percentages sum to 100 across this row; all other percentages are column percentages.

EFFECTS ON WORK-FAMILY CONFLICT

Possible crossover effects of spouses' schedules hold considerable interest. According to Staines and Pleck's (1982) analysis, wives' nondaytime-shift schedule (defined here as a job with any fixed starting time outside the band between 3:30 a.m. and 12:00 noon) positively predicted husbands' level of schedule conflict. The potential parallel effect of husbands' shift work on wives' conflict was absent. However, husbands' regular weekend work was significantly positively associated with wives' reports of work-family conflict concerning schedules. The parallel effect in the other direction was close to zero.

These findings reveal a fascinating asymmetry. Husbands experience schedule conflict when their wives work nondaytime shifts. Wives are not equally sensitive to shift work on the part of their husbands. However, wives experience elevated schedule conflict when their husbands work on weekends, but husbands do not have a similar reaction to wives' weekend work. This asymmetrical pattern—husbands' schedule conflict responding to their spouses' shift work, but wives' schedule conflict responding to their spouses' weekend work—may be interpretable in light of the effects of these schedule character-istics on husbands' time use.

Other analyses not described earlier (see Staines and Pleck, 1982) show that when husbands work nondaytime shifts, they increase their housework, thus taking over some of their wives' traditional family responsibilities. Therefore, wives' conflict is not significantly increased by husbands' shift work. But hus-bands' weekend work does significantly reduce husbands' time in child care and housework, since husbands appear to use weekends to "catch up" on these activities. Thus, when husbands work on weekends, wives' conflicts are increased.

By contrast, wives' weekend work leads to only small, nonsignificant decreases in wives' own time in family roles, and little change in husbands'. Thus, husbands' conflict is not elevated. But wives' shift work appears to increase husbands' time in child care. Though this increment is not statistically significant, it appears to be an additional family responsibility that causes the husband to experience more conflict. Interest-ingly, in both these interpretations, the crossover effect of one spouse's schedule on the other's work-family conflict is medi-ated by the effects of the first spouse's schedule (whether the husband or wife) on husbands' performance of housework or child care.

In other research, Greenhaus and Kopelman (1981) observed no effect of wives' work hours on husbands' total work-family conflict (schedule conflict alone; the same relationships be-tween husbands' hours and wives' conflicts were not exam-ined). Keith and Schafer (1980) found that husbands' number of hours worked predicted employed wives' work-family conflict, but wives' work hours did not predict husbands' conflict (again, a total conflict measure). While these studies used some multivariate techniques, they did not include characteristics of the individual's schedule as controls, while the study by Staines and Pleck did. This may partly account for the discrepancies in findings among these studies.

EFFECTS ON RELATIONSHIPS BETWEEN OWN JOB SCHEDULE AND WORK-FAMILY CONFLICT

Staines and Pleck (1982) established one further relationship: the effects of husbands' nonday and variable shifts on husbands' reports of schedule conflict were significantly exacerbated when the wife also had a nonday or variable shift.[4] That is, it appears that the detrimental impact of the husband's nonday shift is intensified even further when the wife has a nonday or variable shift. Variable shifts worked by husbands, which other analyses showed had no significant effect on husbands' schedule conflict—either overall or when the wife works a day shift—were associated with significantly increased schedule conflict in husbands when the wife works a nonday or variable shift. According to other analyses (Staines and Pleck, 1982; Table 7 of the present report), these combinations of nonday and/or variable shifts with this heightened impact on husbands occurred in 8.9% of all two-earner couples.

DISCUSSION

The case of the dual-earner family raises special issues regarding work schedules (pattern of days, pattern of hours, number of hours) and work-family conflict. This chapter pursues two general approaches to investigating these special issues. In the first place, it contrasts two-earner with one-earner couples to assess the impact of spouses' employment status on work schedules, work-family conflict, and their relationship. The evidence reviewed suggests that wives' employment status affects husbands' work schedules, whereas husbands' employment status may affect wives' work-family conflict. Specifically, compared to husbands of housewives, husbands with employed wives have work schedules that are less stressful in two important respects: Such husbands are more likely to work the conventional pattern of days (that is, a stable set of weekdays only), and they average a shorter work week. On the other hand, compared to those with nonemployed husbands, working wives married to working husbands tend to report higher levels of schedule conflict. The latter finding supports the earlier conjecture that spouses' employment creates an additional form of scheduling conflict (job-job conflict) that proves particularly burdensome to employed wives. Taken as a whole, the data on the effects of spouses' employment status point to an asymmetry along gender lines that represents a potential inequity or source of inequity. That is, within the domain of schedules and conflict, the only demonstrated effect on working husbands of having an employed wife is the positive one of an easier work schedule. In contrast, within this same domain, the only apparent effect on working wives of having an employed husband is the negative one of higher levels of schedule conflict.

The second general approach involves comparisons within two-earner couples. It investigates the effects of one partner's work schedule on the spouse's work schedule, work-family conflict, and their interrelationship. The data give the preliminary indication that spouses' schedules do affect each other in one respect, but not others. In the case of pattern of days worked, spouses tend to work matching schedules, thus supporting the hypothesis of similarity rather than complementarity. Spouses' shift and number of hours worked are not significantly related. In short, the data indicate that spouses in two-earner couples keep their work lives in step in only one of three respects. The strongest determinant of an individual's level of work-family conflict is clearly the individual's own schedule (Staines and Pleck, 1982), yet spouses' work schedules may also affect the individual's work-family conflict. Two such crossover effects emerge, in each case after the effects of the individual's own work schedule have been controlled for. Wives' shift work elevates husbands' schedule conflict, while husbands' weekend work increases wives' schedule conflict. In both instances, the crossover effect may be understood in terms of the effect of spouses' nonstandard schedule on an intervening variable, husbands' contribution to family roles. In addition, the analyses of dual-earner couples produce limited evidence that a spouse's work schedule can affect the relationship between one's own work schedule and one's work-family conflict. Specifically, having a wife who works a shift other than the standard day shift tends to exacerbate the effect of the husband's nonday or variable shift on his own level of schedule conflict.

NOTES

1. This review does not consider the effects of spouses' employment or work schedule on an individual's level of participation in family tasks. For reviews of the effects of the former, see Pleck (1977, 1981, and forthcoming). For a review and analysis of the effects of the latter, see Staines and Pleck (1982).

2. Although data on earnings are available in the 1977 Quality of Employment Survey, the relationship between spouses' employment and own earnings was not examined or controlled for in these analyses.

3. Husbands' and wives' number of days worked per week are, however, significantly positively correlated, so that husbands and wives tend to have similar numbers of days: Husbands working 1-4 days are particularly likely to have wives working 1-4 days, and husbands working 6-7 days have a higher than average rate of having wives also working 6-7 days. Number of days worked per week is moderately correlated with number of hours worked per week.

4. The one exception is that a husband's nonday shift does not have a significantly stronger impact on his schedule conflict when his wife has a variable shift than when she works a regular day shift. Even in this case, however, the effect of the husband's nonday shift is substantially (though insignificantly) elevated.

REFERENCES

Bohen, H. and A. Viveros-Long
    1981   Balancing Jobs and Family Life: Do Flexible Work Schedules Help? Phila-
            delphia: Temple Univ. Press.
Dickinson, J.
    1974   "Labor supply of family members," in J. Morgan et al. (eds.) Five Thousand
            American Families—Patterns of Economic Progress, Volume 1. Ann Ar-
            bor, MI: Institute for Social Research.

Greenhaus, J. and R. Kopelman
  1981   "Conflict between work and nonwork roles: implications for the career
          planning process." Human Resource Planning 4: 1-10.
Hood, J. and S. Golden
  1979   "Beating time/making time: the impact of work scheduling on men's family
          roles." Family Coordinator 28: 575-582.
Keith, P. and R. Schafer
  1980   "Role strain and depression in two-job families." Family Relations 29: 483-
          488.
Lein, L., M. Durham, M. Pratt, M. Schudson, R. Thomas, and H. Weiss
  1974   "Final report: work and family life." Cambridge, MA: Center for the Study
          of Public Policy.
Lopata, H. Z., D. Barnewolt, and K. Norr
  1980   "Spouses' contributions to each other's roles." In F. Pepitone-Rockwell
          (ed.) Dual-Career Couples. Beverly Hills, CA: Sage.
Marsh, L. C.
  1981   "Hours worked by husbands and wives." J. of Family Issues 2: 164-179.
Mooney, M.
  1981a   "Wives' permanent employment and husbands' hours of work." Industrial
          Relations 20: 205-211.
  1981b   "Does it matter if his wife works?" Personnel Administrator (January):
          43-49.
O'Brien, M.
  1980   "Fathers' perceptions of work-home conflicts." Presented at the British Psy-
          chology Society, London.
Pleck, J. H.
  forthcoming   "Husbands' paid work and family roles: current research issues,"
          in H. Lopata and J. H. Pleck (eds.) Research in the Interweave of Social
          Roles, Volume 3: Families and Jobs. Greenwich, CT: JAI.
  1981   "Wives' employment, role demands, and adjustment: final report." Unpub-
          lished monograph, Wellesley College Center for Research on Women. (with
          the collaboration of M. Rustad)
  1977   "The work-family role system." Social Problems 24: 417-427.
Pleck, J. H., G. Staines, and L. Lang
  1980   "Conflicts between work and family life." Monthly Labor Rev. (March):
          29-32.
  1978   "Work and family life: first reports on work-family interference and workers'
          formal childcare arrangements, from the 1977 Quality of Employment Sur-
          vey." Working Papers, Wellesley College Center for Research on Women.
Quinn, R. and G. Staines
  1979   The 1977 Quality of Employment Survey. Ann Arbor, MI: Institute for
          Social Research.
Ross, H. and I. Sawhill
  1975   Time of Transition: The Growth of Families Headed by Women. Washing-
          ton, DC: The Urban Institute.
Staines, G., and J. H. Pleck
  1982   "Work schedules' impact on the family." Unpublished monograph, Rutgers
          University.

5

Hours Worked
by Husbands and Wives

LAWRENCE C. MARSH

Social scientists have long been interested in trying to determine the factors that influence the amount of market work by men and, in more recent years, by women. Wage rates, along with several other socioeconomic variables, have been seen as playing an important role in determining one's hours of market work. In some studies both own wage rate and spouse's wage rate are seen as being influential in determining hours of market work. This last point has been discussed by a number of authors, including Mincer (1962), Cain (1966), Heckman (1971), the authors in Cain and Watts (1973), and several others.

One consideration that has not been explored in explaining hours of market work is that of the spouse's hours of market work. To what extent are the number of hours worked by one spouse influenced by the hours worked by the other? What is the direction of this influence? In other words, do hours of work by one spouse substitute for hours of work by the other, or are their hours of work complementary, where one spouse will work more hours if the other does?

As with past studies in this area, other important influences on hours worked, such as age, education, number and ages of children, and other personal and household considerations, must be taken into account and controlled for to as great an extent as possible in the regression analysis. In addition, a study of hours of market work must allow for relatively tight or slack local market demand conditions by including variables that reflect the relative state of the local economy.

Finally, these relationships may vary for persons in different socioeconomic groups, such as black, white, unionized, nonunionized, salaried, and hourly workers. Consequently, socioeconomic classes must be examined and compared to see if behavior is significantly different for these different groups. Previous studies on this topic have generally ignored socioeconomic class distinctions.

MODEL SPECIFICATION

Before discussing the details of model structure, it is important to note that this is not a study of the labor force participation decision since it involves only couples where both partners are already engaged in remunerative employment. This approach separates the hours worked decision from the labor force participation decision in a theoretical sense,[1] and avoids potential discontinuities due to any fixed costs of starting market work. This does not completely eliminate the censoring problem associated with dependent variables with truncated distributions as in the case of zero hours of market work (see Layard et al., 1980). Past econometric studies have been primarily concerned with obtaining fairly exact absolute elasticities for policy decision purposes, whereas this study will focus on the relative effects of wage rates and spouse's hours of work for different socioeconomic groups. Consequently, ordinary regression methods will be used in this study and the more complicated and expensive tobit analysis methods will be left for future research.

The data for this analysis are from the 1976 panel study of income dynamics by Duncan and Morgan (1976) from the

Survey Research Center of the Institute for Social Research at the University of Michigan, and were collected under the sponsorship of the U.S. Department of Health, Education, and Welfare. A total of 5862 household heads were interviewed for an average of 25 minutes and 3482 wives were interviewed for an average of 22 minutes, providing a broad sample covering the entire United States. About 90% of the interviews were conducted by telephone with the remainder done in person, except for a few distant people who filled out their own questionnaires. This study covered details of work, household, and personal characteristics. Many questions centered on income and labor market activity in addition to the standard socioeconomic questions (sex, race, marital status, and the like). For purposes of this analysis of husbands' and wives' hours of market work, the sample was reduced to less than 2780 respondents by considering only married couples living together who were both actively engaged in remunerative employment.

This model consists of two equations: one for the husband and one for the wife. The husband's equation has as its dependent variable the husband's annual hours working for money (HRSHUS). The first five explanatory variables in both the husband's and the wife's equations are dummy variables representing various occupations to allow for their differences in working hours. These occupations include professional workers (PROFESS), clerical and sales workers (CLERICAL), craft workers (CRAFT), equipment operatives (OPERATOR), and unskilled laborers (LABORER). The next explanatory variable used in this equation is WAGEHUS, which is the husband's wage or salary on an hourly basis. A positive relationship between wages and hourly labor might be expected, as a higher wage rate makes leisure relatively more expensive in terms of opportunity cost and makes work more rewarding by way of the substitution effect. However, if workers find their incomes already adequate to meet their immediate needs, they may be tempted to respond to increases in their wage rates by working fewer hours as this income effect outweighs the usual substitution effect of a wage increase. Also, the wage rate may be less important in determining hours of market work for husbands than for wives to the extent that husbands exhibit less flexibility in their labor force hours of work commitment. Age of husband in years (AGEHUS) might be an important personal characteristic to control for since older workers may be less inclined to work long hours. A negative coefficient would be expected especially if older, semiretired workers cannot increase their hours of work without jeopardizing their social security incomes. Another personal characteristic to take into consideration is the husband's education (EDUCHUS). More education may result in having a more interesting and satisfying job, while greater education itself may reflect to some extent a determination to advance oneself through study and hard work. This would suggest a positive relationship between education and hours worked.

The wife's influence on the hours of work of the husband is seen through the hours of work by the wife and her wage rate, as well as indirectly through her contribution to other family income. The wife's hours of market work may have either a positive or negative effect on husband's hours of work depending upon the complementarity or substitutability, respectively, of husband's and wife's hours of work as already indicated. On the other hand, the wife's wage rate (WAGE-WIFE) should have a negative effect on husband's hours of work from a purely rational, economic perspective since the higher her wage the greater her comparative advantage in market work relative to her husband. However, psychological considerations may override rational, economic behavior in this situation. If the husband feels a psychological need to be the breadwinner in the family, he may work more hours if his wife has a higher wage rate, in order to bring home more money than his wife. If this psychological effect is dominant, then a positive relationship will be seen between wife's wage and husband's hours of work.

Next, it is necessary to control for certain general family influences on the husband's hours of work. In particular, the amount of other income the family gets may influence the need for the husband to work long hours. If the family already has a good income flow from sources other than husband's and wife's income, the husband may not be under as much pressure to work long hours. Consequently, a negative relationship between other family income (OTHERINCH) and husband's hours of work is expected. Also, the number of dependents (DEPEND) that the family must support may affect the husband's hours of work. A positive relationship between the number of dependents and hours of work would be expected. Finally, home ownership may be important for the husband's working hours decision. Home ownership may or may not imply a greater financial burden such as a heavy mortgage obligation depending on rent alternatives, but home ownership more often suggests greater responsibility for upkeep and maintenance and, therefore, more obligation for nonremunerative work at home. In a way, this is analogous to the wife's concern for number and age of children in her working hours decision. The OWNER variable is coded as 1 for families that own or are in the process of purchasing their own home and 0 otherwise.

Finally, market demand considerations must be taken into account in explaining the hours of market work by the husband. A desire to work more hours may be frustrated by a slack economy, or, during boom times, employees may be pressured to work longer hours when the available pool of substitutable workers has all but dried up. Furthermore, more part-time jobs may be available when the economy is expanding. Two variables are used here to control for this effect. The first variable, JOBS, is designed to indicate whether the respondent perceives a shortage or surplus of unskilled workers exists in the respondent's county. Interviewers coded this variable as 1 for situations where there are many more jobs than applicants, and increased it in integer steps as more unskilled workers are unable to find jobs. For example, a 1 indicates many more jobs than applicants, a 2 means simply more jobs than applicants, a 3 means most people able to find jobs, and so on. An increase in this variable can be expected to result in a decrease in the hours of work of the husband on the average. The JOBS variable is more of a perceived or subjective variable, whereas the other demand side variable, UNEMPLOY, is a more objective measure in that increases in its value directly relate to increases in the unemployment rate in the respondent's county. For a more elaborate treatment of the unemployment variable in a labor supply model see Ashenfelter (1980).

The wife's equation is set up in a similar manner, but reflects to some extent the wife's traditional role, emphasizing children and housework in addition to the market work variables used in the husband's equation. The dependent variable for the wife's equation is the wife's annual hours working for money (HRSWIFE). The first five explanatory variables for the wife's equation are the same type of occupation variables as used in the husband's equation: PROFESS, CLERICAL, CRAFT, OPERATOR, and LABORER. The next explanatory variable is the wife's wage rate (WAGEWIFE) which represents the wife's wage or salary on an hourly basis. The coefficient of this variable generally is expected to take on a positive value since the wage rate represents the opportunity cost when not engaging in market work. Also, women may be more likely than men to relate positively to higher wages. As in the husband's case, the wife's age (AGEWIFE) is expected to be negatively related to hours worked (having controlled for children separately). This expectation is supported by Quester (1977), who found that older women, other things being equal, supply fewer hours of labor to the market; this may be due partially to a cohort effect. Furthermore, her education level (EDUCWIFE) should be positively related to hours worked, as explained for the husband's equation. Farkas (1976) has found education to be an important influence on wife's hours of market work. Shaw (1979) found that black married women significantly increased their labor force commitments in response to improvement in their educations. Almquist (1977) contends that education has become a better predictor of a woman's employment than the presence or absence of young children.

The husband's influence on the wife's hours of market work appears through the variables HRSHUS and WAGEHUS in the wife's equation. The HRSHUS variable represents the hours of market work of the husband with a coefficient that may be either positive or negative, depending upon its complementarity with or substitutability for the hours the wife spends working for money. Complementarity would suggest that husbands and wives value their time together more. Substitutability suggests more concern for considering their relative comparative advantage tradeoff in market work. The wage rate of the husband, as defined above, would be expected to have a negative coefficient for the comparative advantage reason described for the husband's equation. Another analogous variable, OTHERINCW, represents income to the family other than the wife's or husband's income from market work. Again, a negative relationship is expected here, since higher other income suggests less financial burden and, therefore, less need to work. This hypothesis is supported by data analyzed by Ryscavage (1979) who found a negative relationship between husband's income and wife's labor force activity. Ewer et al. (1979) consistently found this same relationship.

Special variables of usual importance to the wife include considerations for children and housework. The importance of children in influencing women's market work is obvious and has been demonstrated in numerous studies, including Bowen and Finegan (1969) and Sweet (1973). The children affect the wife's hours of market work both through the age of the youngest child (YOUNGEST) and the number of children under 18 years of age (CHILDO17). Clearly, the YOUNGEST variable can be expected to have a positive effect on the wife's hours of market work since older children are more likely to increase demand for income than for mother's time, while the

CHILDO17 variable can be expected to have a negative influence on the wife's hours of market work. In addition, three variables related to housework are included. These are home ownership (OWNER); the number of rooms in the house (ROOMS); and the annual hours of housework performed by persons other than the wife (HOUSWKO). One final special variable indicates whether or not the family has moved within the last year. This variable could be important whenever the husband has had a job transfer, and the wife either cannot get a job immediately or uses the move as an opportunity to take a vacation or to make other home improvements before resuming market work. In the case of short moves within the immediate area, the MOVED variable would not be expected to be important, but for moves of any substantial distance, a negative association between moving within the last year and the number of hours of market work for the wife would be expected.

Finally, the same market demand variables used for the husband's equation are used for the wife's. Both the JOBS variable and the UNEMPLOY variable can be expected to have negative effects on the hours of market work of the wife as their values increase as defined in the discussion of the husband's equation.

Since in the husband's equation the wife's hours of market work are used to explain in part the husband's hours of market work, and since in the wife's equation the husband's hours of market work are used to explain in part the wife's hours of market work, a simultaneous equation relationship between the husband's and wife's equations is necessary to obtain consistent estimates of the regression coefficients for each equation. This simultaneous equation approach helps sort out the direction and relative strength of the effect of the wife's hours of market work on the husband's hours of market work and vice versa. For example, suppose that the husband's hours of work have a significant positive effect on the wife's hours of work, but at the same time the wife's hours of work have no influence or even a negative influence on husband's hours of work. Two such separate but simultaneous relationships can be sorted out statistically if the husband's equation and the wife's equation are each statistically identified. Identification in a two-equation system requires that there exist in each equation at least one variable (with a nonzero coefficient) that does not appear in the other equation. This allows one of the two regression lines to be separately "moved" by varying its unique variable or variables while the other regression equation line sits still to have the "picture" of its fit to the data points taken. Each equation can be statistically identified in this manner and the two equations' coefficients can thus be estimated simultaneously.

If the two equations were otherwise unrelated, a limited information simultaneous equation estimator such as two-stage least squares would be adequate. However, it is likely that the error terms are correlated across equations since any factors not included, such as additional demand considerations, would be likely to affect both equations to some degree. As a result, a full information simulatenous equation estimator (three-stage least squares) was used to obtain at least asymptomatically efficient coefficient estimates.

INTERPRETATION OF EMPIRICAL RESULTS

The results of the regression analysis are shown in Tables 1 and 2. There are a number of implications which can be drawn from these results.[2]

The intercept value of hours worked for the various occupations is always positive and statistically significant for husbands, although there were too few observations on black hourly professionals to estimate their intercepts. This general result suggests a strong commitment to long annual hours of market work by husbands as opposed to some wives, particularly union wives, who tended to have negative intercepts. Having controlled in this way for differences in working hours of different occupational groups, the analysis can focus on the other explanatory variables.

TABLE 1
Husbands' Equation Coefficient Estimates and t-Statistics
Explaining Husbands' Hours of Market Work

	White Salaried	Black Salaried	White Union Hourly	Black Union Hourly	White Nonunion Hourly	Black Nonunion Hourly
PROFESS	3801.7** (10.01)	3935.2** (8.93)	1830.5** (4.78)	too few cases	1309.6* (2.55)	too few cases
CLERICAL	3416.7** (9.85)	3807.3** (8.85)	1658.8** (4.68)	1352.3** (5.79)	804.8* (2.00)	2440.4** (7.33)
CRAFT	3865.2** (11.22)	4032.5** (10.19)	1970.1** (6.14)	1407.1** (6.24)	1200.0** (2.90)	2494.2** (8.01)
OPERATOR	3685.7** (9.86)	3448.7** (7.23)	1444.4** (4.42)	1559.2** (6.53)	1436.6** (3.65)	2420.35** (7.83)
LABORER	3519.4** (9.26)	3807.7** (9.24)	1983.9** (5.94)	1646.2** (7.41)	1182.6** (2.83)	2277.76** (7.37)
WAGEHUS	−0.86** (−6.91)	−0.91** (−3.55)	−0.18 (−1.13)	−0.76** (−4.12)	−0.51* (−2.50)	−0.11 (−0.43)
AGEHUS	20.00** (4.14)	−3.49 (−0.64)	−0.08 (−0.02)	−3.71 (−1.01)	13.85** (3.81)	−8.44* (−2.30)
EDUCHUS	−19.83 (−1.28)	−22.20 (−1.29)	−4.33 (−0.24)	22.45* (2.11)	61.31** (3.24)	−29.90* (−2.58)
HRSWIFE	−0.32** (−4.82)	0.13 (0.91)	0.04 (0.71)	0.16** (3.63)	0.11 (1.29)	0.16** (3.00)
WAGEWIFE	−0.26** (−3.45)	0.77* (2.53)	0.28** (2.79)	0.74** (3.27)	1.51** (4.99)	0.72* (1.98)
OTHERINCW	0.02 (0.01)	−0.01 (−0.80)	−0.04** (−4.56)	0.00 (0.49)	−0.12** (−7.35)	−0.02** (−2.85)
DEPEND	95.83** (4.26)	−48.58 (−1.57)	39.88* (2.32)	18.32 (1.01)	28.50 (1.10)	12.88 (0.72)
OWNER	−138.08 (−1.38)	287.33** (2.74)	505.03** (6.80)	106.20* (2.00)	131.05* (2.28)	184.37** (2.72)
JOBS	−261.64** (−4.50)	−424.70** (−3.68)	−83.97* (−1.99)	79.36* (2.22)	50.54 (0.98)	−70.95 (−1.58)
UNEMPLOY	−4.40 (−0.14)	159.69* (2.44)	46.84 (1.86)	−29.50 (−1.31)	−135.83** (−4.63)	8.46 (0.28)

*Significant at the .05 level.
**Significant at the .01 level.

The wages paid to the husbands and wives have an interesting effect on the number of hours they work. In general, husbands seem to work fewer hours the more they are paid per hour. This negative wage effect is particularly true for salaried

TABLE 2
Wives' Equation Coefficient Estimates and t-Statistics
Explaining Wives' Hours of Market Work

	White Salaried	Black Salaried	White Union Hourly	Black Union Hourly	White Nonunion Hourly	Black Nonunion Hourly
PROFESS	142.66 (1.13)	322.51** (5.55)	-649.24* (-2.12)	too few cases	-49.53 (-0.12)	too few cases
CLERICAL	356.45** (2.77)	-367.20** (-9.05)	-728.02** (-5.37)	-365.42 (-0.79)	471.10* (2.09)	556.36* (2.42)
CRAFT	too few cases	too few cases	too few cases	-292.05 (-0.62)	too few cases	805.96** (2.97)
OPERATOR	121.30 (0.48)	7.97 (0.13)	205.47 (1.64)	-281.41 (-0.64)	767.36** (3.58)	678.99** (3.10)
LABORER	-784.00** (-4.74)	794.71** (10.82)	-582.58** (-4.32)	-162.30 (-0.36)	424.27 (1.97)	232.40 (1.04)
WAGEWIFE	-0.36** (-4.47)	-0.85** (-10.15)	-0.94** (-7.21)	0.27 (0.93)	0.80* (2.31)	-1.00** (-3.23)
AGEWIFE	19.12* (2.30)	-4.20* (-2.04)	11.78 (1.80)	-8.58 (-1.33)	-21.00* (-2.07)	17.68** (4.13)
EDUCWIFE	9.09 (0.42)	-2.94 (-0.32)	109.14** (3.84)	62.04* (2.30)	118.05** (4.70)	80.57** (5.46)
HRSHUS	0.13 (1.87)	-0.28** (-6.76)	-0.29** (-3.08)	0.62** (5.84)	0.01 (0.15)	0.08 (1.42)
WAGEHUS	-0.09 (-0.36)	-0.16 (-1.14)	0.70* (2.09)	1.25** (3.25)	1.56* (2.56)	0.41 (1.37)
OTHERINCW	-0.02 (-1.56)	-0.19** (-4.24)	-0.02 (-1.45)	-0.05** (-4.19)	-0.14** (-5.07)	-0.02 (-1.68)
YOUNGEST	5.27 (0.40)	-2.85 (-0.49)	8.56 (0.70)	39.30** (3.82)	58.53** (3.49)	5.14 (0.54)
CHILD017	-5.91 (-0.13)	70.06** (3.14)	118.98** (3.41)	64.54* (2.19)	-166.38** (-4.35)	34.13 (1.49)
OWNER	225.00* (2.20)	-116.25** (-3.09)	245.20* (2.13)	7.58 (0.09)	-74.36 (-0.83)	-477.56** (-5.46)
ROOMS	-0.15 (-0.00)	257.00** (13.10)	67.15 (1.84)	-114.85** (-4.31)	189.30** (4.31)	46.86 (1.48)
HOUSWKO	0.17** (2.98)	-0.14** (-5.48)	-0.19** (-3.08)	-0.04 (-0.70)	0.32** (4.14)	0.15** (3.01)
MOVED	97.76 (1.11)	-969.36** (-11.87)	-199.42 (-1.44)	-196.33 (-1.15)	-249.84** (-2.74)	-410.66** (-3.48)
JOBS	223.80** (3.98)	238.82** (6.62)	-31.51 (-0.53)	142.32** (2.82)	-184.00** (-2.86)	-16.35 (-0.35)
UNEMPLOY	-120.90** (-4.00)	186.93** (7.23)	-33.64 (-1.03)	-63.70* (-2.08)	32.85 (0.82)	-83.92** (-2.83)

*Significant at the .05 level.
**Significant at the .01 level.

workers. Wives also appear to work less the more they are paid. The increased market wage rate may enable them to maintain an adequate income while cutting back on their working hours, particularly overtime hours.

Black workers seem to work less the older they become, except for black nonunion hourly wives. Most white workers appear to increase their hours of work with their age.

The level of education of husbands seems to have a negative relationship to their number of hours worked, with the significant exception of black union hourly husbands and white nonunion hourly husbands. On the other hand, wives' education is positively related to their hours of market work for almost all groups. The positive relationship of education to wives' hours of market work may reflect greater opportunities for flexibility in working hours than is available for husbands. Also, the more educated a wife is, the more interest she may have in market work.

Husbands respond differently to the number of hours their wives work. Blacks work more hours if their wives work more hours. White salaried husbands tend to work less as their wives work more. The wives' behavior shows that black union wives work more as their husbands work more, while white union wives and black salaried wives work less as their husbands work more. The analysis also indicates that as the wives' wage rates increase, the husbands usually seem to work more hours.

Wives appear to work more hours the higher their husbands' wage rates, except for salaried wives, who work less. A positive response by hourly workers in general to their spouses' wage rates could reflect one spouse being encouraged by the other spouse's success in attaining a higher wage rate. The variable of "other income" seems to have a negative relationship to the hours both husbands and wives work for almost all groups analyzed, as expected.

The number of dependents and children in the family was examined in several different ways. Husbands, especially whites, seem to work more the more dependents they have. For wives, the age of the youngest child is particularly important. As expected, the older the youngest child, the more likely it is that the wife works more hours outside the home. The more children under the age of 18, the more hours the wife seems to work outside the home. This was not expected and may indicate that for these women the added financial burden of a large family outweighs the added housekeeping burden. The significant exception is white nonunion wives, who reduce their market work.

Home ownership was found to have a fairly strong positive relationship to the number of hours of market work of husbands, which is contrary to the expectation that was expressed above, but may be explained by the greater financial burden of home ownership. The relationship of home ownership to wives' hours of work appears to be positive for whites and negative for blacks, at least where significant.

The number of rooms in the home was analyzed only for wives. It is used as a proxy for housework other than that related to children, although it might also be related to family size and need for income. The regression results show a mixed relationship of number of rooms to the number of hours of the wives' market work, with it having a negative relationship for black union wives while tending to have positive relationship for other wives. The number of hours of housework performed by other persons appears to be significantly positive for market work of nonunion wives and white salaried wives, but negative for other groups.

The effect of the family having moved in the last year also was analyzed only for wives, since they may want or have to settle for part-time work initially after moving. It is found that all groups of wives work fewer hours if they have moved in the past year, except for white salaried wives. This generally negative relationship is especially impressive since it includes both moves within a city and moves between cities. Presumably, the effect between cities would be even stronger, although the data here do not allow for such a test.

The analysis also shows that as the number of job applicants relative to the number of available jobs increases, husbands seem to decrease their hours of market work while wives seem to increase their hours of market work. This phenomenon may reflect situations where the husband faces a decreased demand for his labor and the wife compensates by increasing her supply of labor. An increase in the unemployment level in the county of residence tends to have a mixed but somewhat negative relationship to the number of hours of work, with the significant exception of black salaried workers. This outcome was generally expected since a high unemployment rate reflects a decrease in demand for labor.

SUMMARY AND CONCLUSIONS

For nonsalaried workers the wage rate of each spouse had a positive relationship to the hours worked by the other spouse. This suggests that, other things being equal, as one spouse's wage rate increases the other spouse may feel a competitive need to increase his or her hours of market work in order to maintain the relative contribution to household income. This seems especially true for husbands. At the same time, the own wage relationship is generally negative, especially for husbands. This suggests that an income effect may be dominant and that workers are more interested in getting more leisure time than in increasing their take-home pay in response to an own wage increase.

The relationship of each spouse's hours of work to the other spouse's hours of work was positive in most cases, reflecting complementary work behavior. The only significant exceptions to this result were white salaried husbands, black salaried wives, and white union wives, who appeared to treat their spouses' work as a substitute for their own hours of market work.

NOTES

1. Ben-Porath (1973) has pointed out that this distinction is particularly important if labor force participation rates do not reflect the percentage of time an average woman spends in the labor force, but instead indicate the proportion of women who have made a relatively long-term commitment to labor force employment.

2. Six mutually exclusive sets of regressions were performed, each with two simultaneous equations: one for husbands and the other for wives. The six mutually exclusive sets consisted of white salaried workers, black salaried workers, white union

hourly workers, black union hourly workers, white nonunion hourly workers, and black nonunion hourly workers. The system coefficients of determination, R^2, for these six groups were, respectively: .9334, .9927, .9306, .9744, .9238, and .9369. Although there were about 1000 observations in each equation, some of the occupation groups within each equation did not have enough observations to be estimated. However, the remaining occupation groups had at least 100 observations each.

REFERENCES

Almquist, E. M.
   1977   "Women in the labor force." Signs: J. of Women in Culture and Society 2 (Summer): 843-855.
Ashenfelter, O.
   1980   "Unemployment as disequilibrium in a model of aggregate labor supply." Econometrica 48 (April): 547-564.
Ashenfelter, O. and J. Heckman
   1974   "The estimation of income and substitution effects in a model of family labor supply." Econometrica 42 (January): 73-85.
Ben-Porath, Y.
   1973   "Labor force participation rates and the supply of labor." J. of Pol. Economy 81 (May/June): 697-704.
Bowen, W. G. and T. A. Finegan
   1969   The Economics of Labor Force Participation. Princeton, NJ: Princeton Univ. Press.
Cain, G.
   1966   Married Women in the Labor Force. Chicago: Univ. of Chicago Press.
Cain, G. and H. Watts (eds.)
   1973   Income Maintenance and Labor Supply. Chicago: Markham.
Cramer, J. C.
   1980   "Fertility and female employment: problems of causal direction." Amer. Soc. Rev. 45 (April): 167-190.
Duncan, G. and J. N. Morgan
   1976   A Panel Study of Income Dynamics: Procedures and Tape Codes, Wave IX. Ann Arbor, MI: Institute for Social Research.
Ewer, P. A., E. Crimmins, and R. Oliver
   1979   "An analysis of the relationship between husband's income, family size and wife's employment in the early stages of marriage." J. of Marriage and the Family 41 (November): 727-738.
Farkas, G.
   1976   "Education, wage rates, and the division of labor between husband and wife." J. of Marriage and the Family 38 (August): 473-483.
Fields, J. M.
   1976   "A comparison of intercity differences in the labor force participation rates of married women in 1970 with 1940, 1950, and 1960." J. of Human Resources 11 (Fall): 568-577.

Gronau, R.
    1973   "The effect of children on the housewife's value of time." J. of Pol. Economy Supplement 81 (1973): 168-199.
Heckman, J. J.
    1978   "A partial survey of recent research on the labor supply of women." Amer. Econ. Rev. Papers and Proceedings: 200-212.
    1974a   "Shadow prices, market wages, and labor supply." Econometrica 42 (July): 679-694.
    1974b   "Effects of child-care programs on women's work effort." J. of Pol. Economy 82 (April): S136-S163.
    1971   "Three essays on household labor supply and the demand for market goods." Ph.D. dissertation, Princeton University.
Hood, J. and S. Golden
    1979   "Beating time/making time: the impact of work scheduling on men's family roles." Family Coordinator 28 (October): 575-582.
Layard, R., M. Barton, and A. Zabalza
    1980   "Married women's participation and hours." Economica 47 (February): 51-72.
Lee, L. C. and R. Ferber
    1977   "Use of time as a determinant of family market behavior." J. of Business Research 5 (March): 75-91.
Leuthold, J. H.
    1968   "An empirical study of formula income transfers end the work decision of the poor." J. of Human Resources (Summer): 312-323.
Lobodzinska, B.
    1977   "Married women's gainful employment and housework in contemporary Poland." J. of Marriage and the Family 39 (May): 405-416.
Mincer, J.
    1962   "Labor force participation of married women," pp. 63-97 in H. G. Lewis (ed.) Aspects of Labor Economics. Princeton, NJ: Princeton Univ. Press.
Quester, A. O.
    1977   "The effect of the tax structure on the labor market behavior of wives." J. of Economics and Business 29 (Spring/Summer): 171-180.
Richardson, J. G.
    1979   "Wife occupational superiority and marital troubles: an examination of the hypothesis." J. of Marriage and the Family 41 (February): 63-72.
Ryscavage, P.
    1979   "More wives in labor force have husbands with above average incomes." Monthly Labor Rev. (June): 40-42.
Shaw, L. B.
    1979   Changes in the Work Attachment of Married Women, 1966-1976. Columbus: Center for Human Resource Research, Ohio State University.
Sweet, J. A.
    1973   Women in the Labor Force. New York: Seminary.
Tilly, L. A. and J. W. Scott
    1978   Women, Work and Family. New York: Holt, Rinehart & Winston.

6

Women's Jobs and
Family Adjustment*

CHAYA S. PIOTRKOWSKI
PAUL CRITS-CHRISTOPH

The increasing participation of married women in the labor force has spurred research into the relationship of women's employment to family adjustment in dual-earner families.[1] When women's employment status is considered, current research evidence indicates that, in general, husbands and wives in dual-earner and single-earner families do not differ significantly in level of family—and particularly—marital adjustment (see, for example, Wright, 1978; Nye, 1974; Staines et al., 1978; Booth, 1979; Locksley, 1980). Despite the proliferation of such studies of women's employment, we still know relatively little about the ways women's paid work lives may influence the quality of family relationships. Qualitative studies that have investigated this relationship have limited generalizability because of the small samples utilized and their emphasis on professional and managerial families. Moreover, studies that compare family adjustment in dual-earner and

*The authors would like to thank Faye J. Crosby for her generosity in making available data collected in a study of relative deprivation and working women. This study of relative deprivation was supported by NIMH Grant 1R01-MH31595. Data were collected in 1978. The present study was supported by NIH Biomedical Research Support Grant 5-S07-RR07015 to Yale University.

single-earner families are not designed to explicate the *processes* that link women's jobs to family adjustment.

It is our opinion that, at this time, an especially fruitful approach to the study of women's employment and family adjustment is to deemphasize questions about which family type fares better and to focus instead on the processes linking women's jobs and family relations *within* groups. Because men's and women's roles and experiences in the family differ, such analyses need to be undertaken separately for husbands and wives. The development of an adequate theory for understanding the relationship between work life and family adjustment in dual-earner families ultimately rests on our ability to describe the interactions between husbands' and wives' paid and unpaid work roles as they directly and indirectly influence each family member's adjustment. Such a conceptualization is necessarily complex. Consequently, it is useful to begin with simpler components. In the study report here we consider the relationship of women's employment to women's family adjustment in dual-earner families.

It is important that research on women and their employment treat women's work with sufficient complexity. The pioneering qualitative studies of dual-career families have been able to address the complexity of women's work and family roles by simultaneously considering a host of variables in interaction (see, for example, Rapoport and Rapoport, 1971; Holmstrom, 1972). Quantitative research necessarily must focus on fewer variables and relationships. However, too often, quantitative studies have emphasized the fact of women's employment and attitudes toward and commitment to the work role in general (see Safilios-Rothschild, 1970; Bailyn, 1970; Nye, 1963; Ridley, 1973; Orden and Bradburn, 1969; Locksley, 1980). Unfortunately, such variables do not tell us much about women's *actual* employment experiences and the conditions of their work (Hoffman, 1963), nor do they address the question of whether features of women's *particular* jobs influence their family adjustment. A review of recent quantitative research on the relationship of women's employment to family adjustment reveals that other job-specific variables rarely are examined. Although some studies have considered factors such as women's occupational prestige and job satisfaction (e.g., Ridley, 1973; Gover, 1963; Hoffman, 1963; Richardson, 1979; Yarrow et al., 1962; Harrell and Ridley, 1975), to our knowledge no studies have examined multiple characteristics of women's particular jobs simultaneously.

In the study reported here we utilized multiple regression procedures to investigate the relationship of specific job experiences and conditions of work to family adjustment for a sample of women in dual-earner families. Family adjustment was defined as the degree to which a family member has satisfying relationships with others in the family. More specifically we focused on two general questions:

(1) Is the paid occupational life of women in dual-earner families significantly related to their family adjustment?
(2) Which specific occupational factors are significantly associated with women's family adjustment in dual-earner families, and what is the nature of these associations?

In selecting the work variables to be included in the analysis, we were guided by several considerations: Data were not collected specifically for the purposes of this study; thus the variables available to us were limited. Of the pool of potential variables, we included only those for which we could develop reliable measures. Furthermore, we required that these variables be meaningful for both men's and women's work in dual-earner families. With work life emerging as a significant life role for women, it is fruitful to begin to conceptually integrate research on wives' employment with the literature on men's occupations and family lives. These criteria led us to focus simultaneously on four general features of women's paid work lives that may be related to their family adjustment: job satisfaction, job-related psychological mood, time spent at work, and occupational rewards.

CONCEPTUAL BASIS OF STUDY

Men's satisfaction with the intrinsic features of their work has been viewed as a threat to their family participation and, therefore, to family adjustment (see Rapoport and Rapoport, 1965; Young and Willmott, 1973). This notion is based on the assumption, noted by Marks (1977), that human psychological "energy" is scarce and finite. Consistent with Marks's concept of human psychological energy as expandable and as "created" by satisfying multiple roles, Piotrkowski (1979) alternatively has proposed that job gratification can result in positive emotional "energy" available for family participation. She has further proposed that the intervening link between degree of job gratification and family adjustment is the psychological mood state that results from what one does at work on a daily basis.

Although limited, research on husbands' job satisfaction and their marital adjustment (Ridley, 1973; Kemper and Reichler, 1976) and on mothers' work satisfaction and mother-child relationships (Piotrkowski and Katz, forthcoming; Hoffman, 1963; Yarrow et al., 1962; Harrell and Ridley, 1975) supports the hypothesis that level of gratification carries over into the family from the work place. Data concerning the relationship between wives' job satisfaction and marital adjustment are less consistent (see Locksley, 1980; Ridley, 1973; Staines et al., 1978). The possible influence of job gratification on women's family adjustment remains an important research question.

Amount of time spent at work also has been hypothesized as a possible constraint on adequate family role performance for both men (see Aldous, 1969; Young and Willmott, 1973) and women (see Sweet, 1973). However, this hypothesis generally was not supported by a study of husbands' work time (Clark et al., 1978). Although men's work time may be less important for family relations than previously assumed, family adjustment may be particularly sensitive to women's work time because of their central affective and household roles. Professional and nonprofessional women alike complain of insufficient time with family members (see Rapoport and Rapoport, 1971; Burke and Weir, 1976; National Commission on Working Women, 1979; Heckman et al., 1977; Walshok, 1979). Since full-time employed women differ in the number of hours they are employed, work time was included in our analysis as a possible predictor of women's family adjustment.

The effects of occupational rewards on family life have received a great deal of attention in the literature on men's occupational and family lives. Although recent empirical evidence casts doubt on the continuing importance of husbands' occupational rewards (such as income or prestige) on marriage (Glenn and Weaver, 1978; Jorgensen, 1979), until recently it has been agreed that men's occupational rewards result in increased marital solidarity and happiness (Scanzoni, 1970). On the other hand, instead of enhancing the marital relationship, women's occupational achievements have been viewed as threatening it. As Richardson (1979) has noted, Parsonian functionalist theory predicts that occupational status competition between husbands and wives poses a threat to affectional relations in the marriage. Richardson however found no empirical support for the hypothesis that wives' superior occupational prestige was associated with decreased marital happiness. Safilios-Rothschild (1976) has suggested that a wife's higher occupational status can be tolerated as long as her income is lower than her husband's in those societies where income is the dominant status line. Including measures of women's occupational rewards allowed us to evaluate their relevance for our sample.

There is a small body of literature suggesting that the relationships between occupational factors and family adjustment differ by occupational class. Conflicts between time spent at work and job gratification, on the one hand, and family participation, on the other, have been assumed to be most intense for men in managerial and professional occupations (Rapoport and Rapoport, 1965; Young and Willmott, 1973). In contrast, it has been assumed that lack of job gratification and job involvement for men in working-class occupations leads to a "natural" segmentation of work and family life (see Blood and Wolfe, 1960; Kanter, 1977), to compensatory family involvement (Dubin, 1956), or to the expenditure of unutilized work energy within the family realm (Young and Willmott, 1973). Alternatively, Ridley (1973) and Piotrkowski (1979) have hypothesized that psychologically rewarding jobs enhance family participation and adjustment. Although these propositions have been advanced for men, they may be applied to employed women as well. The existence of such class-conditional relations also was investigated in this study.

METHODS OF STUDY

Participants for this study were drawn from a sample of employed white women from 25 through 40 years of age who participated in a larger study of relative deprivation and working women (Crosby, forthcoming). Respondents for this larger study were obtained through stratified random sampling procedures from the street lists of Newton, Massachusetts. On the basis of occupation, each potential respondent was assigned an NORC status ranking (Davis, 1974). Participants with NORC ratings of 40.0 or below were assigned to the low-status group. Participants with NORC ratings of 61.0 and above were assigned to the high-status group. Included in the study reported here were the 40 low-status and 59 high-status employed married women in dual-earner families who worked 35 hours per week or more. The final volunteer rate of over 84% for the study of relative deprivation increases our confidence that the results of the study are not biased due to sampling procedures.[2]

Research participants were interviewed in their homes for approximately one hour. Interview items tapping conceptually relevant work and family variables were used to create the measures for this study. Occupational rewards were measured by the respondent's NORC *status* ranking (high or low) and by reported *salary*.[3] To provide an indicator of amount of *time* spent at work, respondents also were asked approximately how many hours per week they worked. Multi-item self-report scales measuring satisfaction with various aspects of work life and psychological mood state at work also were created. Scales with a Cronbach's alpha coefficient of .65 or above[4] were factor analyzed to reduce the number of predictor variables. The data reduction procedures resulted in six relevant predictor variables: two self-report measures of job satisfaction (Intrinsic Job Gratification and Job Security), a measure of job-related mood (Positive Job Mood), measures of occupational reward (Status and Salary), and a measure of work time (Time).[5] Cronbach's alpha coefficients for the measures of job satisfaction and job-related mood ranged from .79 to .80.

Three indicators of women's family adjustment were utilized. A scale measuring Marital Satisfaction was composed of eight items asking about satisfaction with relations with spouse and with marriage in general. A second indicator of family adjustment, measuring satisfaction with Family Relations, was composed of two items tapping feelings about family life in general.[6] Finally, a Positive Home Mood score was computed as a measure of mood at home. This measure was included on the assumption that moods experienced at home are, in part, one indicator of the quality of one's relationships with other family members.[7] The procedure used in creating this scale was parallel to that used in creating the Positive Job Mood scale.[8] Alpha coefficients for these three scales ranged from .65 for Family Relations to .88 for Marital Satisfaction.

SAMPLE CHARACTERISTICS

Sample characteristics are presented in Table 1. As the data indicate, the sample was composed of young, highly educated, employed women. As expected, the high-status women were significantly more educated and earned significantly more money than the low-status women. High-status women also tended to be older and to work significantly more hours per

TABLE 1
Demographic Characteristics

		Total Sample (N = 99)	High Status Women (N = 59)	Low Status Women (N = 40)	Group Diffs.
Age (years)	M	32.3	33.3	30.8	p ≤ .004
	SD	4.1	3.6	4.4	
At Present Job	M	47.6	45.5	50.7	ns
(months)	SD	42.4	41.9	43.4	
Hours Worked	M	44.3	47.4	39.7	p ≤ .001
(time)	SD	11.4	13.4	4.7	
Number of Children for those with	M	1.8	1.6 (N = 29)	2.0 (N = 20)	ns
children (N = 49)	SD	1.0	1.0	.9	
Average Age of	M	7.7 (N = 46)	6.7 (N = 27)	9.2 (N = 19)	ns
Children	SD	4.8	4.5	5.0	
Education					p ≤ .001
High School or less	(N)	13 (13.1%)	0 (0 %)	13 (32.5%)	
Some College	(N)	10 (10.1%)	1 (1.7%)	9 (22.5%)	
College Degree	(N)	22 (22.2%)	7 (11.9%)	15 (37.5%)	
Graduate	(N)	54 (54.5%)	51 (86.4%)	3 (7.5%)	
Salary					p ≤ .001
$15,000 or less	(N)	52 (52.5%)	19 (32.2%)	33 (82.5%)	
$16,000 to $30,000	(N)	35 (35.4%)	29 (49.2%)	6 (15.0%)	
$31,000 or above	(N)	12 (12.1%)	11 (18.6%)	1 (2.5%)	
Household Income					p ≤ .001
$15,000 or less	(N)	3 (3.1%)	0 (0 %)	3 (7.5%)	
$16,000 to $30,000	(N)	28 (29.2%)	8 (14.3%)	20 (50 %)	
$31,000 or above	(N)	65 (67.7%)	48 (85.7%)	17 (42.5%)	

NOTE: The Ns may differ slightly because of missing data.

week. These sample characteristics must be taken into account when interpreting results.

DATA ANALYSES PROCEDURES

Status was used as a rough indicator of occupational class, and the data were analyzed separately for each status subgroup to determine whether relationships between women's occupational lives and family adjustment differed by class. Three simultaneous regression analyses were performed for each status subgroup to determine the relation of the five remaining predictor work variables to the dependent measures. In addition, the presence or absence of children under the age of 18 living at home was included as a control variable, as this variable has been associated with marital satisfaction (Nock, 1979). The limited age range in the sample provided some control for length of marriage. Within-group analyses resulted in controlling educational level, as educational level was highly correlated with Status (r = .75; p ≤ .001). Other possible control variables were not included because of limitations in sample size and potential problems of multicollinearity.[9]

To determine the possible effects of occupational prestige on the dependent variables, the high- and low-status groups were combined and regression analyses performed for each dependent variable. Because Status was moderately correlated with Salary (r = .53; p ≤ .001), a hierarchical regression analysis was performed in which Status was entered at Step 2 after the control variable for presence or absence of children. At Step 3 all remaining work variables were entered simultaneously. Entering Status before other work variables allowed for the most powerful test of the hypothesis that Status is a significant predictor of family adjustment. Finally, cross-product interaction terms between Status and other work variables were entered at Step 4 to determine if significant interactions for class existed (see Cohen and Cohen, 1975). Because Positive Job Mood was hypothesized as intervening between job satisfaction and family adjustment, a simultaneous regression analysis also was performed for each status subgroup to determine the effects of Job Security, Intrinsic Job Gratification, Time, and Salary on Positive Job Mood. Age was entered as a control variable because age has been associated with job satisfaction.

RESULTS AND DISCUSSION

Intercorrelations among the major variables are presented in Table 2. Correlated predictor variables can create problems of multicollinearity in the data analyses, thereby reducing our

TABLE 2
Zero-Order Correlations Among Major Variables

	1	2	3	4	5	6	7	8	9
		Low Status Women (N = 40)							
1.		.47**	-.02	-.08	.10	-.28	-.45**	.13	-.10
2.			.01	.07	.13	-.13	-.19	.02	.03
3.				.47**	.28	.37*	.49**	.65***	.03
4.					.35*	.04	.18	.28	.07
5.						.01	.11	.19	.16
6.							.61***	.29	.08
7.								.46**	.09
8.									-.19
		High Status Women (N = 59)							
1.		.08	.10	.15	.17	.04	.06	.11	.08
2.			-.16	-.26*	.18	.16	.07	-.12	-.25
3.				.37**	.11	-.20	-.21	.41***	.18
4.					.14	-.07	.14	.15	.28*
5.						.11	.33**	.21	-.14
6.							.57***	.14	-.30*
7.								.28*	-.26*
8.									.00

*p ≤ .05; **p ≤ .01; ***p ≤ .001
NOTE: 1 = Salary; 2 = Time; 3 = Positive Job Mood; 4 = Intrinsic Job Gratification; 5 = Job Security; 6 = Marital Satisfaction; 7 = Family Relations; 8 = Positive Home Mood; 9 = Presence/Absence of Children (Absence = 1, Presence = 2).

ability to discover significant relationships. Nevertheless, these intercorrelations reflect the real conditions of work life. Piotrkowski (1979) has suggested that mood at work is associated with intrinsic, but not extrinsic, aspects of the job. The zero-order correlations are consistent with this hypothesis. Intrinsic Job Gratification was significantly associated with Positive Job Mood, whereas satisfaction with job security was not. These results lend some support for the validity of the Positive Job Mood scale and suggest that it does not merely tap a tendency to report positive or negative job attitudes. As

TABLE 3
Multiple Regression Analysis Among Low-Status Women (N = 40)

	Beta	Unique Variance	F
Marital Satisfaction			
Presence/Absence of Children	.063	.004	0.17
Positive Job Mood	.463	.163	7.08*
Intrinsic Job Gratification	−.192	.026	1.14
Job Security	−.036	.001	0.05
Time	.008	.000	0.00
Salary	−.275	.057	2.46
Multiple R^2		.243	1.76
Family Relations			
Presence/Absence of Children	.026	.001	0.04
Positive Job Mood	.522	.208	12.30**
Intrinsic Job Gratification	−.127	.011	0.68
Job Security	.046	.002	0.10
Time	.025	.000	0.03
Salary	−.466	.163	9.66**
Multiple R^2		.444	4.40**
Positive Home Mood			
Presence/Absence of Children	−.237	.054	3.54
Positive Job Mood	.666	.336	22.20***
Intrinsic Job Gratification	−.070	.004	0.24
Job Security	.068	.004	0.25
Time	.114	.010	0.65
Salary	−.205	.031	2.07
Multiple R^2		.500	5.50***

*$p \leqslant .05$; **$p \leqslant .01$; ***$p \leqslant .001$
NOTE: Absence of children = 1; presence of children = 2.

expected, the three dependent variables were significantly correlated. Despite the substantial correlations between the Family Relations and Marital Satisfaction scales, they were retained as separate indicators. We assumed that the Family Relations scale tapped more global aspects of family adjustment than Marital Satisfaction.

Results of the major data analyses are presented in Tables 3 and 4. Limited sample size—especially for the low-status

TABLE 4
Multiple Regression Analysis Among High-Status Women (N = 59)

	Beta	Unique Variance	F
Marital Satisfaction			
Presence/Absence of Children	−.265	.060	3.57
Positive Job Mood	−.176	.026	1.56
Intrinsic Job Gratification	.071	.004	0.23
Job Security	.059	.003	0.19
Time	.065	.004	0.21
Salary	.052	.003	0.15
Multiple R^2		.127	1.26
Family Relations			
Presence/Absence of Children	−.248	.053	3.73
Positive Job Mood	−.310	.081	5.75*
Intrinsic Job Gratification	.279	.059	4.17*
Job Security	.293	.076	5.41*
Time	−.021	.000	0.03
Salary	.022	.001	0.03
Multiple R^2		.267	3.16*
Positive Home Mood			
Presence/Absence of Children	−.067	.004	0.26
Positive Job Mood	.392	.130	8.55**
Intrinsic Job Gratification	−.043	.001	0.09
Job Security	.176	.027	1.80
Time	−.118	.012	0.78
Salary	.060	.003	0.22
Multiple R^2		.211	2.31*

*$p \leqslant .05$; **$p \leqslant .01$; ***$p \leqslant .001$
NOTE: Absence of children = 1; presence of children = 2.

women—means results must be interpreted cautiously. The question of whether women's occupational lives are significantly associated with their self-reported family adjustment can be answered with a cautious affirmative for this sample of highly educated women. For each status subgroup, work variables accounted for a significant proportion of the variance in two of the three measures of family adjustment. The data analyses also addressed our second research question of which particular work variables were significant for family adjustment. When compared on the three dependent measures of family adjustment, the high- and low-status groups did not differ significantly. However, when we examined the relationship between specific work variables and women's family adjustment *within* each group, interesting patterns emerged.

For the low-status group (see Table 3), level of Positive Job Mood was positively related to women's reports of Marital Satisfaction, to their reports of satisfaction with Family Relations, and to reported level of Positive Home Mood. These results are consistent with the zero-order correlations reported in Table 1. In the case of Marital Satisfaction, the overall F ratio did not achieve significance and this finding must be interpreted cautiously. Although Intrinsic Job Gratification did not show a direct association with family adjustment, it was a significant predictor of job mood ($F = 7.36$; d.f. = 1,34; $p \leqslant .05$), with the overall F value for this regression analysis almost achieving significance at the .05 level. The fairly substantial correlation between Positive Job Mood and Intrinsic Job Gratification may have obscured any direct association between job gratification and the family variables.

These findings are consistent with the hypothesis that for women in low-status occupations, satisfaction with intrinsic aspects of work influences their family adjustment through job-related mood (Piotrkowski, 1979). Nevertheless, we cannot rule out the hypothesis that influences flow from home to work, an alternative that must be considered in future research. No support was found for the hypotheses that low-status women compensate for lack of gratification at work with increased satisfaction with their family roles or that, for them, work and family are entirely segmented.

For the low-status group, a significant *negative* relationship emerged between Salary and reported satisfaction with Family Relations, a result consistent with their zero-order correlation. This finding lends some support to Safilios-Rothschild's (1976) hypothesis that a woman's income may be especially salient for family adjustment. In contrast, no significant association between Salary and Family Relations emerged for the high-status group (see Table 4). This interaction between Status and Salary achieved significance ($F = 6.34$; d.f. = 1,91; $p \leqslant .05$). The difference between the groups may be attributable to the differing meanings that women's salaries have for the families of high- and low-status women. In the families of high-status women, 85.7% of families earned \$31,000 or more annually (see Table 1). In the low-status group the majority of families earned \$30,000 or less per year. It may be that in lower-income families, wives' increased economic success threatens their husbands' perceptions of themselves as adequate breadwinners. In an affluent family a woman's income may pose no such threat to her husband. A limitation of this interpretation is that, theoretically, a wife's income should pose a threat to the marital relationship. Yet women's incomes were not significantly related to our measure of marital adjustment. Possibly, women's increased incomes in less affluent families may enable them to report general—if not marital—dissatisfaction more freely. The relationship of women's salaries to their family adjustment requires further exploration.

In the high-status group a somewhat different pattern of significant associations emerged (see Table 4). Women's reported marital satisfaction appeared immune to work influences. However, work variables were significantly related to the other two measures of family adjustment. As with the low-status group, Positive Job Mood was positively associated with reported positive mood at home. Satisfaction with Job Security and Intrinsic Job Gratification each were predictors of high-status women's reported satisfaction with family relations. As in the case of the low-status group, Intrinsic Job Gratification also was positively associated with Positive Job Mood ($F = 4.96$; d.f. = 1,53, $p \leqslant .05$), with the overall F value just missing significance at the .05 level. Again, this finding suggests the indirect influence of job satisfaction on family adjustment.

This pattern of results for the high-status group is consistent with the hypothesis that job satisfaction with both intrinsic and extrinsic features of work life influences women's family adjustment. However, an additional finding not consistent with this interpretation emerged as well: For the high-status women, Positive Job Mood was *negatively* associated with satisfaction with family relations. Alone, this finding would suggest a conflict between work enjoyment and family adjustment in this group. The overall pattern of findings suggests alternative interpretations. For the professional or managerial woman, job satisfaction may contribute to her global family adjustment. However, in comparison with a particularly exciting day at work, the family realm may appear mundane and relatively unsatisfying. Her pleasure with her work day also may lead to continued emotional and intellectual involvement with the occupational tasks of the day, causing conflict with the necessity of doing chores, attending to squabbling children and the like. Job involvement and job satisfaction are conceptually distinct, though they may be correlated (Rabinowitz and Hall, 1977). In the high-status group, the measure of job mood may be tapping job involvement as well as intrinsic job gratification. Job involvement may detract from family relations, while job satisfaction may enhance them. Daily work-family conflict due to extreme job involvement may coexist with a carryover of job satisfaction into the family realm, thereby reconciling the apparently contradictory propositions advanced for the relationship between work and family relations among professional and managerial groups.

The interaction between Positive Job Mood and Status achieved significance for women's reported satisfaction with their family relations ($F = 8.36$; d.f. = 1,91; $p \leqslant .01$). For the group of high-status women, Positive Job Mood was negatively related to Family Relations; for the low-status women the association was positive. For a woman in a low-prestige job that may not be intrinsically interesting, feelings of pleasure at work may not imply continuing involvement with the work tasks of the day. Rather, for her the pleasurable feelings at work may contribute to positive family involvement.

Other apparent differences between the two groups also deserve comment. Job Security emerged as a significant predictor of Family Relations for the high-status, but not the low-status women. The women in low-prestige occupations felt more satisfied with their job security than the high-status women (t = 1.77; d.f. = 97; p ⩽ .08), a difference that approached significance. The low-status women were well educated and may have felt secure in the knowledge that they could remain in their jobs or find other, similar ones. Since they were relatively satisfied, their job security may not have been salient for their family lives. On the other hand, the young, high-status women of the sample were employed in jobs with career ladders, so that job security was associated with satisfaction with opportunities for job advancement (r = .55; p ⩽ .001). Thus, for them, concerns about job security may have been particularly salient. This difference between the groups must be interpreted cautiously, as no significant class interaction effect for Job Security and Family Relations emerged in the overall analysis. Sample size limitations also may have attenuated possible associations in the low-status group. Similarly, the apparent difference between groups for Intrinsic Job Gratification as a predictor of Family Relations was not reflected in the test for interaction effects. Further research on larger samples is needed to determine whether or not these apparent group differences are reliable.

Although they must be interpreted cautiously, the nonsignificant findings are as noteworthy as the significant ones. Occupational Status did not emerge as a significant predictor of family adjustment in the regression analysis (see also Richardson, 1979). Time at work also was not directly associated with women's reported family adjustment (see also Clark et al., 1978). There are several possible explanations for this latter finding. Despite women's reports that they find the combination of work and family roles burdensome, they also are socialized to place their family needs before their own. Consequently, when time is scarce, their own personal needs may go unmet. Amount of time spent working also may be too gross an indicator of how work time influences family adjustment. Time itself is a complex variable and includes dimensions such as timing of work hours, synchronization of work and family life-cycle tasks, and so on (Aldous, 1969). Working an eight-hour evening shift may have significantly different effects on family adjustment than eight hours of work during the day (see Mott et al., 1965). Moreover, the influence of time on family adjustment may be indirect. The significant zero-order correlation between time spent at work and Intrinsic Job Gratification in the high-status group (see Table 2) suggests that work time may influence women's family adjustment indirectly, through its effect on their job satisfaction. Future research efforts need to be directed at examining the complexities of time as they may influence family adjustment.

The lack of reliable significant relationships between work variables and women's reports of their marital satisfaction is noteworthy in light of the emphasis on marital adjustment in the literature on dual-earner families. There are several possible explanations of this finding. Our indicator of marital adjustment may have been inadequately measuring those aspects of the marital relationship that are sensitive to women's jobs. We also tested the possibility that role salience moderated the relationship between job satisfaction and marital adjustment (see Ridley, 1973). Examining respondents' scores on two items measuring commitment to the work role, we found that over 85% of the sample reported that they definitely or probably would continue working, even if there were no financial need to do so. Thus, the lack of strong significant relations between work satisfaction and marital adjustment did not appear to be due to the unimportance to these women of their employment role. In her sample of employed married Finnish women, Haavio-Mannila (1971) also found that women's work satisfaction was significantly related to satisfaction with family life in general but not with satisfaction with the spousal relationship. Some research evidence suggests that marital satisfaction is more sensitive to husbands' than to wives' job satisfaction and that both husbands' and wives' work roles must be considered (Bailyn, 1970; Ridley, 1973). Together with the results reported here, these studies suggest that the marital relationship is especially sensitive to husbands' jobs, while family relations in general and relations with children are sensitive to wives' jobs. Future research needs to consider the differential sensitivity of familial subsystems to husbands' and wives' employment roles.

CONCLUSION

The results of this study suggest that women's jobs are significantly associated with their reported family adjustment in dual-earner families. Despite the lack of significant differences in family adjustment in the groups of high- and low-status women sampled, the data analyses revealed significant work-family relationships within groups. Indicators of job satisfaction and job-related mood emerged as particularly important predictors of reported family adjustment. Although possible areas of work-family conflict were identified in both groups, the results generally support the hypothesis that women's experiences of their jobs "spill over" into the family realm. Such spillover was not uniform, for women's marital adjustment appeared to be relatively immune to the work variables considered. Little support was found for the hypothesis of compensatory relations between work and family for the low-status women studied.

Not all work variables were measured in this study, and it is possible that future research including measures of additional job characteristics and experiences will modify the pattern of findings. It should be noted, too, that the data are consistent with influences that flow from the family to the work place. Social desirability factors and common method variance also may have inflated the associations between job and family adjustment measures. Ideally, data about family relations should be gathered from other family members (see Piotrkowski and Katz, forthcoming). Further research is needed to determine the reliability and generality of the results reported here, the association of job characteristics not included in this study with women's family adjustment, and the causal direction of obtained relationships.

Although we lacked specific data on the family adjustment of the husbands of the women studied, the findings are suggestive for further research in this area. The overriding concern with the effects of wives' employment on the marital relationship may obscure other aspects of husbands' and wives' family adjustment that may be more sensitive to women's jobs. Together with other research our finding suggests that women's moods at home and their satisfaction with family relations are associated with their job experiences, and that husbands' moods and general family adjustment are associated indirectly with their wives' jobs. The minimal relationship between job variables and marital adjustment in our sample of work-committed women suggests that husbands' marital adjustment may be relatively independent of their wives' work experiences. Instead, we would hypothesize that husbands' marital adjustment is associated with their own job satisfaction, which indirectly influences their wives.

Whereas the link between wives' subjective work experiences and husbands' family adjustment may be indirect, objective work variables may be directly linked to husbands' adjustment. For example, one interpretation of the negative association between salary level and general family satisfaction in the sample of low-status women is that salary has an indirect impact on wives through its direct effect on their husbands. Thus, the nature of family roles may mediate the relationships between work roles and family adjustment (see Mortimer, 1980). In order to develop an adequate theory of work-family relations in dual-earner families, systematic research into such direct and indirect pathways of influence is needed. The results of this study demonstrate the utility of within-group analyses to investigate the complex processes linking the specific features of wives' occupational roles to family adjustment in dual-earner families.

NOTES

1. The term dual-earner is used instead of dual-worker because this latter term obscures the unpaid housework performed primarily by women.

2. See Faye J. Crosby, *Relative Deprivation and Working Women* (1982) for a complete description of the sample, questionnaire, and results.

3. Respondents were asked, "Approximately how much do you earn yearly?" The twelve available response categories ranged from "nothing" to "over $50,000." These categories were treated as interval data for purposes of analysis.

4. Alpha coefficients were computed from data on all employed married men and women in the larger study (N = 224).

5. The Intrinsic Job Gratification scale was composed of six scaled items such as, "Taking everything into account, how satisfied would say you are with your present job?" Responses ranged on a five-point scale from "very satisfied" to "very dissatisfied." The Job Security scale was composed of four scaled items with questions such as, "Within this last year, how often have you felt some sense of grievance concerning job security?" Responses ranged on a five-point scale from "always" to "never." The Positive Job Mood scale was derived from eleven summed items selected from the Roseman Mood List (see Crosby, forthcoming). Participants responded to the question, "Think for a second about the last two days at work (yesterday and today). Which of the following emotions did you feel at any time during the last two days while at work?" by endorsing any of 38 adjectives describing mood states (such as happy, sad, proud). A comparable negative job mood score was used as a predictor of Positive Job Mood and a residual score for each respondent obtained, in order to control for a possible generalized tendency to report feelings. The residual score was used in the analysis.

6. The Marital Satisfaction scale included items such as, "Everything considered, how happy has your marriage been for you?" Responses ranges on a six-point scale from "nearly perfect" to "extremely unhappy." One item on the Family Relations scale asked, "Now, taking everything into account how would you say you feel about your family life?" Responses ranged on a five-point scale from "very satisfied" to "very dissatisfied."

7. We assume that moods experienced at home are determined by multiple factors, including job experiences and family structure. The effects of work on moods experienced at home may be both direct and indirect, through the influence of jobs on family relationships.

8. See Note 5 above.

9. Age was highly correlated with the presence or absence of children ($r = .61$; $p \leqslant .001$ and $r = .50$; $p \leqslant .001$; low- and high-status groups, respectively), and household income with salary ($r = .52$; $p \leqslant .001$ and $r = .64$; $p \leqslant .001$; low- and high-status groups, respectively), and household income with salary ($r = .52$; $p \leqslant .001$ and $r = .64$; $p \leqslant .001$; low-and high-status groups, respectively).

REFERENCES

Aldous, J.
 1969 "Occupational characteristics and males' role performance in the family."
  J. of Marriage and the Family 31 (November): 707-712.

Bailyn, L.
    1970   "Career and family orientations of husbands and wives in relation to marital happiness." Human Relations 23 (April): 97-113.
Blood, R. O., Jr. and D. M. Wolfe
    1960   Husbands and Wives. New York: Macmillan.
Booth, A.
    1979   "Does wives' employment cause stress for husbands?" Family Coordinator 28 (October): 445-449.
Burke, R. J. and T. Weir
    1976   "Relationship of wives' employment status to husband, wife and pair satisfaction and performance." J. of Marriage and the Family 38 (May): 279-287.
Clark, R. A., F. I. Nye, and V. Gecas
    1978   "Work involvement and marital role performance." J. of Marriage and the Family 40 (February): 9-22.
Cohen, J. and P. Cohen
    1975   Applied Multiple Regression/Correlation Analysis for the Behavioral Sciences. Hillsdale, NJ: Erlbaum.
Crosby, F. J.
    1982   Relative Deprivation and Working Women. New York: Oxford Univ. Press.
Davis, J. A.
    1974   Codebook for the Spring 1974 General Social Survey. Chicago: University of Chicago.
Dubin, R.
    1956   "Industrial workers' worlds." Social Problems 3 (January): 131-142.
Glenn, N. D. and C. N. Weaver
    1978   "A multivariate, multisurvey study of marital happiness." J. of Marriage and the Family 40 (May): 269-282.
Gover, D. O.
    1963   "Socio-economic differential in the relationship between marital adjustment and wife's employment status." Marriage and Family Living 25 (November): 452-457.
Haavio-Mannila, E.
    1971   "Satisfaction with family, work, leisure, and life among men and women." Human Relations 24: 585-601.
Harrell, J. and C. Ridley
    1975   "Substitute child care, maternal employment and the quality of mother-child interaction." J. of Marriage and the Family 37 (August): 556-564.
Heckman, N., R. Bryson, and R. Bryson
    1977   "Problems of professional couples: a content analysis." J. of Marriage and the Family 39 (May): 323-330.
Hoffman, L. W.
    1963   "Mother's enjoyment of work and effects on the child," pp. 95-105 in F. I. Nye and L. W. Hoffman (eds.) The Employed Mother in America. Chicago: Rand McNally.
Holmstrom, L.
    1972   The Two-Career Family. Cambridge, MA: Schenkman.
Jorgensen, S.
    1979   "Socioeconomic rewards and perceived marital quality. A re-examination." J. of Marriage and the Family 41 (November): 825-835.

Kanter, R. M.
    1977   Work and Family in the United States: A Critical Review and Agenda for
            Research and Policy. New York: Russell Sage.
Kemper, T. D. and M. L. Reichler
    1976   "Work integration, marital satisfaction, and conjugal power." Human
            Relations 29 (October): 929-944.
Locksley, A.
    1980   "On the effects of wives' employment on marital adjustment and com-
            panionship." J. of Marriage and the Family 42 (May): 337-346.
Marks, S. R.
    1977   "Multiple roles and role strain: some notes on human energy, time and
            commitment." Amer. Soc. Rev. 42 (December): 921-936.
Mortimer, J. T.
    1980   "Occupation-family linkages as perceived by men in the early stages of
            professional and managerial careers." Research in the Interweave of Social
            Roles: Women and Men 1: 99-117.
Mott, P. E., F. C. Mann, Q. McLoughlin, and D. P. Warwick
    1965   Shift Work: The Social, Psychological and Physical Consequences. Ann
            Arbor: Univ. of Michigan Press.
National Commission on Working Women
    1979   National Survey of Working Women: Perceptions, Problems and Pro-
            spects. Washington, DC: National Manpower Institute.
Nock, S. L.
    1979   "The family life cycle: empirical or conceptual tool?" J. of Marriage and
            the Family 41 (February): 15-26.
Nye F. I.
    1974   "Husband-wife relationship," pp. 186-206 in L. Hoffman and F. Nye (eds.)
            Working Mothers. San Francisco: Jossey-Bass.
    1963   "Marital interaction," pp. 263-281 in F. I. Nye and L. W. Hoffman (eds.)
            The Employed Mother in America. Chicago: Rand McNally.
Orden, S. R. and N. M. Bradburn
    1969   "Working wives and marriage happiness." Amer. J. of Sociology 74
            (January): 391-407.
Piotrkowski, C. S.
    1979   Work and the Family System. New York: Macmillan.
Piotrkowski, C. S. and M. H. Katz
    forthcoming   "Work experience and family relations among working-class and
            lower middle-class families," in H. Z. Lopata and J. H. Pleck (eds.) Re-
            search in the Interweave of Social Roles, Volume 3. Families and Jobs.
            Greenwich, CT: JAI.
Rabinowitz, S. and D. T. Hall
    1977   "Organizational research on job involvement." Psych. Bull. 84: 265-288.
Rapoport, R. and R. Rapoport
    1971   Dual-Career Families. New York: Viking.
    1965   "Work and family in contemporary society." Amer. Soc. Rev. 30 (June):
            381-394.
Richardson, J. G.
    1979   "Wife occupational superiority and marital troubles. An examination of
            the hypothesis." J. of Marriage and the Family 41 (February): 63-72.

Ridley, C. A.
1973 "Exploring the impact of work satisfaction and involvement on marital interaction when both partners are employed." J. of Marriage and the Family 35 (May): 229-237.
Safilios-Rothschild, C.
1976 "Dual linkages between the occupational and family systems: a macro-sociological analysis." Signs 1, 3 (part 2): 51-60.
1970 "The influence of the wife's degree of work commitment upon some aspects of family organization and dynamics." J. of Marriage and the Family 32 (November): 681-691.
Scanzoni, J.
1970 Opportunity and the Family. New York: Macmillan.
Staines, G. L., J. H. Pleck, L. J. Shephard, and P. O'Connor
1978 "Wives' employment status and marital adjustment." Psychology of Women Q. 3 (Fall): 90-120.
Sweet, J.
1973 Women in the Labor Force. New York: Seminar.
Walshok, M. L.
1979 "Occupational values and family roles: women in blue-collar and service occupations," pp. 63-83 in K. W. Feinstein (ed.) Working Women and Families. Vol. 4. Beverly Hills, CA: Sage.
Wright, J. D.
1978 "Are working women really more satisfied? Evidence from several national surveys." J. of Marriage and the Family 40 (May): 301-314.
Yarrow, M. R., P. Scott, L. deLeeuw, and C. Heinig
1962 "Child-rearing in families of working and non-working mothers." Sociometry 25 (June): 122-140.
Young, M. and P. Willmott
1973 The Symmetrical Family. New York: Random House.

7

Marital Effects on Occupational Attainment*

BAM DEV SHARDA
BARRY E. NANGLE

A neglected area in the growing literature on men's and women's status attainment is that of the interaction effects which occur in the context of marriage. It is not surprising that marital effects have been little examined, given that stratification research has only recently progressed beyond an exclusive focus on the status attainment of men. Most research concerned with female status, however, has followed the work of DeJong et al. (1971) in an attempt to determine if the status attainment process differs for men and women. Earlier work failed to reveal substantial differences in stratification or mobility by sex, but later, more detailed analyses have led to the discovery that background factors and achievements affect the socioeconomic attainments of women and men in somewhat different ways (see Rosenfeld, 1978; Hauser et al., 1974; Featherman and Hauser, 1976; Treiman and Terrel, 1975). In all of these studies, however, the overriding concern has been with applying the model of men's intergenerational mobility (Blau and Duncan, 1967) to the careers of women. When *effects* of marriage are considered at all, they are typically

*We are thankful to A. O. Haller and Joseph Conaty for their critical comments on an earlier draft of this article. We also are grateful to A. O. Haller and David L. Featherman for allowing us the use of the data employed in this article.

considered in the context of "marital mobility" (Tyree and Treas, 1974; Taylor and Glenn, 1976), in which women's adoption of the status of their husbands is investigated.

There have been some notable exceptions to the above pattern, though even in studies of individual attainment within marriage the interaction of husbands' and wives' behaviors in labor markets has been little addressed. A number of researchers have brought us closer to a focus on the family in suggesting that both husbands' and wives' socioeconomic attainments should somehow be counted in arriving at household social standing (see Sampson and Rossi, 1975; Ritter and Hargens, 1975). Recently Benham (1974) and Oppenheimer (1977) have attempted to measure the impact of wives' educational and income attainments on family status. These and other findings, though not quite adequate, have heavily informed the formulation of our research problem. The object of our article is not to research the individuals' contributions to family status, which was the focus of these researchers. We wish, however, to further understand the status attainment process of both husbands and wives by asking how the outcome of the process for one partner in a marriage is shaped by the market behavior of the other partner.

MARRIAGE AND MOBILITY

Marriage, though generally regarded by social scientists as an important life-cycle event, has not always been considered an overly important one in the study of status attainment. Typically, the stages regarded relevant to status attainment are the formative years spent in the family of origin, years of formal schooling, first occupation, and current occupation (Blau and Duncan, 1967: Chapter 5). Yet, given that socioeconomic standing is attributed to families as much as it is to individuals, and given that at least income, if not the occupational status itself, is a product of both husbands' and wives' occupations, it seems approporiate to direct our attention to events and relations in marriage which may affect the occupational attainment process. In fact, existing work suggests several approaches one might take in framing the problem of marital effects on individual status attainment.

One approach, exemplified by Benham (1974), is to view certain attainments of both husbands and wives as increments to human capital which accumulates in the household. For example, educational attainments of a wife are seen not only to directly increase her own occupational potential, but also to add to the occupational gains for her husband, such that "the effective stock of human capital for each marriage partner is a positive function of the individual stock of human capital in the household" (Benham, 1974: S58). The implication is that by sharing knowledge, offering incentives to one another and so on, spouses increase the productivity of each other by enlarging their own capital stock. Benham's evidence, however, is not convincing. His demonstration of the effect of wife's education in a regression model of husband's earnings fails to rule out a selective mating interpretation (for example, see Welch, 1974). Nevertheless, Benham was able to show that the association between wife's education and husband's earnings is highly variable at different marriage durations, suggesting that attainment covariance has some component which is not fixed by selective mating.

Another, and somewhat contradictory, approach to the interaction of spouses' attainments is found in Oppenheimer (1977). Oppenheimer's work directly confronts the issue of whether there is a causal connection between the socioeconomic contribution of the wife and her husband's socioeconomic characteristics. She argues that a wife will tend to participate in the labor force *only* if her working enhances the status of that family. In turn, the wife's labor force participation can be substituted for the husband's mobility or, alternately, compensate for his realtively low wages. Her analysis of data for the 1970 Public Use Samples suggests that: (1) within seven broad occupational categories, husbands' earnings are inversely related to both wives' labor force participation and wives' earnings; and (2) working wives are quite consistently found in the same occupational categories as their husbands.

OCCUPATIONAL ATTAINMENT
DURING MARRIAGE: A MODEL

All of this suggests that processes of spouses' occupational attainment are related to one another, but in a complex way. In order to separate clearly "own" and "spouse" effects on individual status, we propose and test a model of the status attainment process for husbands and wives which focuses on phases of the marital stage of their respective life cycles.[1] In essence, our model (Figure 1) incorporates models for both spouses in which current status of each is predicted to be a function of: (1) origin status of marriage; (2) educational attainments within marriage; (3) decisions regarding the timing of children; and (4) occupational and educational attainments of spouse. We expect that education for both spouses will play a significant role in their occupational attainments. Education attained by either spouse after marriage, however, is likely to have an additional effect on the couple's current occupational attainments net of the effect of their educational attainments at the time of marriage. Further, it is our hypothesis that postmarital educational gains will be more significant for wives' status attainments, since postmarital education for wives should signify a more or less conscious decision by couples that both spouses will contribute occupationally to family status (Oppenheimer, 1977).

Postmarital education and occupational attainments of wives may be a drag or a substitute for such attainments on the part of husbands (Benham, 1974), but these effects may be mitigated somewhat by an expected strain toward consistency (Oppenheimer, 1977). For this reason, a wife's postmarital attainments should be positively related to those of her husband. In this article we examine the processes of "consistency maintenance and trading-off attainments" among the

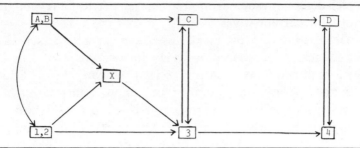

Figure 1: Postmarriage Interaction Model of Status Attainment for Working Couples

A = Educational attainment of husbands at marriage.
B = Occupational attainment of husbands at marriage.
C = Postmarriage educational gain of husbands.
D = Current occupational attainment of husbands.
X = Family planning.
1 = Educational attainment of wives at marriage.
2 = Occupational attainment of wives at marriage.
3 = Postmarriage educational gains of wives.
4 = Current occupational attainment of wives.

working couples. We have also included in our model the fertility behavior of the working wives.

Deferring childbirth, for example, is taken to be an indication of a desire for mobility, probably for both spouses, but especially for the wife. Family planning, should, therefore, predict a wife's education after marriage. Since education in American society is the major vehicle through which occupational status is achieved, postmarital educational gains should also affect current occupational attainment for females (as well as for males).

DATA

The models are estimated using data from a longitudinal study of 341 Michigan men surveyed in 1957 and again in 1972 (for a detailed description of data collection methods and sample, see Otto and Featherman, 1975). In the current analysis we have included items from the follow-up survey, which dealt with socioeconomic characteristics of respondents and their current wives.

Occupational status in all cases is measured by scores on the Duncan Socioeconomic Index for occupations, coded by the 2-digit census occupation codes (Duncan, 1961).[2] Education is measured by number of school years completed, including vocational training, and is apportioned into that completed before and after current marriage. Family planning is simply the interval before the birth of the first child, that is, the year of the birth of the first child minus the year of marriage.

FINDINGS

Zero-order correlations for variables in the model are presented in Table 1. Education at marriage for both spouses is strongly related to both initial and current occupations, though in both cases the relationship is somewhat stronger for men than for women. The correlation of spouses' educational attainments at marriage of .565 suggests high selective mating. Current occupation of wife loses all association with husband's initial occupation, though some zero-order consistency (.171) remains in spouses' current status. Family planning is only weakly related to any of the origin or destination variables.

Postmarital educational gain appears a partial reflection of earlier attainments, but is largely determined by factors not in the model. Wife's postmarital educational gain bears a stronger relationship to husband's initial education than does his postmarital educational gain to her education at marriage. This pattern is suggestive of some "catching up" on the part of wives. On the other hand, spouses' postmarital educational gains correlated with current status do not show the pattern we hypothesized. It is among husbands, rather than wives, that the correlation between postmarital educational gains and current occupation is strongest (.359 versus .285).

The model estimated in Table 2 employs seven reduced form equations which, as in path analysis, predict attainments at

TABLE 1
Coefficients of Correlation Among Variables of Postmarriage Interaction Model

Variables	(1)	(2)	(3)	(4)	(5)	(6)	(7)	(8)
(1) Husband's Education at Marriage								
(2) Husband's Occupation at Marriage	.6461							
(3) Wife's Education at Marriage	.5653	.3825						
(4) Wife's Occupation at Marriage	.4024	.2540	.5570					
(5) Childbirth Interval	.1776	.1797	.1734	.0851				
(6) Husband's Post Marriage Education	.2117	.0261	.1559	.0891	.0973			
(7) Wife's Post Marriage Education	.2408	.1211	.2374	.1316	.2121	.1514		
(8) Husband's Current Occupation	.6440	.6213	.3706	.1456	.0659	.3590	.1751	
(9) Wife's Current Occupation	.2351	.0870	.4901	.5339	.1563	.1022	.2852	.1706

various stages of marriage from own and spouses' attainments at their marriage. In simultaneous equation form:[3]

$$Y_1 = a_1 + b_{11} x_1 + b_{21} x_2 + v_1$$

$$Y_2 = a_1 + b_{12} x_1 + b_{22} x_2 + v_2$$

$$Y_3 = a_3 + b_{13} X_1 + b_{23} x_2 + b_{33} y_1 + b_{43} y_2 + v_3$$

$$Y_4 = a_4 + b_{14} x_1 + b_{24} x_2 + b_{34} y_1 + b_{44} y_2 + b_{54} y_3 + b_{64} y_5 + v_4$$

$$Y_5 = a_5 + b_{15} x_1 + b_{25} x_2 + b_{35} y_1 + b_{45} y_2 + b_{55} y_3 + b_{65} y_4 + v_5$$

$$Y_6 = a_6 + b_{16} x_1 + b_{26} y_2 + b_{36} y_1 + b_{46} y_2 + b_{56} y_3 + b_{66} y_4 + b_{76} y_5 + b_{86} y_7 + v_6$$

$$Y_7 = a_7 + b_{17} x_1 + b_{27} x_2 + b_{37} y_1 + b_{47} y_2 + b_{57} y_3 + b_{67} y_4 + b_{77} y_5 + b_{87} y_6 + v_7$$

where:

X_1 is husband's education at marriage

X_2 is wife's education at marriage

Y_1 is wife's occupation at marriage

Y_2 is husband's occupation at marriage

Y_3 is childbirth interval

Y_4 is wife's postmarital educational gains

Y_5 is husband's postmarital educational gains

Y_6 is wife's current occupation

Y_7 is husband's current occupation

The estimates of these reduced form regressions predicting both the husbands' and wives' postmarital educational gains (Y_5 and Y_4) produce small R^2s (for husbands .0799 and for wives .1032). In the case of husbands, only education at marriage is statistically significant for husbands' postmarital education. No other variable seems to have significant influence. The only other variable that seems to have any sizable negative effect (though not statistically significant) is hus-

TABLE 2
Standardized Regression Coefficients of Postmarriage Interaction Model

Predetermined Variables	Dependent Variable						
	W OCCUP(M)	H OCCUP(M)	CHILD BIRTH INT	W ED(PM)	H ED(PM)	W OCCUP	H OCCUP
H ED(M)	.1339	.6318*	.0619	.1663	.2863*	-.1524	.3655*
W ED(M)	.4705*	.0254	.1180	.1352	.0490	.2916*	.0249
W OCCUP(M)			-.0284	-.0143	-.0201	.4294*	-.2139*
H OCCUP(M)			.1078	-.0661	-.1929	-.1962	.4307*
CHILD BIRTH INT				.1642*	.0563	.0863	-.1113
SPOUSE ED(PM)				.0822	.0849	.0515	-.0014
OWN ED(PM)						.1749	.2825*
SPOUSE OCCUP						.2024	.1381
R^2	.3155	.4182	.0467	.1032	.0797	.4117	.5985

*Unstandardized coefficient is more than twice its standard error.

NOTE: Variables are: H ED(M) = husband's educational attainment at the time of marriage; W ED(M) = wife's educational attainment at the time of marriage; H OCCUP(M) = husband's occupational status at marriage; W OCCUP(M) = wife's occupational status at marriage; CHILD BIRTH INT = childbirth interval; SPOUSE ED(PM) = spouse's educational attainment postmarriage; OWN ED(PM) = own educational attainment postmarriage; SPOUSE OCCUP = current occupational status of spouse; W OCCUP = current occupational status of wife; H OCCUP = current occupational status of husband.

band's own occupation at marriage. Perhaps one could argue that married men who have high-status occupations at marriage are less likely to seek education in postmarital years and that those who have low-status occupations seek decent educational levels. Unlike their husbands, however, wives' postmarital education gains could not be predicted from either wife's or husband's education and occupation at marriage. On the contrary, the only variable that has statistically significant influence on a wife's postmarital educational gain is her family planning efforts. This points out the value of family planning for those women who might like to advance their educations after marriage.

The first stage of our model has, therefore, revealed that while both groups of husbands and wives made some educational gains, husbands' gains follow the familiar paths of career development and social mobility. Wives' only predictable chance for education after marriage, however, is through delaying childbirth.

Disregarding the origin factors (not considered in our model) and concentrating on the marital effects on spouses' occupational achievements as origins in our model, we note that a husband's current occupational status is significantly affected by his own education at marriage, his occupational status at marriage, plus his postmarital educational gains. Wives' education, which Benham (1974) found significantly affected husbands' earnings in his research, does not seem to have affected current occupational status of husbands in our data. The effects of education of wives on husbands' current occupational status is statistically insignificant. Surprisingly enough, however, wives' occupational status at marriage has negatively affected the current occupational status of their husbands (b = -.2139). In sum, therefore, 60% of the variance in the current occupational status of husbands is explained by their own educational achievements, both those which they had at the times of their marriages and the postmarital gains they have made, plus their own occupational status at marriage, *minus* the effects of their wives' occupational status at marriage. This may be interpreted to mean that, other things being equal, a wife's employment in a high-status occupation early in the marriage may be somewhat detrimental to the husband's chances for future occupational mobility.

Though neither husband's occupation nor education at marriage is statistically significant in the equation predicting wife's current occupational gains, they do, however, show negative signs. Previous research has indicated that this might be the case. For example, several occupations traditionally followed by males require the social support of their wives in so formal a way that Papanek (1973) labeled such careers "two-person careers."

Research has indicated that some occupations are so "absorbing" (Kanter, 1977; White, 1952), such as some professional or managerial occupations or those associated with politics, and other occupations so time-consuming—such as those requiring traveling—that work tends to "spill over" to the time that is normally utilized by others for their own family pursuits, especially recreation. This necessitates the occupational role performance at what Weinstock (1963) called the "central" and "peripheral" levels; men typically focus on the "central" roles, leaving most of the "peripheral" roles to be handled by their wives. Since wives have to perform the support functions required of these "peripheral" roles, Papanek's (1973) designation of "two-person career" seems appropriate. One may also add that these "two-person careers" are the consequence of a complex division of labor and the structure of complex work organizations, where an incumbent of a high-status job faces constant competition from well-qualified, better-trained contestants. The incumbent has to remain alert to the possibility of being "weeded out" if he is not aggressively working for his career advancements (Moore, 1962; Tausky and Dubin, 1965; Hall, 1975).[4] Wives, particularly working wives, therefore, have to perform support functions for their husbands at the cost of developing their own careers. We argue that wives in such situations "trade off" their own careers in favor of the careers of their husbands.[5] In fact, such a noncareer-type pattern of wives' employment is exhibited in our own analysis of wives' currrent occupational attainments.

We now turn to the examination of wives' current occupational attainments from the variables of their own educational and occupational attainments at marriage, their spouses' occupational and educational attainments at marriage, their postmarital educational gains, and childbirth intervals. Wives' current occupational attainments are predicted from their own educational achievements and occupational status at marriage. We have reported earlier that family planning is crucial for married women who wish to advance their educations. Family planning, however, does not have any net effects on their current occupational status. Possibly husbands' educational and occupational status at marriage have negative net effects for the reasons discussed above, that is, because wives "trade off" their own status for that of their husbands. It seems plausible that their postmarital educational gains—resulting from their family planning efforts—contribute somewhat to their current occupational status, though the coefficients are not significant. Since *all* the variables in this equation (Y_6), other than wives' occupational and educational attainments at marriage, are statistically insignificant, we cannot rely on whatever small effects we have detected. We conclude, therefore, that wives in our sample follow a "noncareer" pattern of employment—perhaps a compensatory mechanism in developing a "two-person career."

Our findings, therefore, point to rather differential educational and occupational attainment models for working spouses. Husbands continue to advance in their careers by gaining more education after marriage. The postmarital educational gains, however, are a function of their (husbands') own earlier attainments (occupational and educational attainments at marriage). Occupational attainments at marriage tend to put constraints on husbands' occupational mobility patterns. Wives' postmarital educational gains and labor force participation, however, follow *completely* different patterns from those of their husbands. The only variable that explains their postmarital educational gains is that of their own fertility behaviors (via birth control), *but* these small educational gains are not adequately rewarded by the labor market.

DISCUSSION

Earlier studies of the occupational attainment processes of males and females in the United States have found broad similarities (Featherman and Hauser, 1976; Treiman and Terrell, 1975). More recent studies, however, have indicated the relevance of some additional variables for female education and occupational attainment models (Rosenfeld, 1978).

Despite the fact that some women have made postmarital educational gains, the traditional "male mobility model," such as the one utilized here, does not adequately predict these gains. We are left to attribute these gains to random effects of exogenous factors worthy of investigation by future research. Further, that these postmarital educational gains have very little socioeconomic payoff for wives in terms of occupational attainment is rather shocking compared to the significant payoff this variable has for men's own current occupational attainments. This may be the result of significant differences in the career patterns of the men and women of these "two-person career" families. We also suspect that married women are somehow more likely to be allocated to the occupations segregated in the labor market by sex. Several researchers have alluded to distinctions in occupations patterning such career differences by calling them "sex typed" (McLaughlin, 1978a, 1978b). Such occupations typically require much formal education but offer little chance for mobility (Wolfe and Rosenfeld, 1978).

There is yet another explanation. It becomes hard for a married woman to change her job (as it does for a married man) if it requires a physical move. It is well known that wives are more likely to facilitate their husbands' moves for career advancement than they are their own (Duncan and Perruci, 1976). We must, however, add that husbands are not immune from similar forces of "restricted mobility." If employment in "sex typed" occupations and desire to support their husbands causes "restricted careers" for wives, their participation in the active labor force also restricts their husbands' mobility somewhat—especially when the wives are employed in high-status occupations. In examining the husbands' current occupational attainments, for example, we noticed a rather strong and statistically significant negative effect of wives' initial occupational status, net of the positive effects of husbands' own educations (both at marriage and postmarital gains) and their occupations at marriage. This, however, does not conflict with earlier notions that a wife's employment contributes significantly to *family* income and status (Sampson and Rossi, 1975; Ritter and Hargens, 1975; Benham, 1974; Oppenheimer, 1977), which it does. However, our findings indicate that such contributions of wife to family status restrict the chances of occupational mobility of their husbands. Further research is needed to uncover the dynamics of negotiations within the families about employment and mobility. We should, therefore, move away from status attainment models involving individuals and investigate the relationship between family dynamics and the dynamics of the market.

NOTES

1. For a discussion of the life-cycle model of status attainment see Blau and Duncan (1967: Chapter 5), Duncan et al. (1972: Chapter 1), and Sharda (1977: Chapter 1), among others.

2. For a discussion of the appropriateness of Duncan's (1961) SEI scores for comparing the status attainments of men and women, see Treimen and Terrell (1975: 175-176).

3. The equation system assumes simultaneous determination of spouses' attainments during the marital phase of the life cycle. This is reflected by a nonrecursive specification of equations for Y_4 through Y_7. The implication of this specification, of

course, is that the last independent variable in each of the equations will be correlated with the respective variables' error term. This could result in overestimation of the effects of these independent variables (Pindyck and Rubinfeld, 1976: 128).

4. Our discussion of wives' contribution to their husbands' occupational roles is informed by an excellent discussion and summary of the literature by Mortimer et al. (1978: especially pages 291-294).

5. An alternative explanation, however, is that because of sex typing of occupations, working women (wives included) could not be allocated to high-status occupations despite their higher educational gains (McLaughlin, 1978a).

REFERENCES

Benham, L.
    1974   "Benefits of women's education within marriage." J. of Pol. Economy 82: S57-71.
Blau, P. M. and O. D. Duncan
    1967   The American Occupational Structure. New York: John Wiley.
DeJong, P. Y., M. J. Brawer, and S. Robin
    1971   "Paterns of female intergenerational mobility: a comparison with male patterns of intergenerational occupational mobility." Amer. Soc. Rev. 36: 1033-1042.
Duncan, O. D.
    1961   "A socioeconomic index for all occupations," chapter 6 in Albert J. Reiss, Jr. et al. (eds.) Occupations and Social Status. New York: Macmillan.
Duncan, O. D., D. L. Featherman, and B. Duncan
    1972   Socioeconomic Background and Achievement. New York: Seminar.
Duncan, R. P. and C. C. Perucci
    1976   "Dual occupational families and migration." Amer. Soc. Rev. 41: 252-261.
Featherman, D. L. and R. M. Hauser
    1976   "Sexual inequalities and socioeconomic achievement in the U.S., 1962-73." Amer. Soc. Rev. 41: 462-483.
Hall, R.
    1975   Occupations and the Social Structure. Englewood Cliffs, NJ: Prentice-Hall.
Hauser, R. M., D. L. Featherman, and D. P. Hogan
    1974   "Race and sex in the structure of occupational mobility in the United States, 1962." Working paper 74-26, Center for Demography and Ecology, University of Wisconsin, Madison.
Kanter, R. M.
    1977   Work and Family in the United States: A Critical Review and Agenda for Research and Policy. New York: Russell Sage.
McLaughlin, S. D.
    1978a   "Sex differences in the determinants of occupational status." Sociology of Work and Occupations 5 (February): 5-30.
    1978b   "Occupational sex identification and the assessment of male and female earnings inequality." Amer. Soc. Rev. 43 (December): 909-921.

Moore, W. E.
    1962   Conduct of the Corporation. New York: Random House.
Mortimer, J., R. Hall, and R. Hill
    1978   "Husbands' occupational attributes as constraints on wives' employment."
            Sociology of Work and Occupation 5 (August): 285-313.
Oppenheimer, V. K.
    1977   "The sociology of women's economic role in the family." Amer. Soc. Rev.
            42: 387-406.
Otto, L. B. and and D. L. Featherman
    1975   "Social structural and psychological antecedents of self-estrangement and
            powerlessness." Amer. Soc. Rev. 40: 701-719.
Papanek, H.
    1973   "Men, women and work: reflections on the two-person career." Amer. J. of
            Sociology 78 (January): 852-872.
Pindyck, R. and D. Rubinfeld
    1976   Econometric Models and Economics Forecasts. New York: McGraw-Hill.
Ritter, K. V. and L. L. Hargens
    1975   "Occupational positions and class identification of married working wo-
            men: a test of the asymmetry hypothesis." Amer. J. of Sociology 80: 934-
            948.
Rosenfeld, R. A.
    1978   "Women's intergenerational mobility." Amer. Soc. Rev. 43: 36-46.
Sampson, W. A. and P. H. Rossi
    1975   "Race and family social standing." Amer. Soc. Rev. 40: 201-214.
Sharda, B. D.
    1977   Status Attainment in Rural India. New Delhi: Ajanta.
Tausky, D. and R. Dubin
    1965   "Career anchorage: managerial mobility aspirations." Amer. Soc. Rev. 30
            (October): 725-735.
Taylor, P. A. and N. D. Glenn
    1976   "The utility of education and attractiveness for females' status attainment
            through marriage." Amer. Soc. Rev. 41: 484-498.
Treiman, D. J. and K. Terrell
    1975   "Sex and the process of status attainment: a comparison of working women
            and men." Amer. Soc. Rev. 40: 174-200.
Tyree, A. and J. Treas
    1974   "The occupational and marital mobility of women." Amer. Soc. Rev. 39:
            293-302.
Weinstock, S. A.
    1963   "Role elements: a link between acculturation and occupational status."
            British J. of Sociology 64 (June): 144-149.
Welch, F.
    1974   "Comment." J. of Pol. Economy 82: S72-75.
White, R. W.
    1952   Lives in Progress: A Study of the National Growth of Personality. New
            York: Dryden.
Wolfe, W. C. and R. Rosenfeld
    1978   "Sex structure of occupations and job mobility." Social Forces 56: 823-845.

PART III

Within the
Two-Earner Family

This group of articles is concerned with what goes on in families where paychecks come to both her and him. Marital satisfaction has been seen as problematic in such families (Nye, 1974: 186-188). Simpson and England, however, in their comparison of competing theories concerning the relation between wives and husbands being in the paid labor force and marital solidarity, find such couples' role similarity can strengthen the couple relation. Poloma, Pendleton, and Garland, in their longitudinal research, carry on the examination of the marital relation in dual-career couples. The portions of the family cycle when children are present are often periods of career stalemate for women, they find, and among these professional women commitment to the marriage tends to mean less career success. Marital solidarity among this segment of dual earners appears to be associated with husband career priorities rather than dual-career equality.

Model, in her analysis of factors related to husbands participating in household tasks, also finds husbands' jobs given priority. Wives do more around the house despite their jobs outside the home. Only when their earnings approach those of their husbands, so that wives' market productivity is equal to their husbands', does participation in household tasks begin to equalize.

In her examination of parenting roles, Carlson looks at the effects on little boys in those rare families where fathers and mothers share caregiving tasks. Her findings, like those of Simpson and England, do not always support cherished beliefs. Just as two-earner couples can have stronger marriages than one-earner families, so, too, can fathers who are active in child care have sons no less "masculine" than their peers from families with the conventional parental imbalance in family role performances.

REFERENCE

Nye, F. I.
  1975 "Husband-wife relationship," pp. 186-206 in L. W. Hoffman and F. I. Nye (eds.) Working Mothers. San Francisco: Jossey-Bass.

8

Conjugal Work Roles and Marital Solidarity*

IDA HARPER SIMPSON
PAULA ENGLAND

The continuing increase in women's employment outside the home lessens the sex differentiation of conjugal roles. This research explores the effects of this dedifferentiation on marital solidarity. We use cross-sectional survey data to determine how respondents' marital solidarity is affected by whether wives are employed, and the occupationally derived socioeconomic status of both husbands and wives. Our findings dispute both a sex-role differentiation and a bargaining perspective on marital solidarity. We find that marital interaction is enhanced when both spouses are employed, and that marriages do not benefit from the socioeconomic superiority of the male. We propose what we call the role homophily theory of marital solidarity.

THREE THEORIES AND SOME EVIDENCE

Aldous et al. (1979: 242-248) identify two main theoretical perspectives on the linkage between the occupational system

*Authorship is joint and equally shared. We acknowledge helpful comments from Richard L. Simpson, as well as NIMH grant 5T 32 MH 14670 03, which supported Paula England during a 1979-1980 postdoctoral fellowship at Duke University Medical

and the family: the role differentiation theory and bargaining theory. We derive a third from literature on companionship marriage and homogamous mating; we call it *role homophily* (see Lazarsfeld and Merton, 1954). The three perspectives lead to different predictions about the effects of wives' employment and occupational status on marital solidarity. This disagreement of the three theories is mirrored by inconsistent findings of earlier research regarding the effects of wives' employment on marriages. (For a review of literature on the effects of wives' employment, see Rallings and Nye, 1979.) Little research has looked at effects of wives' employment on their husbands' marital satisfaction (Rallings and Nye, 1979), nor has it considered, as an independent variable, wives' occupational status singly or in relation to their husbands'. Our research deals with these neglected areas. Table 1 charts the predictions generated from the three theories.

PARSONS'S SEX-ROLE DIFFERENTIATION THEORY

Parsons (1942, 1949, 1955) saw the family as a reproductive organization based on sex differentiation of roles within and outside the family. The husband's role is in the economic system outside the family domain and is concerned with procurement of resources for family livelihood. The wife's role is centered within the family and is oriented to procreative and sustaining functions. The husband's occupation links the family to the socioeconomic system. The wife adapts her roles to her husband's occupational role; the husband does not adapt to his wife. The sexual division of labor between the husband and wife corresponds to Durkheim's organic solidarity. Role complementarity builds marital solidarity. Parsons saw conjugal relations as a structure that articulates the family system with the economic system of industrial society. His

Center, and Biomedical Research Support Grant 303-3188 to Ida Harper Simpson. Data from the Quality of American Life Survey were made available by the ISR Social Science Archive, University of Michigan. Data from the 1970 Occupation-Industry classification were made available by Kenneth Spenner. We bear full responsibility for our analysis and interpretation of these data.

TABLE 1
Predictions About the Effects of Wives' Employment and Spouses' Socioeconomic Status from Three Theories of Marital Solidarity

Effect of:	Wife's Employment		Wife's SES		Husband's SES		Male SES Superiority[a]		SES Congruity[b]	
Theories / Effect on:	Husbands	Wives	Husbands	Wives	Husbands	Wives	Husbands	Wives	Husbands	Wives
Sex role differentiation	−	−	−	−	+	+	+	+	No prediction	
Bargaining	$-^c$	+	$-^c$	+	+	$-^c$	$+^c$	$-^c$	No prediction	
Role Homophily	+	+	No prediction		No prediction		−	−	+	+

a. Husband's SES minus his wife's (HSES−WSES).

b. Negative of absolute value of husband's SES minus wife's SES (−|HSES−WSES|).

c. These predictions hold only when total resources brought into the family are controlled. Without this control the positive effect of the additional resources for the unit might outweigh the negative effect of having less resource-based personal bargaining power.

concern was the needs of the family system rather than spouses' satisfactions from marital interactions. (For an exposition and criticism of the Parsonian perspective on female employment, see Oppenheimer, 1977.)

An extension of the Parsonian perspective to a consideration of wives' labor force participation posits deleterious effects on marital solidarity. When a wife and her husband both seek success in work, they are competitors. Aldous et al. (1979: 242-243) assess research literature to test the proposition that "marital role differentiation with the husbands performing the occupational role and wives the family caretaker role is positively related to marital stability." At the time when Parsons wrote, data on divorce supported the proposition. But times have changed; it is now normative for wives to work (Rallings and Nye, 1979: 214-215). Some worked when Parsons wrote. About them he said, "The large proportion do not have jobs which are in basic competition for status with those of their husbands" (Parsons, 1942: 608-609). According to the role differentiation perspective, the adverse effects of wives' working should be reduced by their being in occupations that are not in status competition with their husbands' occupations.

Even since the 1950s, when wives began to work in large numbers, some research findings are consistent with Parsons's predictions. Employed women are more apt to divorce if they have relatively high earnings (Ross and Sawhill, 1975: 57) or potential earnings (Cherlin, 1979) and are highly educated (Glick and Norton, 1977). Several studies have also shown that wives' employment adversely affects marital satisfaction and/ or adjustment (Nye, 1961; Gover, 1963; Michel, 1970; Scanzoni, 1970; Bean et al., 1977). Few studies have considered the impact of wives' occupational status on wives' and husbands' perceptions of their marriages (Rallings and Nye, 1979).

BARGAINING THEORY

The bargaining perspective of exchange theory (Homans, 1961) emphasizes the separate interests of the two individual spouses. Each spouse bargains to have decisions made in his or her individual interest. Bargaining power rests on resources one can offer or withhold. Resources may be generated within the marriage through nurturance and sustenance activities, or outside the marriage through socioeconomic rewards. Resources generated from extrafamilial socioeconomic systems give more bargaining power than within-family role contributions such as affection, housework, and child care. The perspective assumes that individuals try to maximize their resources and their bargaining power.

We must deal with an ambiguity in the bargaining theory before making our predictions. Resources are valuable to both spouses and they try to maximize them. Socioeconomic rewards that are a bargaining tool for one spouse are also a resource consumed jointly. The effects of access to shared resources and of one's own relative bargaining power may have counteracting effects on marital satisfaction. While one spouse's high socioeconomic position weakens the other's relative bargaining power, it also increases the resources the other has access to. For this reason, we need to hold constant combined family resources to make predictions about the effects on marital satisfaction of either spouse's contributions.

When we hold constant the level of socioeconomic resources coming into the family, the bargaining theory predicts that marital satisfaction depends on the relation of the spouse's externally generated resources to those of his or her mate. A gain in resources and resulting bargaining power for one entails a loss for the other. Wives' employment should have a positive effect on wives' marital satisfaction, but a negative effect on that of husbands. Two studies have found such a negative effect of wives' employment on husbands' satisfaction, together with a positive effect on wives' satisfaction (Scanzoni, 1970, 1972; Burke and Weir, 1976). (See also Ferree, 1976, who found that wives' employment increased their marital satisfaction; no data on husbands were gathered.) The effects of one spouse's socioeconomic status on the other have not been studied as far as we know. But the general notion that a couple is happier when the family's total financial, educational, and status resources are greater is supported by many studies (Terman, 1938; Blood and Wolfe, 1960; Gurin et al., 1960; Renne, 1970; Scanzoni, 1970; Miller, 1976). This notion is compatible with all three theories.

ROLE HOMOPHILY THEORY

We propose a perspective which we term role homophily. Its basic tenet is the opposite of that of the role differentiation theory. It is based on the argument that similarity of roles builds marital solidarity. When the home and the socioeconomic system are each the locus of a role for each spouse, spouses bring similar objective interests into their marriages. The problems of one spouse can be more readily appreciated by the other. Similar locations promote commonality in social outlooks. An effect of this commonality is to enhance marital communication and companionship. Marital solidarity is also increased when wives and husbands share responsibility for the family livelihood. Both spouses must contribute inputs if solidarity is to be maximized; neither of them, alone, can bring inputs sufficient to compensate for a lack of inputs by the other. Conjugal interests that grow from congruity of their socioeconomic positions are not reducible to the constituent parts. Our view of role homophily corresponds to Durkheim's notion of mechanical solidarity.

Our perspective is consistent with findings from several bodies of research. The notion that shared world views enhance solidarity is compatible with the theory of homogamous mate selection, as well as with research showing that communication is the social-psychological variable that best predicts marital satisfaction (Navran, 1967; Snyder, 1979). Sex-role differentiation has divisive effects; it separates the worlds of husbands and wives and this separation impedes mutual understanding and companionship. At a time when instrumental functions of the family have given way to companionate functions (Hicks and Platt, 1970; Nye, 1974), mechanical solidarity arising from role congruity becomes increasingly important for marital solidarity. The kind of marital structure that we predict will be experienced most positively by husbands and wives corresponds to the "symmetrical family" that Young and Willmott (1972) see as having emerged recently in industrial societies.

Our contention that role congruity enhances marriage takes support from the U-shaped curve of marital satisfaction over the life cycle; the greatest satisfaction occurs before child rearing and after children are launched from the home (Bernard, 1934; Terman, 1938; Gurin et al., 1960; Burr, 1970; Rollins and Feldman, 1970; Rollins and Cannon, 1974; Aldous, 1978: 202; and Schram, 1979). The dip in satisfaction may simply indicate the rigors of child rearing, but we find it suggestive that the greatest satisfaction coincides with those periods with the least sex-role differentiation. The enhancing effect of role congruity is shown more directly in studies that show that marital satisfaction benefits from equality of power (Bean et al., 1977) and flexible sex-role differentiation (Michel, 1970).

Our theory deals with marital solidarity, not the survival and disolution of marriages. It is ironic that while role congruity occasioned by the wife's employment enriches marital interaction, the wife's work may also give spouses the independence to dissolve the marriage if a bad situation arises. When wives lack financial independence, they cannot afford to dissolve marriages, even when they are dissatisfied with them; many such marriages remain intact (Cuber and Haroff, 1965; Levinger, 1965).

Some studies support none of the three theories of marital solidarity we have described; they find no effects on marriages of the socioeconomic status of either spouse (Glenn and Weaver, 1978; Jorgensen, 1979) or of wives' employment (Blood and Wolfe, 1960; Campbell et al., 1976; Booth, 1977; Glenn and Weaver, 1978; Wright, 1978).

RESEARCH PROCEDURES

DATA

To test our predictions from the three theories we have used data from the Quality of American Life Survey conducted by Campbell, Converse, and Rodgers in 1971 (described in Campbell et al., 1976). From their national probability sample of 2164 adults we selected all white, married respondents with children (including those whose children had left home). We restrict our study to whites because black women have a work tradition different from that of whites. The restriction to married persons with children is made because Parsons's theory attributes the sex differentiation of roles to the procreative function of the family.

Our subsample averaged 43 years of age. The husband respondents had a mean age of 44.2 years and the wife respondents 42.5 years. Slightly over 60% of the families represented by husband and wife respondents had children under 18 living at home (61% of the husbands and 63% of wives), and nearly 40% were in the postparental stage. The average education of husbands and wives was a little less than 12 years. Wives were employed in 40% of the families. Around one-half of the families in the sample had combined family incomes over $10,000. The average employed wife (respondent and spouse of husband respondent) earned considerably less than her husband—$3000 versus $8000 in 1971. But spouses differed little in occupational prestige and education requirements of their jobs. Wives exceeded their husbands' status about as often as husbands exceeded that of their wives. This reflects the concentration of wives in white-collar clerical and sales work; these jobs had higher prestige and educational requirements than many predominantly blue-collar ones held by husbands, but had lower earnings.

DEPENDENT VARIABLES

The dependent variables in our analysis are indicators of what we call marital solidarity; we divide these into four categories of variables: mutuality, marital commitment, marital satisfaction, and family satisfaction. The questionnaire items in each category are listed below.

Mutuality:

How often do you disagree with your husband/wife about how much money to spend on various things?—very often, . . . never (5 categories);

How well do you think your husband/wife understands you— your feelings, your likes and dislikes, and any problems you may have: Do you think he/she understands you not well at all, . . . very well? (4 categories);

How well do you understand your husband/wife?—not well at all, . . . very well (4 categories);

How much companionship do you and your husband/wife have— how often do you do things together?—hardly ever, . . . all the time (5 categories).

Marital commitment:

Have you ever wished you had married someone else?—never, . . . often (5 categories);

Has the thought of getting a divorce ever crossed your mind?— never, . . . often (5 categories).

Marital satisfaction:

How much satisfaction do you get from your marriage?—none, . . . a very great deal (7 categories). (This item is asked amid questions on satisfaction from a variety of life domains, such as work, hobbies, and so on.)

Family satisfaction:

How much satisfaction do you get from your family life?—none, . . . a very great deal (7 categories). (This question is asked amid questions on satisfaction from a variety of life domains, such as work, hobbies, and so on.)

INDEPENDENT VARIABLES

Our independent variables include wives' employment status and several measures of the occupationally derived socioeconomic status of each spouse. Wives' employment status was dichotomized as employed or not employed.[1] We did not take into account the number of hours wives worked because this information was not obtained from male respondents about their wives. For this reason we cannot examine the effects of the number of hours wives worked on husbands' perceptions of their marriages. Since we want our analyses of husbands and wives to match, we will not use the information available on hours worked for wives. The fact that these data are missing is unfortunate. Some past research has found that the effect of wives' employment depends on whether it is part-time or full-time (for a summary, see Rallings and Nye, 1979). The data we use show no differences in female respondents' perceptions of marital solidarity between those employed full- and those employed part-time (Campbell et al., 1976: 440).

Our second set of independent variables consists of occupationally derived socioeconomic characteristics of husbands and wives. The Quality of American Life data provide few measures of occupational characteristics. To get these, we merged two socioeconomic attributes of respondents' occupations into the file. Codes of two occupational characteristics were provided by Spenner (1977): the occupation's requirement for formal schooling, measured by the *Dictionary of Occupational Titles* (DOT) scale of general educational development, and occupational prestige, measured by Temme's (1975) scale. Our third socioeconomic indicator is income. The income information is in the Quality of American Life data set. Respondents were asked about their family incomes and personal incomes. For a measure of spouse's income, we subtracted respondent's income from family income.

ANALYSIS PROCEDURE

We use the partial Pearson correlation coefficient to test our predictions. Since financial resources affect marital solidarity, we have controlled family income in all analyses so that we can isolate the effects that are predicted differently by the theories. In examining the effect of each spouse's socioeconomic status, we control the status of the other spouse. When we assess the impact of differences between husbands' and wives' socioeconomic status, we control for the husband's status level.

Since marital understanding and satisfaction are curvilinear over the life cycle of a family (see Aldous, 1978: 202 for a summary of research), we do all of our analysis within life-cycle stages or control for age and presence of children at home as proxies of family life cycle. We consider only the parental and postparental life-cycle stages: parental with children in the dwelling unit and the youngest under 6 years of age; parental with children in the dwelling unit and the youngest aged 6 to 17; and postparental with children, but none 18 or younger in the dwelling unit. (The Quality of American Life data set does not distinguish children 18 and over who live at home from those who do not.)

In interpreting our findings, we take into account problems inherent in the measures of quality of life in the data set. Campbell et al. (1976) report two limitations of these items, including the marital solidarity ones. The variance in each item is small and the responses are skewed toward the positive end. They surmise from this that respondents adjust the scale to their circumstances rather than rate their subjective feelings on an objective scale. They found low correlations of demographic variables with the quality of life items. Indeed, few correlations reached .20. These limitations were not unique to marriage but were true for all subjective measures of quality of life. For these reasons, we decided to consider the directions of correlation coefficients when they had probability levels of .25 or less. Our tables report numerical coefficients significant at the .05 level and signs (but not numerical values) of coefficients with probabilities from .05 through .25. Since we have multiple indicators of marital solidarity, we use the sign test to infer statistical significance from a consistent pattern of same-signed coefficients, even if the single correlations are not significant at the .05 level. We use one-tailed tests of significance throughout, since all our predictions involve signs.

FINDINGS

WIFE'S EMPLOYMENT

The sex-role differentiation theory predicts that employment of the wife impairs marital solidarity; the role homophily theory predicts that it enhances solidarity. The bargaining theory predicts that it benefits the wife's marital situation but adversely affects the husband's. Our findings on the effects of the wife's employment on wives' and husbands' perceptions of marital solidarity within life-cycle stages are given in Table 2. They show that employment of the wife has salutary effects on marital solidarity as perceived by both husbands and wives.

All significant relationships between wives' employment and marital solidarity are positive; most of the signs of nonsignificant coefficients are positive as well. Out of 24 coefficients estimating the effects of wives' employment on wives' perception of marital solidarity, 10 are positive with a significance level at or below .25. Of the 24 effects of wives' employment on husbands, 15 are positive and significant at or below .25. If we look at each of these coefficients as an independent test of the relationship between wives' employment and marital solidarity, we would expect only one-fourth to be positive and significant at the .25 level in a population with no relationship. A (binomial) sign test indicates that the number of pluses with significance levels of .25 or below for wives (10 out of 24) has a probability of .055 of occurring by chance. For husbands, the 15 out of 24 can be expected to occur by chance less than 5% of the time. The total for husbands and wives combined (25 of 48) also would occur by chance less than 5% of the time. Although interpretation of the sign of any one nonsignificant coefficient entails a greater than 5% risk of Type I error, the consistent pattern of positive signs of the nonsignificant coefficients, in combination with the several significant positive correlations, gives us confidence in concluding that wives' employment helps marital solidarity.

Wives' employment serves both husbands and wives, but it is more beneficial for husbands, particularly during the parental stages. The effects on the spouses differ most when they have

TABLE 2

Partial Correlations[a] Between Wives' Employment and Marital Solidarity, Controlling for Family Income

	Wives			Husbands		
Marital Solidarity Indicators[b]	With child under 6 years	With ≥1 child, but none under 6 years	Post-parental (no child under 18 at home)	With child under 6 years	With ≥1 child, but none under 6 years	Post-parental (no child under 18 at home)
Mutuality						
Disagree about spending	+	+	−	+		+
Spouse understands respondent		+			+	
Respondent understands spouse		+	−	.23	+	
Companionship				.18	.16	−
Marital Commitment						
Wished married someone else	−			.15	−	
Thought of divorce		+	.13	+		−
Satisfaction						
Satisfaction from marriage		+	.14	+	+	+
Satisfaction from family life		+	.17	+	+	.13
N[c]	127-130	129-131	208-213	115-116	106-107	206-208

a. A sign without a correlation coefficient in this table and the one to follow indicates that the relationship is not significant at the .05 level, but $p \leq .25$.
b. All correlations in this table and the one to follow reflect scaling of variables such that greater marital solidarity receives a higher score. Positive coefficient means that employment of the wife increases marital solidarity.
c. Ns within a column within this table and the one to follow vary because missing values differ between marital solidarity items.

children under 6 years old in the home. During this period, wives' employment exerts a positive effect on husbands' marital experience, but its effects on wives are almost nil. This sex difference in the timing of the effects of wives' employment may reflect sex differentiation of domestic responsibilities. When children are under 6, child-care responsibilities are very time-consuming and cannot be scheduled to suit the convenience of the parent. Since wives do the preponderance of domestic work even when employed (Walker, 1970; Meissner et al., 1975; Robinson, 1977; Berk and Berk, 1979; Pleck, 1979), our findings suggest that a domestic work overload may cancel out positive effects of employment for wives. It is significant, however, that during this time of heavy child-care responsibilities, employment does not adversely affect wives' perceptions of their marital solidarity.

As children age, the employment of wives comes to affect them in more nearly the same way as it affects husbands. When the youngest child is between 6 and 17, and in the postparental stage, the patterns of influence on wives and husbands are very similar. But the effects differ for both spouses between the two life-cycle stages. In the postparental stage, the point in the family life cycle when marital satisfaction reverses an earlier downward slope and begins to rise (Aldous, 1978: 202) and parenthood is no longer a basis of sex differentiation between spouses, wives' employment no longer promotes mutuality for husbands and wives. Spouses' worlds within the family are now more similar; perhaps this dedifferentiation of family roles serves mutuality earlier served by wives' employment. Wives' employment continues to aid marital and family satisfaction in the postparental stage. (Of our coefficients, three are positive and significant at the .05 level.)

All in all, our findings show that the wife's employment benefits marital relations the most during the parental stage of the family, when marital and parental relations compete, and that husbands are the main beneficiaries. Why might this be? A wife's employment links her to collective life. This link is particularly important for marital solidarity from the view of husbands during the stage of preschool children. The extra-familial work role seems to keep wives' interests from narrowing to an exclusive concern with children. Without this institutionalized link that employment provides, demands of child rearing could more easily lead to an overabsorption in the mother role. The employed wife may well have more "wifely" vitality than the full-time mother. She shares an extrafamilial role with her husband to make her world more like his. Husbands benefit much from their wives' work roles.

Our findings on wives' employment support the role homophily theory and disconfirm the bargaining and sex-role differentiation theories of marital solidarity. Wives' employment has a stronger positive effect on husbands than on wives, just the opposite of what bargaining theory would predict. The salutary effect of women's employment on both husbands and wives is consistent with the role homophily theory that we advance. Communication and commonality are facilitated when wives' worlds are similar to husbands' because both work outside the home.

SOCIOECONOMIC CHARACTERISTICS OF SPOUSES

The effects of socioeconomic status on the perception of marital solidarity differ for husbands and wives. For wives, marital solidarity is increased by having a high-status occupation as well as by having a husband with high status. Table 3 shows that all 14 significant coefficients for wives are positive and most of the signs of the coefficients we consider are also positive. A sign test of such an occurrence of positive coefficients shows a probability below .05. In contrast, husbands' marital perceptions are little affected by their own status or that of their wives. Husbands and wives differ more in the effects of income than in the effects of other status attributes. An increase in the wife's or her husband's income improves her perception of her marriage, but a wife's income has less effect on her husband than his own income, and any effect is negative. The differences between husbands and wives are also striking with respect to occupational prestige. The wife's prestige benefits both spouses more than the husband's (see Simpson and Mutran, 1981).

Again, our findings are inconsistent with both the bargaining theory and role differentiation theory. In Parsons's theory, a high-status wife is competing with her husband in his role as provider. Parsons's perspective suggests positive effects on both spouses' perceptions of marital solidarity when the husband has high status, but negative effects on both spouses' perceptions of the marriage when the wife has high occupational status. This latter prediction is contradicted by our findings. Bargaining theory predicts a positive effect on either spouse of his or her own socioeconomic status, controlling for the total level of family resources. It is the prediction of a negative effect of one's spouse's socioeconomic status that our analysis challenges; we find a positive effect on wives of their husbands' socioeconomic status and essentially no effect on husbands of their wives' status. Role homophily theory makes no prediction about the direction of effects of either spouse's socioeconomic status on marital solidarity. The finding that women are more affected by their own and their spouses' status than men are is not predicted by any of the three theories. Future research should seek to explain this sex difference.

A more direct test of the predictions of the role differentiation and bargaining theories compares the socioeconomic status of the spouses. We construct a difference score by subtracting the wife's status from her husband's; a high score indicates the husband's socioeconomic superiority and a low score indicates the wife's superiority. The role differentiation theory predicts that the husband's socioeconomic superiority enhances marriage for both spouses; the bargaining theory predicts that husbands' ascendancy improves husbands' perceptions of their marriages but detracts from that of wives. The findings do not support either theory. (These data are not reported.) Using the sign test we find that husbands' higher status does reduce wives' perception of marital solidarity, as bargaining theory predicts, but it does not improve the

TABLE 3

Partial Correlations Between Socioeconomic Status and Marital Solidarity, Controlling for Respondent's or Spouse's SES,[a] Age, Children in Household,[b] and Family Income[c]

	Wives						Husbands					
	Income[d]		Educ. Requirement of Occupation		Occupational Prestige		Income[d]		Educ. Requirement of Occupation		Occupational Prestige	
Marital Solidarity Indicators	Respondent	Spouse's	Respondent	Spouse's	Respondent	Spouse's	Respondent	Spouse's	Respondent	Spouse's	Respondent	Spouse's
Mutuality												
Disagree about spending	.08	.08		+		+	+					+
Spouse understands respondent	+	.08	+	.13	+	+	+		.13	+	+	+
Respondent understands spouse	+			.13	+	+			+		+	+
Companionship	+	.09	+		+	−				+		
Marital Commitment												
Wished married someone else	+		.19	+	.14		−					+
Thought of divorce	−		.15	.13	.16		−					+
Satisfaction												
Satisfaction from marriage	+	+	.15		.13	−				+		
Satisfaction from family life	.07	+	+							+		
N	575–580	575–580	202	190	202	202	531–535	531–535	199	185	199	199

a. Spouse's score on a given SES indicator is controlled in correlation with own score on that indicator and vice versa. For example, own income is controlled in the correlation between spouse's income and marital solidarity; spouse's income is controlled in the correlation between own income and marital solidarity.

b. Dichotomized so respondents with children in the dwelling unit are scored 1; others are scored 0. Since we have removed nonparents, only postparental respondents (those with no child under 18 at home) are scored 0.

c. Family income in this table cannot be controlled for in correlations with own and spouse's income since it is a linear function of these variables.

d. Persons with no income in the year prior to the survey are scored as having 0 income; they are not missing cases. Persons not employed last year are treated as missing cases in correlations with occupations' educational requirements and prestige.

marriage for husbands. The failure of husbands' higher socioeconomic status to enhance marriages as viewed by husbands and wives contradicts the prediction of role differentiation theory.

We have not yet given a direct test of the predictions of role homophily theory with respect to socioeconomic status. Such a test requires a measure of spouses' status similarity to each other. We measure the similarity of status by taking the negative of the absolute value of their difference score used above. If socioeconomic similarity improves marital solidarity, as the homophily theory posits, similarity should correlate positively with marital solidarity. Since the similarity score does not distinguish which spouse is higher, neither bargaining nor role differentiation theory makes a prediction about its effects on marital solidarity. We computed partial correlations of this similarity measure with the indicators of marital solidarity, controlling for age, presence of children, and family income. The findings show only 4 of 48 coefficients significant. Of the 24 signs of effects on males, 19 are negative; a sign test shows the chance probability of this patterning to be less than .05. There is no consistent pattern of the signs of the effects on women of socioeconomic congruity. (These data are not reported here.) These findings do not support the role homophily prediction that socioeconomic congruity aids marriage.

We speculate that as women's employment becomes increasingly continuous and norms that prescribe similar work careers for both sexes become more widespread, socioeconomic congruity will increasingly benefit marriage. But at this point in history the relevant role similarity for a theory of homophily is that both spouses have jobs. Wives' employment makes the worlds of husbands and wives more symmetrical; they both have extrafamilial and familial roles.

DISCUSSION

We have considered three theories on the effects of dedifferentiation of spouses' work roles on marital solidarity. Our findings are not consistent with either of the two prominent theoretical perspectives on marital and occupational linkages. We find partial support for a third hypothesis, role homophily. We suggest a need to reassess the view that role differentiation promotes marital solidarity and the notion that one's marital satisfaction depends on one's bargaining position relative to one's spouse.

We show that wives' employment supports marital solidarity as perceived by both husbands and wives. This finding supports the role homophily theory but contradicts predictions derived from the bargaining and role differentiation theories. We suggest that the similarity of wives' and husbands' worlds when both have extrafamilial roles promotes marital solidarity.

But when we look for possible effects of husbands' and/or wives' positions in the socioeconomic system on the perceived solidarity of their marriages, we find little support for any of the three theories. Bargaining theory predicts high satisfaction when one's own status is higher than one's spouse's. Role differentiation theory predicts that marriage is enhanced when the husband's status is high, absolutely and relative to his wife's. Role homophily theory predicts that marriage is enhanced when spouses have similar socioeconomic status. In fact, our findings show that wives' perceptions of their marriages benefit from high socioeconomic status regardless of whether it is derived from their own or their husbands' occupations. But husbands' perceptions of marital solidarity are little affected by either their own or their wives' socioeconomic status. None of the theories offers predictions about the effects of socioeconomic status on marital solidarity that are consistently upheld.

In summary, we derived hypotheses from role differentiation, bargaining, and role homophily theories to explain the effects of spouses' linkage to the occupational system on marital solidarity. Our findings consistently support only one of the predictions. The wife's employment enhances marriage as perceived by both the husband and wife. This prediction comes from role homophily theory. We conclude that the role homophily theory is the best supported of the three.

It is appropriate to reflect on why the bargaining and role differentiation theories have led to erroneous predictions about the effects of wives' employment on marriage. Parsons's theory of sex-role differentiation suffers from an overemphasis on the functional and consensual aspects of arrangements that were current at the time he wrote. The theory posits a *particular* normative structure that relates the family to the socioeconomic system. It is a static conception, and fails to take account of the fact that the normative structure it posits rests on a historically specific complex of societal conditions. Those conditions have changed (Young and Willmott, 1972). Wives leave their homes along with their husbands to go to work and, like their husbands, bring the influence of their work into their marriages. This change in wives' roles has paralleled a shift from instrumental to companionate family functions. The isolation and subordination of wives inherent in Parsons's views on sex-role differentiation impair the companionship that couples now seek. Parsons is correct that the sex-differentiated nuclear family is one way to articulate child rearing with the economic system, but it is only one way and one that is rapidly fading.

The atomistic individualism assumed by bargaining theory gives a very incomplete view of marriage. To be sure, spouses sometimes have conflicts of interest which lead to bargaining for individual gain. But when the quality of the process of interacting is as important to spouses as any limited benefits that can be extracted and taken away from an interaction, there is no such thing as zero-sum game; what one gains at the expense of the other will detract from the "public good" of marital solidarity. Work changes people in ways that affect their empathy, vitality, and the commonality of their marital interaction. It is the contribution of these qualities to marital solidarity that bargaining theory is unable to predict.

Our theoretical reassessment and empirical analysis have led us to propose a theory of role homophily. The theory posits that women's employment increases the role congruity of husbands and wives and thus has positive effects on both husbands' and wives' perceptions of marital solidarity. Our findings support this view. Socioeconomic congruity appears unrelated to marital solidarity; perhaps this is because occupational sex segregation is so pervasive (England, 1981) that congruity of socioeconomic status still means substantially different kinds of work for husbands and wives.

Our analysis of the effects of wives' employment on marriages joins a large literature riddled with conflicting findings. In response to the question of why the reader should believe our conclusions when they conflict with those of other empirical analyses, we point out four assets of our study that recommend its findings. We have used a survey which is more nationally representative and has a larger number of respondents than those used in some past studies. Because we have used multiple indicators of both marital solidarity and socioeconomic status, we can identify consistent patterns in the effects even when the effects are too small to be significant when taken one by one. The most important way in which our analysis differs from many we have reviewed is in statistical partialling to remove spurious effects of variables the literature suggests as important controls. Many of the studies we cite did not control for either life-cycle stage or family income. Finally, our analysis has considered the effects on marriage of wives' employment *and* the status of their jobs; few past studies have dealt with the effects of women's occupationally derived socioeconomic status on subjective indicators of marital solidarity.

We began this article with reference to our interest in the macrosocial effects of sex-role dedifferentiation. Our findings have implications for that question. Since current sex-role change is increasing the number of dual-worker families, our findings suggest a positive aggregate impact of such changes on marital solidarity.

NOTE

1. The question on spouses' employment simply asked men if their wives were doing any work for money now. Housewives, students, or those who were unemployed

were all coded together as not employed. Respondent's own employment status was coded in more detail, distinguishing housewives from students and the unemployed. But for comparability we used the dichotomous coding both for female respondents' reports of their own employment status and for male respondents' reports of their wives' employment status. To see the effects of this coding decision we recomputed the effects on wives in Table 2, counting only housewives as not employed, and counting students and the unemployed as missing values. This change in coding had negligible effects on the results.

REFERENCES

Aldous, J.
    1978   Family Careers: Developmental Change in Families. New York: John Wiley.
Aldous, J., M. W. Osmond, and M. W. Hicks
    1979   "Men's work and men's families," pp. 227-256 in W. R. Burr et al. (eds.)
            Contemporary Theories about the Family: Research Based Theories. Volume I. New York: Macmillan.
Bean, F. D., R. L. Curtis, Jr., and J. P. Marcum
    1977   "Familism and marital satisfaction among Mexican Americans: the effects of family size, wife's labor force participation, and conjugal power." J. of Marriage and the Family 39 (November): 759-767.
Berk, R. and S. F. Berk
    1979   Labor and Leisure at Home. Beverly Hills, CA: Sage.
Bernard, J.
    1934   "Factors in the distribution of marital success." Amer. J. of Sociology 49 (July): 49-60.
Blood, R. O. and D. M. Wolfe
    1960   Husbands and Wives: The Dynamics of Married Living. New York: Macmillan.
Booth, A.
    1977   "Wife's employment and husband's stress: a replication and refutation." J. of Marriage and the Family 39 (November): 645-650.
Burke, R. and T. Weir
    1976   "Relationship of wives' employment status to husband, wife and pair satisfaction and performance." J. of Marriage and the Family 38 (May): 279-287.
Burr, W.
    1970   "Satisfaction with various aspects of marriage over the life cycle: a random middle class sample." J. of Marriage and the Family 32 (February): 29-37.
Campbell, A., P. Converse, and W. Rodgers
    1976   The Quality of American Life. New York: Russell Sage.
Cherlin, A.
    1979   "Work life and marital dissolution," pp. 151-166 in C. Levinger and O. C. Moles (eds.) Divorce and Separation: Context, Causes and Consequences. New York: Basic Books.

Cuber, P. and J. Haroff
  1965   Sex and the Significant Americans. New York: Viking.
England, P.
  1981   "Assessing trends in occupational sex-segregation, 1900-1976," pp. 273-295
          in I. Berg (ed.) Sociological Perspectives on Labor Markets. New York:
          Academic.
Ferree, M.
  1976   "Working class jobs: housework and paid work as sources of satisfaction."
          Social Problems 23 (April): 431-441.
Glenn, N. D. and C. N. Weaver
  1978   "A multivariate, multisurvey study of marital happiness." J. of Marriage
          and the Family 40 (May): 269-282.
Glick, P. C. and A. J. Norton
  1977   "Marrying, divorcing, and living together in the U.S. today." Population
          Reference Bureau 32 (October): 3-38.
Gover, D. A.
  1963   "Socio-economic differentials in the relationship between marital adjust-
          ment and wife's employment status." Marriage and Family Living 25 (No-
          vember): 452-456.
Gurin, G., J. Veroff, and S. Feld
  1960   How Americans View Their Mental Health. New York: Basic Books.
Hicks, M. W. and M. Platt
  1970   "Marital happiness and stability: a review of the research in the sixties."
          J. of Marriage and the Family 32 (November): 553-574.
Homans, G. C.
  1961   Social Behavior: Its Elementary Forms. London: Routledge & Kegan Paul.
Jorgensen, S. R.
  1979   "Socioeconomic rewards and perceived marital quality: a re-examination."
          J. of Marriage and the Family 41 (November): 825-835.
Lazarsfeld, P. F. and R. K. Merton
  1954   "Friendship as a social process," pp. 18-67 in M. Berger et al. (eds.) Freedom
          and Control in Modern Society. New York: Litton.
Levinger, C.
  1965   "Marital cohesiveness and dissolution: an integrative review." J. of Mar-
          riage and the Family 27 (February): 19-28.
Meissner, M., E. Humphreys, S. Meis, and W. Scheu
  1975   "No exit for wives: sexual division of labor and the accumulation of house-
          hold demands." Canadian Rev. of Sociology and Anthropology 12: 424-
          439.
Michel, A.
  1970   "Wife's satisfaction with husband's understanding in Parisian urban fami-
          lies." J. of Marriage and the Family 32 (August): 351-360.
Miller, B. C.
  1976   "A multivariate developmental model of marital satisfaction." J. of Mar-
          riage and the Family 38 (November): 643-657.
Navran, L.
  1967   "Communication and adjustment in marriage." Family Process 6 (Septem-
          ber): 173-184.

Nye, F. I.
   1974   "Emerging and declining family roles." J. of Marriage and the Family 36 (May): 238-245.
   1961   "Maternal employment and marital interaction: some contingent conditions." Social Forces 40 (December): 113-119.
Oppenheimer, V.
   1977   "The sociology of women's economic role in the family." Amer. Soc. Rev. 42 (June): 387-406.
Orden, S. R. and N. M. Bradburn
   1968   "Working wives and marriage happiness." Amer. J. of Sociology 74 (January): 715-731.
Parsons, T.
   1955   "The American family: its relations to personality and to the social structure," pp. 3-33 in T. Parsons and R. F. Bales (eds.) Family, Socialization and Interaction Process. New York: Macmillan.
   1949   "The social structure of the family," pp. 173-201 in R. Anshen (ed.) The Family: Its Function and Destiny. New York: Harper & Row.
   1942   "Age and sex in the social structure of the United States." Amer. Soc. Rev. 7 (October): 604-616.
Pleck, J.
   1979   "Men's family work: three perspectives and some new data." Family Coordinator 28 (October): 481-488.
Rallings, E. M. and F. I. Nye
   1979   "Wife-mother employment, family and society," pp. 203-226 in W. R. Burr et al. (eds.) Contemporary Theories about the Family: Research Based Theories. Volume 1. New York: Macmillan.
Renne, K. S.
   1970   "Correlates of dissatisfaction in marriage." J. of Marriage and the Family 32 (February): 54-67.
Robinson, J.
   1977   How Americans Use Their Time. New York: Praeger.
Rollins, B. C. and K. L. Cannon
   1974   "Marital satisfaction over the family life cycle: a re-evaluation." J. of Marriage and the Family 36 (May): 271-282.
Rollins, B. C. and H. Feldman
   1970   "Marital satisfaction over the family life cycle." J. of Marriage and the Family 32 (February): 20-28.
Ross, H. and I. V. Sawhill
   1975   Time of Transition. Washington, DC: Urban Institute.
Scanzoni, J.
   1972   Sexual Bargaining. Englewood Cliffs, NJ: Prentice-Hall.
   1970   Opportunity and the Family. New York: Macmillan.
Schram, R. W.
   1979   "Marital satisfaction over the family life cycle: a critique and proposal." J. of Marriage and the Family 41 (February): 7-12.

Simpson, I. H. and E. Mutran
　　1981　"Women's social consciousness: sex or worker identity," pp. 335-350 in
　　　　R. L. Simpson and I. H. Simpson (eds.) Research on the Sociology of
　　　　Work, Volume 1. Greenwich, CT: JAI.
Snyder, D. K.
　　1979　"Multidimensional assessment of marital satisfaction." J. of Marriage and
　　　　the Family 41 (November): 813-823.
Spenner, K. I.
　　1977　"From generation to generation: the transmission of occupation." Ph.D.
　　　　dissertation, University of Wisconsin, Madison.
Temme, L. V.
　　1975　Occupations: Meanings and Measures. Washington, DC: Bureau of Social
　　　　Science Research.
Terman, L. M.
　　1938　Psychological Factors in Marital Happiness. New York: McGraw-Hill.
Walker, K.
　　1970　"Time spent by husbands in household work." Family Economic Rev. 2
　　　　(June): 8-11.
Wright, J. D.
　　1978　"Are working women really more satisfied? Evidence from several national
　　　　surveys." J. of Marriage and the Family 40 (May): 301-313.
Young, M. and P. Willmott
　　1972　The Symmetrical Family. London: Routledge & Kegan Paul.

9

Reconsidering the Dual-Career Marriage

A Longitudinal Approach*

MARGARET M. POLOMA
BRIAN F. PENDLETON
T. NEAL GARLAND

Over a decade has elapsed since Rhona and Robert Rapoport published their seminal research report on dual-career marriages (Rapoport and Rapoport, 1969). Since this time at least two dozen other empirical studies have been completed on this topic, giving family scholars a better grasp of the issues and alternatives involved in dual-career marriages. (For reviews of studies through 1978, see Rapoport and Rapoport, 1978, and Mortimer, 1978. Other edited collections of relevance are Bryson and Bryson, 1978, and Peterson et al., 1978.)

As Rapoport and Rapoport (1978) note, the nature of research on dual-career families has moved into more mature stages. The first generation of work in this area identified strains and rewards associated with dual-career families and processes through which this kind of family is sustained. Some determining factors were isolated and explored and beginning attempts were made to suggest ways of removing certain

*This chapter is a revision of a paper presented at the Southern Sociological Society Meetings, Knoxville, Tennessee, March 1980.

negative features associated with dual-career families. A second generation, according to Rapoport and Rapoport (1978), found research drawing from better data banks and looking at families in different stages of the life cycle and different social classes and national/cultural settings. Comparisons were made between the married professional woman and her single counterpart with some initial applications to social policy and strain reduction.

The purpose of this current study is to further investigate concerns found in the second generation of research and, particularly, to meet the request made by Rapoport and Rapoport (1978) that longitudinal studies be used to investigate the consequences of having a dual-career marriage. More specifically, the intent of the current study is to use longitudinal data better to understand the dual-career phenomenon through a developmental approach relating careers to stages in the family life cycle.

METHOD

Original data were collected in 1969 by two of the authors from 53 dual-career couples through the use of separate but simultaneous in-depth interviews. Questions were designed to elicit qualitative information. In 1977, 45 of the 53 wives from the original study responded to a mailed questionnaire constructed from the original, qualitative schedule.[1] The 1977 questionnaire contained mostly Likert-fashion items with responses ranging from "strongly agree" to "strongly disagree," although there were five open-ended questions. All of the women in the study were attorneys, physicians, or university professors employed in the Cleveland, Ohio, area during 1969, the year of the original study. Of the 45 who responded to the questionnaire, 42 identified themselves as being employed in 1977. (One physician had retired, one college professor taught an occasional course, and one attorney did some legal work from her home.) Of these women 40 were able to list promotions and awards they had won during the 1969-1977 period. These included elected judgeships, a university chair, promotions and headships of university departments, partnerships in law firms, and numerous other honors and distinctions. The 5 women who did not report any professional achievements were either retired (1 case), past retirement age but still employed (1 case), or still involved in caring for small children (3 cases). Husbands (who possibly were far more advanced in their careers in 1969 than were their wives) did not experience such clear patterns of career achievements.[2]

In spite of the success records of our respondents, Hughes's (1975: 215-221) observation also is apparent: Married women's career lines are different from most men's. They need not follow the dominant male pattern of professional school right after college, an uninterrupted career line that builds to a pinnacle, reaches a plateau period, and then is followed by retirement.[3] Discussed next is the married woman's career line, using previous literature and the data from this study.

THE DUAL-CAREER MARRIAGE AND MOTHERHOOD

In her longitudinal study of 226 professional women, Yohalem (1979: 55) reports:

> While husbands and children can be sources of great personal satisfaction, marriage and motherhood were not conducive to the maintenance of enduring career commitments. The amount of time devoted to career development by the abnormally large minority of respondents who have never married was considerably in excess of that of ever married women, and childless wives tended to have had a greater employment continuity than mothers.

It appears first that the presence of children has a moderating effect on career development. Second, and related to the marital relationship, is the problem of coordinating the careers of both the wife and the husband. Discussed below with our longitudinal data are these two major costs for women in dual-career marriages: motherhood and geographic mobility.

DEMANDS OF MOTHERHOOD

Of our 45 follow-up respondents, 42 were combining motherhood with career responsibility. Although 14 of these women did not permit motherhood to interrupt their careers, many commented on the negative effects that the family had on their career development. Most frequently noted were limited career involvements, the need to turn down promotions with increased responsibilities, and the need to limit hours to part-time work. Comments similar to this female physician's (#47)[4] were frequent: "My career progression has been slower than my husband's because of the demands of family and home. However, this is really my choice. I love the job I currently have."

Most mothers acknowledged that as long as the children are at home career demands must be somewhat limited. One female professor (#4), unusual in that she expressed regret but not atypical in her situation, noted: "My family has had one effect on my career. I turned down a chance for an administrative, 11-month, time-consuming job to keep the flexibility of a normal academic year—on behalf of my spouse and children. It was my decision, and I regret it."

Some women in our sample dealt with the demands of motherhood and profession by limiting themselves to part-time positions. They readily saw costs of the family demands on their career. One physician (#10) employed three days a week commented: "Inasmuch as I have been employed only part-time, my professional achievements have been hindered." Another physician (#11), employed full-time until the birth of her first child, reduced her work load 50% at that time. With the birth of the second child, she took a 6-month leave then returned to 20% time. Now that the children are in elementary school, she is working half-time. She observed: "Time off with my children has curtailed my professional development."

The reports of our respondents support Yohalem's (1979: 56) conclusions:

> Most of the mothers were satisfied with the way they had apportioned their time between work and home. Of those who had reservations, the great majority wished they had spent more time in career development. Asked to give advice to the younger generation about combining family and career, respondents most commonly recommended this course of action but with certain reservations. It was clear that they generally supported the combination in theory but reality intervened to cast doubts upon its feasibility under all circumstances.

In the present study, as in Yohalem's, most of our respondents wanted children and liked the mix of the two sets of demands offered by motherhood and a career.

LIMITED GEOGRAPHIC MOBILITY

One of the greatest difficulties in effectively coordinating two careers is the problem of geographical mobility. Both spouses may share this "cost" if the couple agrees, and is able, to remain geographically fixed. The wife usually assumes the "cost" in the event of either a forced or a voluntary move. Our data suggest that the role the wife's career plays in such a decision is negotiated and not always predictable.

In 1969, the time of our original interviews, couples were divided according to the role the wife's career should play in a decision to move. The one "equalitarian" couple and the 27 "neotraditional" couples gave equal or nearly equal weight to both careers (Poloma and Garland, 1971a). Subsequent events, however, were not easy to control. In the follow-up study, 15 women reported unplanned changes, ranging from marital problems and divorce to either a husband's or wife's job dissatisfaction or unplanned termination, that modified their activities. One childless college professor took a leave of absence to remain with her physician husband as he sought to meet his military obligations. After a month he was offered a discharge and had no difficulty returning to the hospital of his residency. While the wife was able to regain her university position, she had to wait out one academic year before her return. Other couples were not so fortunate. One professor wife who had earlier refused to follow her husband to a position where she did not have a position assured, found herself denied tenure a year later. She followed him to a new position and waited three years until she could find employment. She wrote on our 1977 questionnaire: "My husband went on a sabbatical overseas. I could not go with him due to my commitment to X University, and he found someone else." Of the 45 follow-up respondents, 10 were involved in at least one geographic move from 1969 to 1977. In *no case* was a move made to enhance the wife's career opportunities.

In the event of a geographic move, except in exceptional circumstances, someone's career has to "give." Supported by the societal norm of the male as chief breadwinner and provider, married women tend to place their careers second in importance to their husbands'. One woman (#32), who already was well established as an attorney in 1969, subsequently divorced and moved to the city of her new husband upon remarriage. She expressed it matter-of-factly: "The change in location meant that I had to start being known again in the legal community. I am just beginning to achieve that."

The question may arise, "What about the woman who refuses to make such a move?" While we do not assert that disillusionment is typical, the written comment of one divorced university professor (#41) who was formerly committed to the dual-career family speaks for itself:

> Another pessimism toward the workings of a dual-career family comes from recent involvement with another man. We were seriously considering commitment to each other, and he wanted me to continue work—but could not understand the concept of a career for a woman. I was to follow him, picking up whatever jobs I could acquire where he went, and was to ask

nothing of him regarding career or time sacrifices so that I could be employed. For a time we tried to combine careers spending weekends together when possible, but any time he took off from his job to spend more time with me was considered pressure from me (even though he had volunteered that time with me). Although I was expected to give up my job at X University and the benefits and retirements I was contributing to, and was expected to find a new job near him at a lesser salary and with lesser benefits, I was still to contribute my half and was not to be his beneficiary in retirement or insurance.

May I summarize by saying that I passionately believe intellectually in the dual-career family situation. However, on the practical level, I'm really doubting as to whether it is often possible. It takes an unusual type of man to give himself as required. It probably also takes an unusual type of woman— maybe a super-achiever, who can coordinate and integrate all facets together into a well-functioning whole. Looking back on my own marriage, which at the time I considered a model, I see that it had serious flaws and worked less well than I thought.

The problems of coordinating two careers are persistent but variable. While problems of mobility are potentially present for all couples, regardless of the stage of the family life cycle, the demands of motherhood are lessened as years go by. One of our respondents (#26) noted at the end of the structured items on the 1977 questionnaire: "I may have answered these questions differently when in my 40s than now that I am in my 60s." Her personal observation is in line with our thesis that both career activities and attitudes do change; and, as another respondent (#30) noted: "At some developmental stages, family needs are overwhelming." We will now consider these developmental stages and their relations to career type.

FAMILY AND CAREER DEVELOPMENT

The combining of a career with marriage and motherhood is done in a number of ways by American women and may be related to stages of the family life cycle. Duvall (1971) has identified eight major stages of the family life cycle:

(1) beginning families (married couples without children)
(2) childbearing families (oldest child under 30 months)
(3) families with preschool children (oldest child 30 months to 6 years)
(4) families with school-age children (oldest child 6 to 13 years)
(5) families with teenagers (oldest child 13 to 20 years)
(6) families as launching centers (first child gone to last child leaving home)
(7) families in the middle years (empty nest to retirement)
(8) aging families (retirement of both spouses)

Briefly considered below are each of these stages in relation to our data for dual-career wives.

Women whose families are in the first stage, or who are permanently childless, do not find that marriage alters their career development. Other research (for example, Simon, 1967; Martin et al., 1975) suggests the contrary: that married career women may be more productive than their single sisters. The major problem facing women at this stage, as in all stages, is a lack of geographic mobility.

Marriage does not affect a woman's career line as seriously as having a family. Judging from our small sample, where only one couple out of our original sample of 53 claimed to be voluntarily and permanently childless,[5] most choose to combine a career with child rearing. This characteristic of our sample coincides also with one of Yohalem's (1979: 191) major findings. She reports:

The presence of a disproportionate representation of never married women among the respondents contributed to the high degree of career continuity exhibited by the group. Relatively few married women remained childless and it was primarily the presence of children that acted as a brake upon careers.

Depending upon their stamina (some were able to get by on 4 or 5 hours of sleep per night) and their own philosophies of child rearing, women in stages 2 and 3 of the family cycle tended to reduce career involvement. Some interrupted their careers while others reduced their hours to part-time employment. It was not unusual for attorneys and physicians to set up practices from their homes during this period. Even those retaining full-time positions, however, cut back (or cut out) professionally related travel, research and publications, speaking engagements, and other professional "extras" that they had enjoyed.

Stages 4 and 5 witnessed an increase in career involvement, with women noting frequently that teenage children were proud of their accomplishments. While some were concerned that their careers may be having a harmful effect on their children, seeing these children develop as young adults alleviated any still unresolved guilt. As one successful attorney (#32) volunteered on our follow-up questionnaire:

> My children, a son 18 and daughter 16, are reasonable, straight people. They are very well adjusted and normal. My son loves my having a career because it keeps him from being overprotected. My daughter and I are very close. She would like to have me home more than I am, but adjusts to the schedule. We take "extra treats" for ourselves, like lunch in Palm Springs, lots of tennis together and good talks.

In stages 6 and 7 the professionally employed wife enters the height of her career. One very successful regular career line professor divided her career into the "job stage" and the "career stage" when we originally interviewed her in 1969. Other successful career women might acknowledge a similar division. As the children are launched, the married career woman has increased opportunity for research, writing, professional organizations, and travel. Yet it is significant that even here family demands may curtail career development. We have seen how one wife took a two-year leave of absence to care for her aged parents. Another couple had a severely retarded and handicapped adult child which kept her physician-mother's career involvement at half time (#27). The latter woman noted:

> Ours is a rather unusual situation and I probably would have worked more and in a somewhat different area had it not been

for our youngest child. However, having a profession and work that I enjoy has made our life with our little handicapped child much easier to cope with. Partly, I am sure, because I have trustworthy and competent help and can be out of the house, we have truly taken pleasure in our child.

Little is known about the eighth stage of dual-career families. Only one respondent (a physician) had retired, and she had always been employed on a part-time basis (#20). Her husband still retained his medical practice. Another respondent's husband had retired while the wife (who is seven years his junior) continued teaching at the university. She reported that her husband helped more with domestic responsibilities since his retirement (#37). Another professor had been widowed, noting that her career involvement helped get her through this trying time (#40). Yohalem (1979: 82-83) inquired about retirement plans in her longitudinal study of professional women, and she makes the following observation:

> The interest shown by respondents in working after reaching the age of 65 suggests that many of these women welcome the recent extension of the statutory retirement age to 70 years, especially those who have reentered the work force and wish to compensate for lost time. The prevailing sentiment was in favor of part-time employment during these years [Yohalem, 1979: 206].

In conclusion, the manner in which the demands of motherhood and mobility are handled varies, and, as suggested by our early discussion on the woman's career development, the career line for a married woman is quite different from that of a married man. It appears that patterns of career development, based primarily on the experiences of married career men, while helpful in understanding career development for married women, need to undergo drastic modification before patterns of career development for women can accurately be explored. As a first step in this direction we offer the following fourfold typology illustrated by patterns in our respondents' career histories.

MARRIED PROFESSIONAL WOMEN
AND CAREER TYPES

We are able to identify four major career types: regular, interrupted, second, and modified-second career lines. A *regular career* is one where the person pursues professional training immediately after graduating from college or shortly thereafter. Upon receipt of the professional degree, the person begins work and continues without, or with minimal, interruption. Regular careers usually involve full-time employment. We have found that part-time regular careers are also frequent among physicians and attorneys who have the freedom to set up, limit, and build private practices. The regular career type, with training being completed before marriage, aligns best with the stages delineated by Duvall (1971). The career is integrated with each of the stages of child rearing with minimal interruption. An *interrupted career* is one that begins as a regular career, but which is interrupted for several years, usually for child rearing. The sequence would display a pattern similar to the following: career training (plus some experience) followed by Duvall's stages 1 and 2, with the career resumed in stages 3 or 4 and other stages following. *Second careers* are those in which training for a profession only occurs after or near the time the children are grown and about to leave, or after a divorce. In these cases Duvall's stages 1 through 5 would occur in order, with career training beginning usually in stage 4 and actual career activities beginning in stages 5 or 6. A *modified-second career* begins earlier and may be defined as the case where professional training and subsequent career involvement occur after the last of the children is deemed old enough not to need full-time mothering, usually between the ages of 3 and 7. In this type, stages 1 and 2 are followed by career training, with career involvement beginning in stage 4 or 5.

These are intended to be ideal types within which there are other variations. We will briefly consider each of these career lines, illustrating from our data how each has served as a viable adaptation for combining a career and marriage.

REGULAR CAREER LINE

Of the 45 women who responded to our follow-up questionnaire, 17 (38%) had regular career lines with full-time employment. Of these, 3 were childless (1 voluntarily; 2 reportedly involuntarily), and the remaining 14 had from 1 to 5 children. While the career pattern in these cases most closely approximates what we might expect of males in these professions, the women still perceived costs to their careers brought about by the two-career situation. The costs were expressed largely in terms of geographic limitations and family demands noted earlier.

There is evidence that some of these women were able to see a difference between what they viewed as the "job" stage of their work and the later "career" stage that developed as family demands lessened. While their work patterns resembled those of many male colleagues, almost without exception married professional women with children found it necessary to compromise some of the "extras" of professional demands because of the family. Lectures, evening work, travel, and annual meetings often could not be integrated into their hectic schedules. They found their professional involvement greatly curtailed when their children were younger, gradually increasing as they got older, and leading to greater involvement—with the rewards of professional honors—only after the children had been launched.

INTERRUPTED CAREER LINE

In the pattern of the interrupted career line, as with the regular career line, professional training is completed immediately after college or with minimal interruption, usually followed by some work experience. There comes a break in the career usually for childbearing and child rearing. Of the 45 respondents, 16 (36%) had an interrupted career line.

Of these, two respondents listed themselves as unemployed due to the responsibilities of childbearing and child rearing in 1977, although one worked intermittently by teaching a course at a local university and the other did some legal work from her home. Both appeared to want part-time employment ideally, and only circumstances of employment opportunities seemed to separate them from the part-time regulars. A professor-mother (#46) of two grade-school-age children commented: "I would prefer to work part-time. The kids and their education are demanding. Financially we are better off now, so part-time work would satisfy me." A young attorney (#19), mother of two children, while doing legal work from her home, stated: "I'm home raising babies 'til both are in school all day. I'm out of the main stream of things during this time. My husband— male of the family—continues to do his thing."

Another illustration of an interrupted career may be found in the attorney (#13) who worked full-time until the birth of her two children. She remained home, not seeking any employment, for five years, and only then returned to full-time work. "I lost about five years of professional growth and promotion opportunities," she observed, "due to an extended leave of absence to be home with our small children." Back in the labor force, this attorney is not noticeably different from her sisters with a regular career line.

Some respondents modified their careers by substituting part-time work for full-time involvement. In 1969 one young professor (#46) stated:

> I would like to have a few more children. And with more than one child it would be difficult to continue working full time. So if I did have a few more children, I would wait until the youngest is in kindergarten before returning to work.

In our follow-up, this wife reported having another baby in 1971 and subsequent part-time employment. While she would prefer to secure a full-time position, she has not been able to. As she wrote in response to our follow-up:

> I still prefer to work—at least part-time. The kids and their education are more interesting and demanding now. Financially, we are better off, so part-time work satisfies me pretty well for now.

Nearly half of our 45 follow-up respondents reported changes in their career involvements from 1969 to 1977. Of these, 14 were more involved and 7 were less involved; for 24 of our respondents there was no change.

SECOND AND MODIFIED-SECOND CAREERS

There were 12 respondents (27%) who had either second careers or modified-second careers, either choosing or circumstances permitting them to put the heaviest demands of early childbearing years behind them before embarking on professional training and then a career. After a late start in their careers, these women follow a pattern of career involvement not unlike those of regular careers. Like regular careers, they may be either full- or part-time and may also be interrupted for other family demands. Because this is a follow-up study, all second careers were begun before 1969.

One woman who earned her Ph.D. in psychology after one child and a subsequent divorce remarried and had two more children. Now a practicing psychologist, she limits the hours per week that she works: "I work in my practice about 20 hours per week. I still have two children at home (ages 10-1/2 and 9) and I feel I can meet their needs only if I restrict the hours I work" (#5).

A professor who pursued a Ph.D. and a career at the university only after her child was in high school took a two-year leave of absence to care for aged parents. After the deaths of her parents, she returned once again to the university to head a special program she was in the process of setting up when she responded to our questionnaire.

Most modified-second careers appear to start slowly to accommodate family demands that are still present and increase momentum as the children grow older, while second careers are able to start out with more momentum due to the family life cycle and continued advancing. Of the seven modified-second careers in this sample, five might be indistinguishable in terms of achievements (promotions) from those of their sisters who had earlier career starts but slowed down career involvements to respond to family demands. Nor is there any appreciable difference in career accomplishments of the five second career respondents. One is a partner in a large law office and four are tenured associate professors with numerous publications at large universities. Second career accomplishments of the respondents were impressive, without any sign of burnout that may accompany lifelong career involvement.

DIVORCE

It is important to note that divorce is possible during any stage of the family life cycle discussed earlier, and is a characteristic of each career type offered in this study. Of our 45 follow-up respondents, 8 were involved in second marriages when originally interviewed in 1969. Some had embarked on their careers during the interim between divorce and remarriage, supporting Yohalem (1979: 191) in her assertion that divorce acted "to propel non-workers into the labor force and to spur career progress." Of these 8 women 2 were either separated or divorced at the time of the follow-up, but neither had remarriage plans. Also, 5 other respondents had either separated or divorced during the study period, with only one having remarried. In only a single case did the respondent acknowledge that her career helped to precipitate the divorce, although in other cases it was implied. One respondent described her situation as follows:

I am currently in the process of divorce. It was my decision. The career allows one to ignore, deny marital problems. For years I was too busy; I did not want to admit the truth. Work is very sustaining in the midst of divorce turmoil. . . . My career has advanced more rapidly than my husband's which has been the source of some tension (never verbalized though). As I have established professional identity, become more independent and sure of myself, my expectations of marriage have changed; i.e., dependency-head. I wish for sharing intimacy which I find is no longer there. Professional training has made me critical of my husband [#11].

Those involved in divorce noted two things: (1) a career made them financially independent, making "divorce possible without serious change in the standard of living," and (2) "having demanding work to do is great therapy during times of stress" (#28). The career itself may or may not have been a factor in the decision to divorce.

Upon remarriage, the new couples may be placed once again in the family life cycle depending upon the age of the youngest child. Most of our 1969 remarriage cases did not have children during the second marriage. It appears unlikely that any experiencing post-1977 remarriages will decide to have another child, which would place additional career restrictions on the wife due to family demands.

SUMMARY

Rapoport and Rapoport (1976: 343-358) have suggested that the dual-career family of the 1970s and 1980s may develop differently from the pattern they found in the 1960s. Indeed it may. Our follow-up data suggest, however, that the structure of the American family makes it virtually impossible for married career women with children to have career lines like those of their male counterparts. As we have seen, these women have benefited from recent legislative and ideological developments. And regardless of their levels of career involvement, most have done well in their professions on those levels. One young pediatrician (#17), however, spoke for others when she wrote:

My thoughts on the two-career family were well summarized by a young lawyer who spoke at the Harvard University commencement last June. She stated that a mother in today's society cannot compete with men or single women without family responsibilities. She added, "The world is full of fathers who rarely see their children (because of their careers); for mothers to follow the same course is not the answer."

This may help to explain a recent finding by Holahan and Gilbert (1979: 451), where high career aspirations were negatively related to role conflict for husbands but positively related to role conflict for wives. Currently the pressure of the married career woman is twofold: family responsibilities and career obligations (see Holahan and Gilbert, 1979; Gass, 1974).[6] An understanding and helping husband (as most women in our study had) helps to alleviate only a few of the family pressures, and cannot eliminate them. Our data suggest that married women do make significant career contributions, but may make them somewhat later in life. This fact should be recognized in hopes of alleviating career pressure on the young woman already overloaded with stresses of family responsibilities.

It seems probable, as implied by Hughes (1975) and confirmed here, that the eight major stages of the family life cycle sponsored by Duvall (1971) need to be extensively modified for women in dual-career marriages in general, and again for those with children and those without. While it is well known and accepted that the pressures on the married career woman are twofold, this study, in conjunction with others, seems to indicate that marriage alone is somewhat dysfunctional for the career-oriented woman, and that the combination of marriage and children creates a highly dysfunctional and pressure-prone situation for the career woman given our contemporary cultural habits. In addition, the career line pinnacle typically reached at a later age by the career woman shortens the woman's career life and may necessitate later ages for forced retirement should current trends continue.

NOTES

1. The findings from the 1969 study are reported in dissertations by Poloma (1970) and Garland (1971). Articles from the original study include Poloma and Garland (1971a, 1971b), Poloma (1972), and Garland (1972). Findings from the 1977 follow-up

study have been reported in Poloma and Garland (1980) and Pendleton et al. (1980a, 1980b).

2. Yohalem (1979), in another longitudinal study of professional women originally interviewed in 1963 and restudied in 1974, had similar findings. She reports, "The finding of the research was that the career commitment of this group of women was variable in intensity, but was rarely extinguished" (Yohalem, 1979: 190). More than four out of five respondents with careers were rated as good or high achievers, demonstrating career advancement (1979: 141).

3. Bailyn (1970) has pointed to the importance of knowing how the husband fits his work and his family into his life in order to adequately evaluate the married woman's resolution of the "career-family dilemma." Husbands in Bailyn's sample varied in placing career first or family first, with a few assigning importance to neither career nor family. Yet she did not find such an easy description of women's career-family patterns. She notes:

> The diversity of educated women's lives makes it particularly difficult to find a meaningful way of describing their career orientation at an early stage of their family life. For the men in the sample, all of whom are married and working and, presumably, expecting to continue this double pattern, the relative contribution of these two realms to their satisfactions in life is a meaningful way of assessing career-family orientation. But these conditions do not hold for the women [Bailyn, 1970: 99-100].

The focus of this chapter is the career pattern of women, which is much more diversified than married men's.

4. Numbers in parentheses accompanying respondents' quotations refer to case numbers assigned couples in 1969 and used again on the 1977 questionnaires.

5. This respondent wrote a note on the 1977 questionnaire stating, "Your questionnaire was maddening. When are you going to do a study of childless two-career families?" One of the authors of this article has been involved in a study of childless couples (Nason and Poloma, 1976). Combining this research with the present research, we would like to suggest that, for the most part, it is not high-status career women who have voluntarily chosen the childless state. The couples in the childless couple study were all of lower status than those of the present dual-career family study, indicating that high-status dual-career couples can better afford the "luxury" (financially) of having both children and two careers. More research is needed to either confirm or refute this tentative observation.

6. It seems the mass media also are beginning to recognize this (see Berk, 1980).

REFERENCES

Aldous, J., R. W. Osmond, and M. W. Hicks
    1979   "Men's work and men's families," pp. 227-256 in W. R. Burr et al. (eds.) Contemporary Theories about the Family. Volume 1. New York: Macmillan.
Bailyn, L.
    1970   "Career and family orientations of husbands and wives in relation to marital happiness." Human Relations 23, 2: 97-109.

Berk, A.
1980   "Modern woman's double life." Newsweek (September 29): 17.
Bryson, J. B. and R. Bryson
1978   Dual Career Couples. New York: Human Sciences.
Duvall, E.
1971   Family Development. Philadelphia: J. B. Lippincott.
Garland, T. N.
1972   "The better half? The male in the dual profession family," in C. Safilios-
        Rothschild (ed.) Toward a Sociology of Women. Lexington, MA: Xerox
        Publishing.
1971   "The forgotten men: husbands of professionally employed women." Ph.D.
        dissertation, Case Western Reserve University.
Gass, G. Z.
1974   "Equitable marriage," Family Coordinator 23: 369-372.
Holahan, C. K. and L. A. Gilbert
1979   "Conflict between major life roles: women and men in dual career couples."
        Human Relations 32, 6: 451-467.
Hughes, H. M.
1975   "Women in academic sociology, 1925-1975." Soc. Focus 8 (August): 215-
        221.
Martin, T. W., K. J. Berry, and R. B. Jacobsen
1975   "The impact of dual-career marriages on female careers: an empirical test
        of a Parsonian hypothesis." J. of Marriage and the Family 37: 734-742.
Mortimer, J. T.
1978   "Dual-career families—a sociological perspective," pp. 1-30 in S. Peterson
        et al. (eds.) The Two-Career Family: Issues and Alternatives. Washington,
        DC: University Press of America.
Nason, E. M. and M. M. Poloma
1976   "Voluntary childless couples: the emergence of a variant lifestyle." Beverly
        Hills, CA: Sage.
Pendleton, B. F., M. M. Poloma, T. N. Garland
1980a   "Scales for investigation of the dual-career family." J. of Marriage and the
        Family 42: 269-276.
1980b   "An approach to quantifying the needs of dual career families." Presented
        at the annual meeting of the Midwest Sociological Society, Milwaukee,
        April.
Peterson, S. S., J. M. Richardson, and G. V. Kreuter
1978   The Two-Career Family: Issues and Alternatives. Washington, DC: Uni-
        versity Press of America.
Poloma, M. M.
1972   "Role conflict and the professionally employed woman," in C. Safilios-
        Rothschild (ed.) Toward a Sociology of Women. Lexington, MA: Xerox
        Publishing.
1970   "The married professional woman: an empirical examination of three
        myths." Ph.D. dissertation, Case Western Reserve University.
Poloma, M. M. and T. N. Garland
1980   "Family life cycle and career: the dual-career family revisited." Presented
        at the annual meeting of the Southern Sociological Society, Knoxville,
        Tennessee, March.

1971a   "The married professional woman: a study in the tolerance of domestica-
        tion." J. of Marriage and the Family 33: 531-540.
1971b   "The myth of the egalitarian family: familial roles and the professionally
        employed wife," pp. 741-761 in A. Theodore (ed.) The Professional Wom-
        an. Cambridge, MA: Schenkman.
Rapoport, R. and R. N. Rapoport
1978   "Dual-career families: progress and prospects." Marriage and Family Rev.
        1, 5: 1-12.
1976   Dual-Career Families Re-examined. New York: Harper and Row.
1969   "The dual-career family: a variant pattern and social change." Human
        Relations 22, 1: 3-30.
Simon, R. J.
1967   "The woman Ph.D.: a recent profile." Social Problems 15: 221-336.
Yohalem, A.
1979   The Careers of Professional Women. Montclair, NJ: Allanheld Osmun.

10

Housework by Husbands

Determinants and Implications*

SUZANNE MODEL

The handicaps women face at home and on the job become more apparent as females increase their participation in education and employment. The women's movement has heightened awareness of sexual inequality (Mason et al., 1976), yet women remain at a disadvantage. Home obligations detract from their ability to seek top jobs and command high wages. Working hours, commuting distance, overtime demands—all must be minimized to allow time and energy for housework and child care.

The research reported here indicates that the sexual nature of the division of labor is not changing. Although women's labor force activity creates substantial overload, husbands are unlikely to relieve the strain. Under optimal conditions, we note the wife doing five times as much domestic work as her spouse and usually more. When husbands contribute, they do so with the understanding that they are operating in "female territory."

Many investigators have examined the division of conjugal roles. Two disparate interpretations arise in these studies. The first opinion is that low-income families are more likely to

*The author wishes to thank Professor David Goldberg for his invaluable assistance in pursuing the research and preparing the manuscript for this study.

193

observe sex-role segregation. Whether this behavior is a result of strong kin involvement (Bott, 1957), committed homemakers (Rosser and Harris, 1965), or sex-role socialization (Perrucci et al., 1978), lower-class men are not inclined to domesticity (Schneider and Smith, 1973).[1]

Other studies contradict these propositions. Blood and Wolfe (1960) report significantly greater husband housework effort in blue-collar than in white-collar homes, as, more recently, do Ericksen et al. (1979). Both these research investigations also indicate that the employment status of the wife is an additional factor inducing husband's household participation.

Studies of more egalitarian relationships, such as those by Rapoport and Rapoport (1976), note that husbands of high-status career women are quite active in family chores. This finding raises the possibility that not only do time limitations created by the wife's employment influence male outputs at home (Blood and Wolfe, 1960), but that the greater her contributions to the provider role, the more help she receives. Scanzoni (1978) observes that the wife's bargaining power in sharing household tasks is associated with the meaning of her work. Women who are career-oriented, self-confident, and continuous in labor force participation are both more likely to contribute a substantial increment to the family living standard and to share housework with their spouses.

The operationalization of such a relative resource balance between mates has varied. Ericksen et al. (1979) found both a positive association between wife's educational achievement and husband's household help, and a negative relation between husband's earnings and his home efforts. These results suggest a relative resource explanation but do not demonstrate one. Farkas (1976) examined wage rate ratios but did not take into account actual earned resources. Scanzoni (1978) explored the effect of husband-wife income ratios among couples 22 to 33 years of age. He found that as the wife's relative income rose, so did male participation in cooking and dishwashing.

Our analysis concludes that attitudes, wife's employment status, husband's income, and stage of the family life cycle each contribute to explaining variance in husband's efforts. When scrutiny is directed at an equal earner subsample, an additional effect is noted. The smaller the income differential between spouses, the greater male housework participation becomes. Since high-paying positions are overwhelmingly held by males, this differential is larger in more affluent families. Implications will be addressed following a discussion of our general results.

ANALYSIS OF DATA

The data set studied comes from the 1978 Detroit Area Study conducted by University of Michigan students and staff. A stratified sample of 650 women within the Detroit metropolitan area was interviewed.[2] All respondents were currently married; only about 8% were black.

While not the main focus of the investigation, several questions on conjugal role division were asked. Five dependent variables and their relationships are here reported. These include wives' sex-role ideology and four measures of husband housework participation, as reported by the wife.

BELIEFS

A number of attitude statements were included in our survey, the centrally relevant one being, "There is some work that is men's and some that is women's, and they should not be doing each other's." Respondents reacted to this judgment, hereafter labeled SHARATT, from "strongly agree" to "strongly disagree" on a five-point scale. Since the statement as worded reflects a traditional outlook, higher scores indicate a more modern viewpoint. The mean response was 3.52, with a standard deviation of 1.20.

In devising a model to explain variance in SHARATT, a number of hypotheses were incorporated. First was the inclusion of influences stemming from women's domestic investments. Large family size or the presence of young children was expected to confirm traditional values. Another perspective posits an achievement-oriented determinant. High levels of education and labor force participation were thought to promote liberalism. Finally, attitudes about conjugal role division may be influenced by individual factors such as age, ethnoreligious commitments, and social class. It was anticipated that younger, higher-status, later-generation women would hold the more modern views.[3]

Data analysis confirmed the hypothesis of a traditional impact associated with the two domestic constraints, but this effect disappeared with the introduction of controls. Social class, operationalized as husband's income, contributed no understanding to the variance in SHARATT, nor did the other personal factors. The persistent and meaningful dimension was that of women's achievement: work status, income, and education. Further, the introduction of multivariable techniques deleted all but two predictors of SHARATT views: wife's labor market participation and her education. The standardized equation is:

$$\hat{Y} = .128 \ X_1 + .215 \ X_2 \qquad N = 650 \qquad R^2 = .0756$$

where $\hat{Y}$ is SHARATT, X_1 is wife's employment status, and X_2 is her education. Both coefficients are significant at the .01 level. It must be admitted, however, that the great majority of variance in SHARATT remains unexplained.

BEHAVIOR

We created four different measures of male housework contribution from our survey material. Respondents were asked, "For each household task, tell me how many times it was done by the wife alone, the husband alone, or the husband with someone else." The tasks were: grocery shopping, laundry, dinner preparation, dinner dishwashing, and vacuuming. The variable HEALON is the sum of all efforts the husband undertook by himself in these household areas. We wondered if some men engaged more in shared than in solitary tasks. We thus added the number of husband activities done only with some-

TABLE 1
Weekly Male Household Tasks: Summary Statistics

Parameter	N	Mean	Standard Deviation	Range	% Husbands Not Involved
HEALON	650	1.51	2.68	0-18	58.8%
HEWITH	650	1.26	2.47	0-22	58.4%
HISSUM	650	2.14	3.24	0-21.5	40.6%
HIS%	650	10.9%	17.02	0-82.9%	40.6%

one else, creating the measure HEWITH. An assumption which the data substantiate has been that the husband's primary coworker is his wife. We judged husband's total contribution to home maintenance by adding each man's HEALON score to half that of HEWITH. We label this result HISSUM.

Finally, families vary in the amount of housework they perform. As Slocum and Nye (1976) illustrate, the household division of labor is frequently measured by the relative rather than absolute contribution of each spouse. To control for the variance in fastidiousness between homes, we devised HIS%. HIS% is the ratio of HISSUM, the husband's share of the work, to the total number of household jobs in areas recorded by the interviewer. A summary of the four above-described measures is presented in Table 1.

In selecting a model to explain husband's household chore contributions, we anticipated, first, that the sex-role attitudes of our female respondents would have relevance. In addition, the domestic, achievement, and environmental factors cited above in the explanatory model of attitudes merited reexamination. Finally, when analyzing behavior, theory suggests the incorporation of temporal contingencies. Available time may determine the choice of actor for some household jobs. A listing of the significant predictor variables for the four male housework measures, as well as their net coefficients, is found in Table 2.[4]

A number of attitude items were analyzed for effects on behavior. The positive feeling toward domestic activity suggested by Rosser and Harris (1965) was operationalized as the

TABLE 2
Husband Household Participation: Standard Net Coefficients

| Parameter | SHARATT | Coefficient[a] | | | R^{2}[b] | N |
		Husband's Income	Wife's Work Status	Family Life Cycle[c]		
HEALON	.0912	−.1413	.1434	−	.0943	580
HEWITH	.1177	0	0	−	.0386	625
HISSUM	.1134	−.1334	.1540	−	.1160	580
HIS%	.1431	−.1136	.1828	−	.1501	580

a. All coefficients are significant at the 0.01 level.
b. R^{2} is the squared multiple correlation with all significant contributors, including family life cycle, in the equation.
c. Since there are six different vectors, their relative effects are presented separately in Table 3.

response to a question, "When you consider your feelings about household tasks, would you say that you liked all, most, a few, or none of them?" Replies showed no relation to husband housework efforts. The only attitudinal variable demonstrating an impact, though small following the introduction of controls, was SHARATT.

Among the domestic factors tested, only life-cycle stage made a contribution to understanding husband's household behavior. A comparison of the coefficients reveals the continued salience of these shifts on responsibilities in the female domain, as suggested by Spanier et al. (1979). Greater male participation is usually associated with newlywed and retired status, lending support to our suspicion that the wife is the husband's major housework partner. When children are available as substitutes, the smallest contribution is made by their fathers on all measures.

From the vantage point of personal achievement, only employment status held explanatory value. A weak relationship between wife's years of labor force participation and husband's helpfulness disappeared under multiple regression procedures.

TABLE 3
Life Cycle Coefficients for Husband Housework

Parameter	Life Cycle Coefficient[a]					
	Newly Wed	Pre-School Parent	Latency Parent	Teen Parent	Children Grown	Retired Couple
HEALON	−.0158	.1402	−.3639	−.3981	.0560	1.547
HEWITH	.7059	−.1339	−.5910	−.3018	−.0640	1.060
HISSUM	.2331	.0853	−.3973	−.5624	−.0107	2.265
HIS%	3.997	1.468	−2.325	−4.477	.3761	13.09
N	23	124	116	184	112	66

a. These coefficients have been recalculated to include the category eliminated to obtain the regression estimate. All values are expressed as deviations from the grand mean of their measure.

For this sample, wife's education level had no impact whatsoever, nor did husband's.

In accordance with the findings of Blood and Wolfe (1960) and Aldous (1969), time serves as a constraint. When wives have more free hours, they accomplish more work around the home both absolutely and relative to their husbands. Male participation is mildly associated with shorter working hours for the husband and longer ones for the wife. This effect, as well as a weak trend favoring the older husband, disappears under multiple regression.

To test the thesis that ascriptive loyalty reinforces a sexual division of labor, as suggested by Harrell-Bond's (1969) work, we correlated generations in the United States, intensity of ethnic identification, religiosity, ethnic group, and religious affiliation with household activity. While wife's religiosity had a small gross effect, none of these variables made any net contribution in explaining the variance.

The validity of Bott's (1957) hypothesis, that the more connected the wife's social network, the more segregated the family roles, was explored in the survey setting. Respondents listed their three closest friends and stated whether or not these were good friends of one another. Networks were scored from unconnected to completely connected. This scale showed no relation to husband's housework participation. A similar measure of consanguinity addressed the possibility that a greater preponderance of relatives in the friendship network was associated with traditionalism in the division of labor. This proposition failed as well.

While no relation was found between husband's income and SHARATT, a negative association obtains for husband's earnings and most of our housework behavior indicators. The liberal effect of education on attitudes is neutralized by high male income, which mitigates sharing behavior for our respondents. Support for a conjoint resource exchange theory, to be outlined below, begins to appear.

Our results lend no confirmation to theories of pronounced conjugal role segregation among working-class couples. Both absolute and relative involvement of husbands fit the model of Blood and Wolfe (1960). Tests for interaction among explanatory variables were negative. As male income went up, husband's chore involvement generally went down. Wife's employment status, sex-role ideology, and the family life stage all add pressure for spouse effort. The determinants of shared housework are less clear, with only attitude and life stage making contributions in this analysis.

DISCUSSION

THEORETICAL APPROACHES

As thinkers in the functionalist tradition, Blood and Wolfe (1960) interpret their results in terms of systemic strain. Female job activity decreases time available for home chores. This tension may result in an increase in husband efforts. However, they too note the lower performance by white-collar husbands.

The status of the high-income man, however, does not become a causal factor. According to their view:

> Not that successful husbands disdain household tasks—they are just too busy being successful to have the time [Blood and Wolfe, 1960: 61].

While most women endorse husband's success, the double-duty day is not so functional for working wives.

According to Scanzoni (1972), the resolution of this conflict will be to the advantage of the spouse with the stronger bargaining power. In reviewing studies similar to ours, he proposes a comparative resource theory. He labels the wife a "junior partner." Despite her level of ability, she is almost always dependent on her husband for the major part of the family income. Most women do not engage in careers, regardless of the number of hours or years worked. Unless women are able to draw equally from that major source of position in our society, income, they cannnot hope to move beyond the rank of junior partner.

A link between this exchange process and the temporal constraints noted by functionalists is provided by Berk and Berk (1978). The American husband most often earns at a higher wage rate than his wife. To maximize the family's monetary gain under conditions of household and financial demand, the husband, rather than the wife, belongs in the workforce. It is rational for the wife to spend more of her hours in domestic work than market work, since the monetary loss incurred by the family is thereby minimized. Again, the implied remedy is equal earning power.

EMPIRICAL TRENDS

We sought to determine if sex-role relationships were affected by equality in the marketplace. Defining egalitarian earnings very broadly as wife's income of not more than $1000 per annum below that of her husband, we were only able to generate 55 cases.

TABLE 4
Mean Male Household Help in Egalitarian Income Homes

		Mean Effort[a]	
		Each Spouse	Each Spouse
	Total	Earns < $15,000	Earns > $15,000
Parameter	Subsample	Annually	Annually
HEALON	2.55	3.07	1.36
HEWITH	2.20	1.60	3.53
HISSUM	3.65	3.88	3.12
HIS%	21.7%	22.3%	20.2%
N	55	38	17

a. Statistical testing for group mean differences between all egalitarian households and the remainder of the sample yielded t values significant at the 0.01 level for all four indicators.

On all measures we developed, this subsample shows higher husband participation. Not unexpectedly, the majority of equal-income families were in the low-income range. Wage and education differentials are usually smaller between spouses of this group. It is the wife of the more successful husband who is more likely the status inferior. Only in three of our egalitarian households did each spouse succeed in earning $20,000 or more annually, a reflection of the low salaries offered females.

Informal study of the data shows that high-income men contribute more to housework if they are married to equal-earning wives. Otherwise, they rank lowest. The 146 husbands whose annual earnings were $25,000 or more averaged a housework contribution of 6.39%. Conversely, working-class husbands exhibit a high level of participation regardless of wife's status. There were 100 husbands with incomes of $10,000 or less who shared 18.3% of the household chores included in our survey. As Table 4 indicates, an additional increment of help is associated with egalitarian earnings at lower levels as well. Unfortunately, the meager case base following the introduction of additional controls on this subgroup makes detailed analysis impossible.

The high HEWITH mean noted among better-income couples is intriguing. Although it cannot be carefully investigated in so small a population, it could indicate a togetherness commitment within the dual-career family, as expected by Rapoport and Rapoport (1976). Of course, more joint efforts might be an artifact of the life-cycle shifts noted above. The newly married, more-educated woman, for example, may more easily achieve wage parity with her husband *before* she drops out of the labor market to have children.

LIMITATIONS OF THE STUDY

Many larger samples of equal-earner spouses from all classes, ages, and backgrounds are necessary for investigators to sort out the causally relevant phenomena. Weighting HEWITH by half when creating HISSUM and HIS% may underestimate husbands' contributions to household endeavor. Some joint tasks, such as grocery shopping, take almost as long done individually as together.

We have not done a time budget study. We have relied on wives' impressions rather than husbands' or joint reports. We have neglected to tap many necessary jobs. Of course, there is no standard method for measuring housework. We believe our approach, based on reported behavioral incidence rather than estimates of frequency, provides a sound empirical basis for conjugal role analysis.

CONCLUDING REMARKS

Buying her way to equal partnership is no easy task for a woman. A segregated labor market employs most women in lower-paying, poor-status posts. In our sample alone, full-time working women's mean earnings were only 46% of those of the men. Surely one of the reasons women do not have careers is because of their family duties. Pleck (1977: 423) explains:

> For women, the demands of the family role are permitted to intrude into the work role. . . . For husbands, the work-family role boundary is likewise asymmetrically permeable, but in the other direction. Many husbands literally "take work home."

These norms further the husband's status and earnings, while concurrently limiting the wife's.

Regretfully, little relief is in sight. Labor force participation among all women continues to grow. But married women who work for the second income so common in our inflationary economy are likely to accept a smaller salary, the more so the more successful the husband. Unknowingly, such women have reinforced their second-class status at home. They remain in a weak bargaining position with respect to their husbands. Their caretaking chores at home simultaneously legitimize their weak labor market position. Prospects for disrupting this vicious circle are not very bright.

NOTES

1. In Bott's (1957) research, the connectedness of the wife's social network, that is, whether she had an interacting group of friends, was the primary determinant of sex-role segregation between spouses. The connected network, however, was more common in working-class households. Similarly, for Rosser and Harris (1965), the central determinant of household sex-role behavior was a very favorable attitude in the wife toward being a homemaker. Again, a strong commitment to domesticity was reported as more common among blue-collar wives.

2. The stratification procedure involved components of geography, race, marital status, and socioeconomic position.

3. Variables used in this part of the analysis are coded as follows: six education and seven income intervals were determined by a combination of their distribution in the data and their meaningfulness. All interval values were then coded at the midpoint. For example, cases of completion of grades 9-11 were combined and coded 10. Age was entered as raw data. Employment status and family life cycle were dummy variables. The latter was constructed following Blood and Wolfe (1960), who view couples as occupying one of six stages, depending on the age of their oldest child. Childless couple stages were categorized by years of marriage and retirement status of husband. Of the wives, 286 were employed, 178 full-time.

4. Additional coding procedures are as follows: wife religiosity was rated on the basis of frequency of church attendance, scaled 1 (weekly or more) to 6 (never). Years of wife's employment were reduced to four categories, while both spouses' hours were trichotomized.

REFERENCES

Aldous, J.
    1979   "Occupational characteristics and males' role performance in the family." J. of Marriage and the Family 31 (November): 707-712.

Berk, R. and S. Berk
  1978   "A simultaneous equation model for the division of household labor." Soc.
         Methods and Research 6 (May): 431-467.
Blood, R. and D. Wolfe
  1960   Husbands and Wives: The Dynamics of Married Living. New York:
         Macmillan.
Bott, E.
  1957   Family and Social Network. New York: Macmillan.
Ericksen, J., W. Yancey, and E. Ericksen
  1979   "The division of family roles." J. of Marriage and the Family 41 (May):
         301-313.
Farkas, G.
  1976   "Education, wage rates, and the division of labor between husband and
         wife." J. of Marriage and the Family 38 (August): 473-483.
Harrell-Bond, B.
  1969   "Conjugal role behavior." Human Relations 22 (February): 77-91.
Mason, K., J. Czajka, and S. Arber
  1976   "Change in U.S. women's sex-role attitudes, 1964-1974." Amer. Soc. Rev.
         41 (August): 573-596.
Perrucci, C., H. Potter, and D. Rhoads
  1978   "Determinants of male family-role performance." Psychology of Women
         Q. (January): 53-66.
Pleck, J.
  1977   "The work-family role system." Social Problems 24 (April): 417-427.
Rapoport, R. and R. Rapoport
  1976   Dual Career Families Re-examined. New York: Harper & Row.
Rosser, C. and C. Harris
  1965   The Family and Social Change. London: Routledge & Kegan Paul.
Scanzoni, J.
  1978   Sex Roles, Women's Work, and Marital Conflict. Lexington, MA: D. C.
         Heath.
  1972   Sexual Bargaining: Power Politics in the American Marriage. Englewood
         Cliffs, NJ: Prentice-Hall.
Schneider, D. and R. Smith
  1973   Class Differences and Sex Roles in American Kinship and Family Struc-
         ture. Englewood Cliffs: NJ: Prentice-Hall.
Slocum, W. and F. Nye
  1976   "Provider and housekeeper roles," pp. 81-99 in F. Nye (ed.) Role Structure
         and Analysis of the Family. Beverly Hills, CA: Sage.
Spanier, G., W. Sauer, and R. Larzelere
  1979   "An empirical evaluation of the family life cycle." J. of Marriage and the
         Family 41 (February): 27-38.

11

Preschoolers' Sex-Role Identity, Father-Role Perceptions, and Paternal Family Participation

BONNIE E. CARLSON

Married women, including those with young children, continue to enter the labor force (Hoffman, 1979). Although the majority of employed women may not have very young children, the number of dual-career families[1] with preschool-aged children is increasing. As women begin to expect and demand equality in the home as well as in the workforce, some of these dual-worker couples will elect to depart from the traditional sex-based division of labor and perform family roles in a nontraditional manner, with husbands taking increasing responsibility for child care and/or housekeeping. To date, very little work has been done on the impact of this natural experiment on the children who live in these pioneering families. Some have expressed concern about these alternative family structures, fearing that children will be neglected or will grow up without a solid sense of their own gender identities. Others feel that the increased involvement of fathers will have

*This research was supported in part by grants from the Center for Continuing Education of Women and the Rackham School of Graduate Studies, the University of Michigan, Ann Arbor, Michigan. It was part of a larger study, of which Dr. Norma Radin was Principal Investigator.

salutary effects both on the fathers themselves and on their children. Many have assumed that children's perceptions of sex roles will be altered when they have observed alternative models in their homes. At this point in time, the accuracy of these varied predictions cannot be assessed due to the meager research on this topic. This study was conducted in order to explore the relationships between different levels of paternal involvement in child-care and household tasks and (1) children's perceptions of the father role and (2) boys' masculinity, in dual-career and more traditional families.

THE CHILD-CARE AND HOUSEKEEPING ROLES

The child-care role, which is concerned primarily with custodial care and physical maintenance of the child,[2] has been associated traditionally with the mother rather than the father (Blood and Wolfe, 1960; Nye and Gecas, 1976). What happens to enactment of the child-care role when the mother is employed? Some have asserted that "the division of labor between husband and wife is affected by maternal employment" and that "husbands of employed women help more in household tasks *including child care*" (Hoffman, 1974: 206, italics added).

However, several empirical studies employing diverse methodologies have found little or no sharing of the child-care role under conditions of maternal employment. For example, two major time-budget studies have obtained data by asking large numbers of respondents to keep time diaries of their activities for the previous day, recorded in small units, such as 15-minute intervals. Both studies found the best predictor of women's child-care time to be the age of the youngest child. However, when this factor was held constant, maternal employment outside of the home was found to have only minimal effects on time spent on family care. Several studies based on interview data have similarly found that regardless of the child care task investigated, even in dual-career families, few instances of total paternal responsibility for a task, or even sharing of it, were identified (Ericksen et al., 1979; Gecas, 1976; St. John-Parsons, 1978; Weingarten, 1978).

Thus, a general consensus does seem to emerge that mothers, regardless of employment status or number of hours worked, have assumed the majority of responsibility for child care. Despite the fact that there has been a great deal of discussion about fathers getting more involved in child rearing, and the assumption that fathers take more responsibility for child care when their wives are in the labor force, these changes do not seem to be reflected to any appreciable extent in recent time-use, questionnaire, or interview data (Ericksen et al., 1979; Gecas, 1976; Robinson, 1977; St. John-Parsons, 1978; Walker and Woods, 1976; Weingarten, 1978).

The situation with regard to the housekeeping role closely parallels that of the child-care role. There is controversy among family experts regarding the extent to which the traditional division of labor, with the wife performing the overwhelming majority of housework, is altered in families where the wife is employed and has a career.

There is agreement that when wives are not employed, their husbands perform very few household tasks, and that those they do perform tend to be limited to the traditional male realms, such as car and yard maintenance, general repairs, and the like (Robinson, 1977; Walker and Woods, 1976). There is also consensus on the fact that when wives are employed the amount of time they spend on household work decreases (by about one-half), but this by no means compensates completely for the increased number of working hours they expend as a result of employment outside of the home. The question is, do husbands of employed wives take greater responsibility for performing household chores than husbands of nonemployed wives? The data bearing on this question are equivocal. Some studies report small increases (such as 10-12%) in husband participation when the wife is employed (Blood and Wolfe, 1960; Perrucci et al., 1978; Robinson, 1977). However, other studies have failed to report noteworthy increases in husband participation in response to maternal employment (Bryson et al., 1976; Stafford et al., 1977; Walker and Woods, 1976).

But there is agreement that even if the husband does increase participation in response to employment of the wife, the increase is almost negligible, the participation tends to be confined to domains traditionally defined as male, and the wife is left to perform the majority of housekeeping tasks. And yet, we know that there are some "role-sharing" couples, and it is important to consider the impact, if any, of such role sharing on the children who experience and observe it. Some child development experts (such as Biller, 1971) have expressed concern about the impact of paternal performance of the traditional feminine family roles, although no published work bearing directly on this issue could be identified.

PERCEPTIONS OF PARENT ROLES

Most of the studies on children's perceptions of parent roles have focused on the functional aspects of adult roles, that is, what men and women actually do and what roles they perform. The conclusions are highly consistent. Children, even as young as age 3, can clearly distinguish between male and female functional adult roles and can identify a wide range of behaviors which are culturally associated with one adult sex role or the other. Mothers are seen as homemakers, actively engaged in child care and household chores, whereas fathers are seen as economic providers (Dubin and Dubin, 1965; Finch, 1955; Hartley, 1960; Vener and Snyder, 1966; Williams et al., 1975).

More recently, a number of researchers have investigated the question of whether actual parental behaviors, such as employment outside of the home and participation in household tasks, are related to the ways in which children perceive adult roles.

Three studies were found which examined young children's perceptions of parent roles in relation to employment status of the mother. Vener and Snyder (1966) found no relationship between mothers' employment status and children's knowledge about adult sex roles in a sample of 120 preschoolers. Miller (1975) compared 17 kindergarten daughters of employed mothers with a matched control group of girls with nonemployed mothers. Daughters of working mothers tended to see parent roles in a less stereotypical way than daughters of nonworking mothers. Marantz and Mansfield (1977) examined two types of stereotyping in relation to both maternal employment status and father participation in household chores (as reported by the mother) among girls in three age groups: five- to six-year-olds, seven- to eight-year-olds, and nine- to eleven-year-olds. Among the youngest girls, employment status of the mother was unrelated to scores on the activity-stereotype measure. However, at all ages, daughters of employed mothers were found to hold fewer qualitative, personality-trait stereotypes than daughters of full-time homemakers. Levels of paternal participation in domestic chores, although associated with maternal employment status, were unrelated to sex-role stereotyping scores.

On the basis of the studies reviewed, it can be concluded that young children can correctly identify culturally prescribed sex roles, and therefore should also be able to identify deviations from stereotypical patterns of adult sex-role behaviors in their own families. However, the limited empirical evidence suggests that direct observation of family experiences, by young girls at least, may have little impact on the way in which they perceive adult sex roles. No data on preschool-aged boys in homes with nontraditional enactment of parent roles were found, and so no conclusions can be drawn with regard to their perceptions. The data suggest that maternal employment, in the absence of increased paternal participation in stereotypically female family tasks, may not affect children's perceptions. It may be the case that a father's departure from the traditional male role would be more salient to a young boy than it would be to a young girl, particularly during the preschool-age period (Marantz and Mansfield, 1977). Therefore, it is conceivable that boys' perceptions of the paternal role might be more affected by observing a nontraditional father, while those of young girls would be less affected or unaffected.

DEVELOPMENT OF MASCULINITY IN BOYS

Because of the concerns expressed by some parents and child development experts that nontraditional performance of the male family role might have deleterious effects on young boys, the relationship between paternal behaviors and sons' masculinity was explored. This should not be interpreted as an assumption on the part of the author that masculinity is more desirable than feminine traits, or exclusively desirable, for young boys.

Studies on masculine development center on five aspects of paternal behavior which have been found to be present in the fathers of boys who are highly masculine: nurturance, punitiveness, masculinity, availability, and dominance. The overall conclusion reached in most empirical studies on this issue is that both paternal dominance and masculinity facilitate masculine development in boys.

With regard to masculinity, there is concern that when fathers engage in "maternal-like" behavior it may inhibit the development of masculinity in their sons (Biller, 1971). According to Biller (1971: 24), it is not the paternal participation in housework per se that causes problems, but rather "the father's surrendering of the masculine role in the family (e.g., decision making) and/or a relative parental role reversal." In fact, it has been said that the most important characteristic of the father in relation to development of boys' masculinity is his role in family leadership and decision making (Biller and Borstelman, 1967).

These conclusions are largely based on a study of 186 middle-class kindergarten boys and their parents. Two measures of parental dominance were employed: (1) children's subjective perceptions of the dominant parent were obtained;

and (2) parents were given a decision-making problem in the area of children's behavior to resolve in a laboratory setting, wherein the relative dominance of each parent was assessed. Both measures were found to be significantly related to sons' sex-role orientation and preferences. On the basis of this, it was concluded that if the mother does not permit the father to be dominant in the family, the father may become excessively dominant with his son, although it was not noted that the boys in the mother-dominant homes were less masculine than other boys (Biller, 1969).

Hetherington (1965) found in a similar study that boys' sex-role preference scores were more masculine in father-dominant than mother-dominant homes. However, it should be noted that the dominance measure used in the Biller and Hetherington studies was obtained in a highly contrived situation and may not be a valid indicator of actual dominance in the home.

On the basis of this review of the literature, the following hypotheses were generated:

(1) there will be an inverse relationship between paternal participation in child care and children's stereotyping of the father role;
(2) there will be an inverse relationship between paternal participation in household tasks and children's stereotypes of the father role;
(3) there will be an inverse relationship between paternal participation in household tasks and sons' masculinity; and
(4) there will be a positive relationship between paternal influence in family decision making and sons' masculinity.

METHOD

THE SAMPLE

To investigate these hypotheses, an exploratory study was conducted using a self-selected sample of 60 families, each having a child between the ages of three and six, all of whom lived in or near a midwestern university community. All but two of the families were white. In general, parents were young, highly educated, and held professional jobs, if employed. To ensure homogeneity with respect to social class, only families which fell into the top two social strata on Hollingshead's Four Factor Index of Social Status (Hollingshead, 1970) were included in the sample. The families were divided into three groups of 20 each on the basis of two variables, maternal employment status and level of paternal responsibility for child care. The groups were matched on sex (12 boys and 8 girls in each) and age of child (mean = 54 months at time of interview).

The *Mother Primary Caregiver* group (Group 1) consisted of families in which the father was employed on a full-time basis, but the mother was not employed outside of the home for more than 10 hours per week, and assumed primary responsibility for child care. Fathers' child care responsibilities were minimal.

In the *Dual-Career, Mother Primary Caregiver* group (Group 2) both parents were employed outside of the home, in school full-time, or full-time combination of both. The mother took primary responsibility for child care, with fathers assuming minimal responsibility.

In the *Dual-Career, Shared Caregiving* group (Group 3) both parents were employed full-time outside of the home, in school full-time or a full-time combination of both. Responsibility for child care was shared approximately equally.

PROCEDURE

Families were interviewed in their homes by the author, trained graduate students in social work, or advanced undergraduate psychology majors. Usually fathers were interviewed first, followed by mothers, with child testing sessions scheduled last. Parents' interviews were audiotaped and lasted from one to one and one-half hours. All interviews were completed within a period of one year.

MEASUREMENT OF PARENT VARIABLES

The questionnaire administered explored the following: extent of involvement in parenting tasks and household chores; feelings about own involvement and spouse's involvement in both parenting and household tasks; family decision making; and availability of each spouse to the child.

In order to obtain a more valid estimate of the father's participation in child care than the global estimate used initially to screen families and assign them to groups, an index was constructed called the Paternal Involvement in Child Care Index (PICCI). The index is computed independently for each spouse and consists of five sections derived from questionnaire items: (1) the *statement of involvement* with the child; (2) an estimate of participation in four *child care* tasks; (3) an estimate of involvement in four *socialization* tasks; (4) influence in family *decision making* associated with child rearing; and (5) *availability* of the father to the child. These five areas were selected on an a priori basis.

Each respondent could obtain a maximum of 12 points on each of the five sections, except for the statement of involvement, which was worth a maximum of 24 points. Fathers were asked about their own involvement with their children, while mothers were asked to rate their spouses' participation. Thus, a Father Total on the PICCI and a Mother Total were obtained for each family. These two scores were summed to obtain the PICCI Grand Total, which was then used to assign families to one of the three groups. Means and standard deviations for the child-care variables are shown by group in Table 1.

To assess the division of labor regarding household chores, the Index of Spouse Participation in Household Tasks was constructed. In the questionnaire, queries were made about nine household tasks: dishwashing, cooking, laundry, cleaning house, paying bills, buying groceries, taking out garbage, small household repairs, and yard maintenance. Each respondent was asked both how frequently the task was performed in his or her household, and what percentage of the time it was

TABLE 1
PICCI[a] Means and Standard Deviations, by Group

PICCI[a] Variable	Mother Primary Caregiver		Dual-Career, Mother Primary Caregiver		Dual-Career, Shared Caregiving	
	X	SD	X	SD	X	SD
Involvement	13.02	1.83	14.22	2.63	18.03	1.45
Child Care	3.18	1.35	3.54	1.51	5.79	1.28
Decision Making	6.45	1.10	6.00	.84	6.45	1.30
Availability	7.70	1.23	8.00	1.65	9.75	1.30
Total	33.97[b]	3.84	35.42[b]	5.48	44.68[b]	3.73

a. Paternal Involvement in Child Care Index.
b. Share Caregiving significantly greater than Dual-Career Mother Primary Caregiver ($t = 7.34$, $p < .00001$, $df = 38$) and Mother Primary Caregiver ($t = 9.24$, $p < .00001$, $df = 38$).

performed by the respondent, his or her spouse, or some other person.

The nine tasks were grouped into two categories based on a well-documented, sex-based household division of labor. Dishwashing, cooking, laundry, cleaning house, paying bills, and buying groceries correspond closely to what Nye and Gecas (1976) have labeled the *female* "housekeeping role." The remaining three tasks, taking out garbage, small household repairs, and yard maintenance can be seen as constituting the *male* household role (Blood and Wolfe, 1960). The index yields separate scores on these two subscales (Female household role and Male household role) for self, spouse, and other. Grand totals are obtained by summing the two subscale scores for self, spouse, and other.

Family decision making was assessed in the interview by asking respondents how decisions were made in the following areas: when children were old enough to try new things; when they should be disciplined; when to make major purchases; how much to spend on food, clothing, and so on; where the family should live; and decisions concerning the husband's and wife's jobs. Response categories were: husband always (1), husband more than wife (2), husband and wife equally (3), wife more than husband (4), and wife always (5). Two scores are of interest in the current study: the total, summed across all seven items, and decision making in regard to the children (the sum of the first two items).

MEASUREMENT OF CHILD VARIABLES

Child measures were administered by trained undergraduate psychology majors during a separate testing session with the child in his or her home. Standardized verbal (Peabody Picture Vocabulary Test—PPVT) and nonverbal (Ravens Coloured Progressive Matrices Test) tests were employed to ensure that the three groups of children were comparable with regard to intellectual ability.

The Parent Role Perception Test (PRPT) is an instrument developed by the author and others using a format similar to that of the IT Scale (Brown, 1956). It measures children's perceptions of adult family roles as they are associated with objects most families have present in or around their homes (an iron, tires, a hammer, dishes, and so on). The objects are represented by means of 16 colored photographs presented to the child in two parts. The child can choose all the items, none of them, or some of them as being used by either parent. Separate totals for fathers and mothers were obtained and labeled the Paternal Role Stereotyping Score (PRSS) and Maternal Role Stereotyping Score (MRSS). Scores ultimately ranged from 0 to 120, with higher values representing a high degree of sex-role stereotyping and scores near zero reflecting a role reversal situation. Complete information about wording and scoring of questions, as well as reliability and internal consistency, can be obtained from the author.

To assess the child's sex-role preference and orientation, a revised version of the IT Scale (Brown, 1956) was used, employing modifications suggested by Biller (1969) and Kohlberg and Zigler (1967).

TABLE 2
Correlations Between Paternal Child Care and Children's
Perceptions of the Father Role

Child Care Measure	Total Sample (N = 53-58) PRSS[b]	Boys (N = 31-34) PRSS	Girls (N = 21-24) PRSS
PICCI[a] Total	−.32*	−.33	−.38
PICCI Involvement	−.40**	−.28	−.55**
PICCI Child Care	−.29*	−.35*	−.26
PICCI Availability	−.15	−.17	−.18

*p < .05; **p < .01
a. Paternal Involvement in Child Care Index.
b. Paternal Role Stereotyping Score.

FINDINGS

Correlations between the four paternal child care variables and measures of children's perceptions of the father role are shown in Table 2. All of the correlations were in the expected direction. In the sample as a whole, only paternal availability was unrelated to stereotyping of the father role. However, when the data are examined by sex a different pattern emerges: Among boys, only PICCI Child Care was significantly related to stereotyping (the more paternal participation, the less stereotyping), although the Total and Involvement scores approached statistical significance. Among girls, PICCI Involvement was highly and significantly related to paternal stereotyping in the predicted direction: The more involved fathers reported themselves to be, the less stereotyped were their daughters' perceptions of them. Thus, Hypothesis 1 received partial support.

Findings pertaining to Hypothesis 2, which predicted an inverse relationship between paternal responsibility for housework and children's stereotyping, are shown in Table 3. Relationships between children's stereotyping and paternal responsibility for household tasks were all in the predicted direction. The more responsibility the father takes for total

TABLE 3

Correlations Between Paternal Participation in Household Tasks
and Children's Perceptions of the Father Role

Household Tasks	Total Sample (N = 52-57) PRSS[a]	Boys (N = 31-34) PRSS	Girls (N = 21-23) PRSS
Female	−.40**	−.50**	−.35
Male	.01	−.01	.02
Grand Total	−.37**	−.49**	−.30

**p < .01

a. Paternal Role Stereotyping Score.

household chores, the less his children are likely to perceive him in a stereotypical fashion on the PRSS. However, it is clear that it is his involvement with traditionally *female* chores, such as cooking, cleaning, and buying groceries, that is responsible for the inverse relationship with the Grand Total. Although the magnitude of the correlations for boys on the Female tasks and Grand Total is larger, as is the sample size, the pattern of relationships between boys and girls is similar. Partial support was therefore obtained for Hypothesis 2.

Correlations between sons' masculinity based on the IT Scale and paternal participation in Female tasks, Male tasks, and Total Household tasks are −.55 (p < .0007), .16(ns), and −.41 (p < .01), respectively, thereby providing support for the inverse relationship predicted in Hypothesis 3. Once again, it appears that it is paternal participation in the traditionally female realm that is related to sons' masculinity. However, it should be noted that in Group 3 (Dual-Career, Shared Caregiving) where fathers perform significantly more household chores than fathers in Groups 1 and 2,[3] mean scores on the IT Scale (M = 54.36, SD = 18.57), although lower than in the combined Mother Prime groups (M = 62.78, SD = 16.96), were not *significantly* lower, based on t values.

The last hypothesis predicted a positive relationship between paternal influence in family decision making and sons' masculinity. Because the decision-making variable is scored in the reverse direction, a significant negative correlation is necessary to obtain support for Hypothesis 4. Correlations between sons' masculinity and Total Decision Making as well as PICCI Decision Making were both small, nonsignificant, and not in the predicted direction ($r = .15$ and $.06$, respectively). Thus Hypothesis 4 was not supported, and it cannot be concluded that self-reported paternal influence in family decision making and sons' masculinity are related on the basis of these data.

DISCUSSION

The limited literature focused on actual parent behaviors and children's stereotypes about adult roles has not yielded strong evidence indicating that these two variables are related among young children. The data reported here provide beginning evidence that paternal behaviors in the realms of household tasks and child care are associated with the perceptions young children hold of the father role. Although the magnitude of the relationships varies as a function of sex of child and the specific aspect of paternal behavior considered, it is clear that children whose fathers assume greater responsibility for child care and housework are significantly less likely to see their fathers in sex-stereotypical terms.

But despite the significant relationships observed between paternal behaviors and children's stereotypes, most of the variance in those perceptions still remains unaccounted for. Given the extent to which sex-role stereotyping pervades the entire culture, it seems likely that children learn such stereotypes on the basis of diverse experiences across many different settings. For example, there is ample evidence to document the pervasiveness of sex-role stereotyping both on television (Freuh and McGhee, 1975) and in children's books (St. Peter, 1979). It is also possible that children, including those from relatively nontraditional families, learn stereotypes from substitute caregivers in settings such as day care homes and preschools, or from babysitters. Little, if any, systematic investigation along these lines has been published.

Thus, it would appear that factors outside of the child's immediate home environment, as well as behaviors observed within the child's family, will have some effect on developing sex-role attitudes and perceptions. It seems safe to conclude that paternal participation in child-caring activities and household tasks contributes *independently* to reductions in children's stereotyping of the functional, behavioral aspects of the father role, as can be seen in the correlations depicted in Tables 2 and 3. On the basis of the data, it also appears that observation of paternal behaviors has similar effects on boys and girls, although in several cases the magnitude of the correlation coefficients was higher (though not significantly) for boys. This is an area that warrants further investigation, especially in light of the fact that no other studies of young boys' sex-role perceptions were identified.

The significant relationship between father responsibility for household tasks and children's stereotyping is somewhat surprising in light of the fact that Marantz and Mansfield (1977) did not find such a relationship among the 6- to 12-year-old girls they studied. However, their measures of both paternal participation in domestic chores and stereotypes were different from the ones employed here. The activity-based stereotype inventory, which would correspond most closely with the PRPT, was in fact broader in the types of activities presented as compared with the PRPT used here. In addition, the measure of paternal housework was obtained from mothers, whereas in this study the measure was obtained directly from fathers.

Support was found for an inverse relationship between sons' masculinity and paternal participation in household tasks, consistent with literature cited (Biller, 1971; Biller and Borstelman, 1967). Although many parents, particularly those who are experimenting with nontraditional family role distributions, would view this as desirable, or at least not see it as problematic, this finding might be interpreted as support for the fear that observing a father perform the "maternal" role may inhibit the development of boys' masculinity.

However, it is puzzling that despite the inverse relationship, the mean scores on the IT Scale for boys in the Shared Caregiving group (where fathers not only performed significantly more housework than fathers in the other two groups, but also significantly more than their own wives, on average[4]) were *not* significantly lower than the means of the other two groups of boys. Thus, at this age at least, observation of a father who takes substantial responsibility for both child care and household tasks, while associated with boys' sex-role preferences, does not seem to have resulted in a group of nonmasculine boys.

The predicted relationship between paternal dominance in family decision making and sons' masculinity was not obtained; this was true both in the case of decision making specific to the domain of child rearing and in relation to a broader measure of family decision making across several different areas. How can this be reconciled with the findings of Biller (1969), Hetherington (1965), and others? Methodological differences in measurement of dominance between the current study and others were substantial, even though the children studied were the same age. The key to understanding this may revolve around the method used to assess paternal dominance, specifically whether one uses a measure based on children's perceptions, one based on observed parental interaction either in the home or in a laboratory setting, or a self-reported measure obtained from the father himself, as was the case here. Biller (1969) himself found that the perceived measure was more highly associated with IT Scale scores than was the observational measure ($r = .46$ versus $r = .27$), although no Z tests were reported. Lynn (1974: 124) has also observed that "a boy's subjective judgment of which parent dominates in the family may be more closely related to his sex-role development than an outside observer's judgment." Unfortunately, perceived dominance was not assessed in this study. In any event, the conclusion that fathers must dominate family decision making in order to ensure their sons' masculinity does not seem warranted. However, it may be the case that if fathers largely opt out of family decision making, by the time their sons reach adolescence there may be problems in the realm of sex-role identity.

Although few definitive conclusions have been reached, it is hoped that this exploration of complex and changing family relationships will stimulate and pave the way for future research on alternative family forms using larger, more diverse, and more representative samples. Caution should be exercised in generalizing from findings obtained here due to the self-selection of the sample and its unknown representativeness.

NOTES

1. The definition of dual-career families used here was borrowed from Rapoport and Rapoport (1976: 9):

The term "dual-career families" was coined to designate a type of family structure in which both heads of household—the husband and wife—pursue active careers and family lives. "Career" is sometimes used to indicate any sequence of jobs, but in its more precise meaning it designates those types of job sequences that require a high degree of commitment and that have a continuous developmental character . . . [C]areers have an intrinsically demanding character.

2. The distinction between child care and child socialization made by Gecas (1976) will be observed here. While he acknowledges that there is some behavioral overlap in the two roles, he states that they tend to be "conceptually distinct activities," which are even sometimes carried out by different persons. The child socialization role involves the teaching of knowledge, values, attitudes, and the "development of the child's social and psychological capabilities," rather than the physical care of the child (Gecas, 1976).

3. Based on one-way analysis of variance, $F(2,56) = 32.13$, $p < .0001$.

4. $T = 4.18$, df = 32, $p < .0002$.

REFERENCES

Biller, H. B.
1971   Father, Child and Sex Role. Lexington, MA: D. C. Heath.

1969   "Father dominance and sex-role development in kindergarten-age boys." Developmental Psychology 1: 87-94.

Biller, H. B. and L. J. Borstelman
1967   "Masculine development: an integrative review." Merrill-Palmer Q. 13: 253-294.

Blood, R. C. and D. M. Wolfe
1960   Husbands and Wives. New York: Macmillan.

Brown, D. G.
1956   "Sex role preference in young children" Psychological Monographs 70: (Whole).

Bryson, R. B., J. B. Bryson, M. H. Licht, and B. G. Licht
1976   "The professional pair: husband and wife psychologists." Amer. Psychologist 31: 10-16.

Dubin, R. and E. R. Dubin
1965   "Children's social perceptions." Child Development 36: 809-847.

Ericksen, J. A., W. L. Yancey, and E. P. Ericksen
1979   "The division of family roles." J. of Marriage and the Family 41: 301-313.

Finch, H. S.
1955   "Young children's concept of parental roles." J. of Home Economics 47: 99-103.

Freuh, T. and P. McGhee
1975   "Traditional sex-role development and amount of time spent watching television." Developmental Psychology 11: 109.

Gecas, V.
1976   "The socialization and child care roles," pp. 33-59 in F. I. Nye (ed.) Role Structure and Analysis of the Family. Beverly Hills, CA: Sage.

Hartley, R. E.
1960   "Children's concepts of male and female roles." Merrill-Palmer Q. 6: 83-91.

Hetherington, E. M.
1965   "A developmental study of the effects of sex of the dominant parent on sex-role preference, identification and imitation in children." J. of Personality and Social Psychology 2: 188-194.

Hoffman, L.
1979   "An updated look at the effects of maternal employment on child development." Presented at a meeting of the Society for Research on Child Development, San Francisco.
1974   "Effects of maternal employment on the child—a review of the research." Developmental Psychology 10: 204-228.

Hollingshead, A. B.
1970   "Four factor index of social status." Department of Sociology, Yale University, New Haven, Connecticut.

Kohlberg, L. and E. Zigler
1967   "The impact of cognitive maturity on the development of sex-role attitudes in the years 4-8." Genetic Psychology Monographs 75: 84-165.

Lynn, D. B.
1974   The Father: His Role in Child Development. Belmont, CA: Wadsworth.

Marantz, S. A. and A. F. Mansfield
1977   "Maternal employment and the development of sex-role stereotypes in 5-11 year old girls." Child Development 48: 668-673.

Meyer, B.
  1980   "The development of girls' sex-role attitudes." Child Development 51: 508-514.
Miller, S. M.
  1975   "Effects of maternal employment on sex-role perceptions, interests and self-esteem in kindergarten girls." Developmental Psychology 11: 405-406.
Nye, F. I. and V. Gecas
  1976   "The role concept: review and delineation," pp. 3-14 in F. I. Nye (ed.) Role Structure and Analysis of the Family. Beverly Hills, CA: Sage.
Perrucci, C. C., H. R. Potter, and D. L. Rhoads
  1978   "Determinants of male family-role performance." Psychology of Women Q. 3: 53-66.
Rapoport, R. and R. Rapoport
  1976   Dual-Career Families Re-examined: New Integrations of Work and Family. New York: Harper & Row.
Robinson, J.
  1977   How Americans Use Time: A Social-Psychological Analysis of Everyday Behavior. New York: Praeger.
St. John-Parsons, D.
  1978   "Continuous dual-career families: a case study." Psychology of Women Q. 3: 30-42.
St. Peter, S.
  1979   "Jack went up the hill, but where was Jill?" Psychology of Women Q. 4: 256-260.
Vener, A. M. and C. M. Snyder
  1966   "The preschool child's awareness and anticipation of adult sex roles." Sociometry 29: 159-168.
Walker, K. E. and M. E. Woods
  1976   "Time use: a measure of household production of family goods and services." Washington, DC: American Home Economics Association.
Weingarten, K.
  1978   "The employment pattern of professional couples and their distribution of involvement in the family." Psychology of Women Q. 3: 43-52.
Williams, J. E., S. M. Bennett, and D. L. Best
  1975   "Awareness and expression of sex-stereotypes in young children." Developmental Psychology 11: 635-642.

PART IV

A Research Agenda

The last words in this book are left to Rapoport and Rapoport, who labeled and had much to do with opening up the dual-career research area. Here they look at dual-earner families in general and research priorities concerning them that are arising in our changing world. Studies in the present volume can make their case. The continuing gender inequity in household and occupational roles to which they point is an issue raised in the research of Model, Sharda and Nangle, and Pleck and Staines. Rapoport and Rapoport also discuss the necessity of looking at two-earner families over the family life cycle—the focus of Poloma, Pendleton, and Garland's research and Carlson's chapter on boys' gender-role identity—and fathers' child-care participation fits into the priority of family structure and children's personality.

Rapoport and Rapoport's list of priorities indicates how the situation has changed since their initial dual-career research, published a decade ago. No longer do writers have to devote space to presenting a rationale for two-earner families. Despite continuing concerns, such as those expressed by Hunt and Hunt, the number of these families (which Hayghe documents) suggests they are becoming normative. This last chapter indicates where we need to be looking in order to make what is normative less difficult to sustain.

12

The Next Generation in
Dual-Earner Family Research

RHONA RAPOPORT
ROBERT N. RAPOPORT

The reassertion by Joan Aldous in this volume of the historical rootedness of the dual-earner family phenomenon is useful. Married women have contributed to the economy from time immemorial, and this should not be forgotten. Christopher Turner (1971) has drawn the analogy between dual-earner families and semisubsistence farm families in eighteenth-century New England. Hanna Papanek (1973) developed the concept of the "two-person career" and showed how it applied not only to missionaries, traders, and schoolmasters of yore, but also to many occupations down to the present day. The small family business—the "Mom and Pop" shop—is a modern example of the dual-worker couple operating a single enterprise.

What we are reminded of in the present volume is important theoretically. Families continuously change, but they change in the manner of the moral rather than the technical order, to use Redfield's (1953) distinction. The moral order evolves in quite a different way from the technical order. The latter evolves stepwise, and as a society develops technologically it harnesses increasing amounts of physical power. This increase of power allows greater numbers of people to inhabit a given locality and/or to devote less effort to accomplish a given task.

229

This is illustrated by the burst of populations and the growth of cities following industrialization and in the modern home, with its many machines and labor-saving devices, as described by Young and Willmott (1973) and others. The moral order, on the other hand, evolves by readapting similar elements. Contemporary families consist of similar numbers of individuals with similar roles to those in preindustrial society, though their value orientations, activity patterns, and relationships have changed.

Peter Laslett (1972), in his research on the history of family structure in Britain, has documented this empirically. He concluded that the changes in size and composition of domestic units from preindustrial times to the present have been exaggerated. They consist now, as they did then, of relatively small numbers of people—with fewer live-in servants now, to be sure—and with relatively small shifts in fertility and component roles. The comparison with the technological changes experienced over the same period is inevitable, the basic social structure is less affected than the physical home. We do not know how much family *dynamics* have changed.

We agree, therefore, that dual-earner families were here before, but that this assertion emphasizes the similarities between past and present family structures. It does not preclude the possibility that there are also differences. The expression "plus ca change, plus c'est la meme chose" emphasizes the element of continuity. Social science analyses such as Mary Jo Bane's *Here to Stay* (1976) and Theodore Caplow's *Middletown's Families* (1982) provide an empirical basis for this emphasis. But we would emphasize the possibility that there have been important changes: in gender-role conceptions, in the role of children, in the linkages between families and their social environments, and in the conception of the family itself. These are no less important because they are "mere ideas" or because they are statistically minority patterns. Perhaps the greatest shift is toward the perception that different family structures are personal/social options rather than products of fate, inheritance, or divine decree.

Perspective on these points may be gained by recounting the historical context of our research on dual-career families. The study of dual-career families as one type of dual-earner family was prompted by the concern in post-World War II Britain with the need to make maximum use of human resources. With the loss of cheap natural resources of the Colonial Empire, Britain recognized that it was a country that must make efficient use of its human resources for its future survival and well-being. The principal human resources it had that were not sufficiently harnessed were the working classes and women. The reform of the educational system, making it more open and accessible through "socializing" education, was aimed at drawing talented working-class people into the educated elite. The study of highly qualified women's careers was a step in the direction of understanding how the potential human resources embodied in women could be better harnessed in the occupational structure. Women who had high qualifications and skills were regarded among the most valuable "wasted" human resources in British society. It was they who were the objects of our investigation in the study, *Women and Top Jobs* (Fogarty et al., 1971). In that study, dual-career families were regarded as a special case of dual-worker families. Their occupations were very demanding and had a developmental sequence. The dual-career families studied had taken on the difficult task of combining careers with raising children, unlike some of their predecessors, such as the Webbs and the Mills. Occupationally active women in the 1960s wished to have both careers and children. This wish is shared by younger couples, and this is one of the reasons for the continued growth of interest in the phenomenon of dual-career families, as we pointed out in our paper, "Three generations of research on dual career families" (Rapoport and Rapoport, 1980). The research in this field has evolved with increasing precision of instruments for measurement and designs using enlarged samples and systematic comparisons.

One of the early findings we noted, as did some of our colleagues, was that although many dual-career families subscribe to egalitarian ideals, few of them lived up to them in practice (Poloma and Garland, 1971). The need to refine our understanding of this phenomenon has been a source of considerable speculation and continuing research. To what extent, for example, is the discrepancy due to differences in male and female value orientations or to differences in the structural constraints of the workplace and different occupations? Whatever the determinants may be, existing research shows that both gender-role conceptions and behavior are changing; but conceptions, behavior, and relationships change at different paces.

Joan Aldous's emphasis on the term "dual-earner families" is useful not only because it avoids the implications of the term "dual-*worker* family" that women's occupation at home is not work, but also because it forces reconsideration of the terms and what they cover and do not cover. The new term, while alerting us to an important definitional element, contains some of its own difficulties. In an era of high unemployment, early retirement, and the need to think flexibly of the patterning of work in one's life, there is the danger that a nonearning worker will be excluded. Many people do voluntary work, and others may work for a time unpaid while trying to relocate themselves. They may even be working at the same kind of job in which they had previously earned. The variety of family types encompassed under the umbrella of "dual-worker families" was recognized to be great. But we are now aware that they do not form a continuum (Gowler and Legge, 1982).

It has become increasingly apparent that classification issues should relate to the larger field, "work and family" (Piotrkowski et al., forthcoming). The work-and-family field has developed since the 1960s. For many years social scientists polarized research in this field, separating work from family studies (Rapoport and Rapoport, 1965). In 1977 Rosabeth Kanter, in her Monograph, *Work and Family in America*, observed that there was a challenging *interface* between work and family. As increasing numbers of women, particularly married women with children, entered the workplace, it was no longer possible to preserve the "myth of two worlds," as Piotrkowski (1978) dubbed the earlier polarity. The two worlds are linked, and what happens in one affects the other. This cross-influence is not only sporadic or confined to disturbance, but also systematic, on a wide scale, and with both positive and negative elements. The study of these cross-influences is now an established *field*.

The field can be seen as having several levels. At the *macroscopic level* is the kind of effort represented by the National Academy of Sciences Conference on Families and the Economy (Nelson, 1982). At this level the aim is to analyze data from which one can draw implications for government social policy. Aggregate demographic, historical, and statistical data are prominent. A *middle level* is exemplified in studies of organizations in relation to maternity benefits and other practices facilitating the opportunity for women as well as men to participate in the labor market (Kamerman and Kahn, 1981; Kamerman and Hayes, 1982). The study by Bohen and Viveros-Long (1981) on flexitime is another example. The *grass-roots level* concerns itself with how families manage the stresses they personally experience, such as on the job. This is exemplified in the research by Piotrkowski (1978) and many of the dual-worker family researchers, including the authors. The Vienna Center Project on Changes in Family Life Patterns in Europe is systematically examining the interaction between the levels in a dozen Eastern and Western European countries.

There are many factors involved in setting research priorities: issues that stem from particular disciplines, issues that stem from the urgencies of particular work organizations with their own costs and benefits, and issues that stem from different political and economic systems. Our own statement, therefore, should be seen in this perspective and taken extremely cautiously. We envision seven areas of priority in research on dual-earner families in the 1980s. Because of the multiplicity and indeterminacy of many of the factors involved in supporting actual research, we state these as "needed" priorities rather than as predictions.

1. *Studies are needed on the impact of current economic changes on family-work roles.*

Macroscopic changes currently under way in the economy are likely to have far-reaching effects on the patterning of work for families. There is likely to be increased general unemployment. There are some signs that women may be less vulnerable to this than in the past. The meaning of gender differences in unemployment patterns will need to be studied, particularly in relation to the family. But in this regard, there may be a new range of patterns, including part-time work and early retirement. There is likely to be experimentation with job sharing and other responses to crisis. These may be motivated by the wish not so much to create equal opportunities for women as to preserve jobs. There may also be an increase in nonrecorded economic activity that will affect both the formal economy and internal family dynamics. Studies are made in how the different types and sectors of economic participation affect and are affected by family factors. As with the experimental introduction of flexitime, there may be a discrepancy between intention and consequences of change.

2. *Studies are needed of the impact of new microtechnologies on family-work patterns.*

Another aspect of current economic and technological changes is the introduction of a new generation of microtechnology. Young and Willmott (1973), in their study of the "symmetrical family," indicated that the miniaturization of household machines had increased the possibility for women to have time to leave the home to take up an occupation outside. Current technological changes may have the reverse effect. It may be possible for women to spend more time at home while participating in the economy. They may choose to master the new skills required to operate remote computer terminals and other apparatus of the new microtechnological advances. Paradoxically, women may be in a better position to take up this new challenge through becoming unemployed in the current recession. Many women who had mobilized themselves and their support systems to work only to find themselves thrown out of their jobs as the labor force is trimmed may be strongly motivated to continue the work patterns they have so recently acquired. They may be well placed in many cases to take up new lines of work in microelectronics fields.

There are indications of a new shift toward home-based work. As this is being adopted by men as well as women, it may not automatically create a stunning reversal of gender roles, nor need it entail a return to the "sweatshop conditions" of nineteenth-century cottage industry or the "captive wife" conditions of the mid-twentieth. There may be situations conducive to advances toward the goal of equality of opportunity, and these need to be identified and studied.

Unemployment is stressful and can be demoralizing, as we know from the studies of the Great Depression. We also know, as Elder's (1974) study highlighted, that it can mobilize newly unemployed men and women, as well as unemployed youth, to search for outlets for activity in social-psychologically meaningful work, even if they are unremunerative in the conventional earning sense. This may have consequences for gender-role definitions and therefore on the structure of dual-earner families. As men seek community or home-based activities, they may find that their wives, who have been the linking persons between home and the local neighborhood, are instrumental in finding work. Women may know who needs work locally and how to operate the information networks that allow men to find channels for doing this work. A new generation of "Mom and Pop" home-based industries may develop in which a relatively egalitarian management structure could evolve. Some of the work by Ray Pahl (1980) and colleagues in England suggests this possibility.

3. *Research is needed on the linkages between macroscopic social processes and the functioning of dual-worker families.*

The current situation of drastic changes offers possibilities for creative research—on the relations between macro- and microprocesses, between social and psychological processes, and between cultural ideals and behavior. Miller and Swanson (1958) related the child's orientation to whether the father worked in a "bureaucratic" or "entrepreneurial" work organization. The conceptualization of the dual-worker family as a distinctive family structure impels us toward examining family structures as an intervening variable. Both parents' occupations have *prima facie* relevance, but this needs specification and detailed study.

Some of the chapters in the present volume point the way. Poloma and her colleagues outline some of the stress points; Carlson introduces the importance of the child's perspective as representing an active force rather than simply a passive response; Model indicates the importance of obtaining new data on the implications of wives' work for husbands' domestic roles. Piotrkowski and Crits-Christoph outline the need to consider various pathways of influence on the child as we come to appreciate the varieties of interactive processes between life on the job and family life.

4. *Studies are needed on the relation between family structure and the personality of the child.*

Research in earlier generations related to the dual-earner family tended to concentrate on the impact of women's work (Hoffman, 1963). The preoccupation was with whether maternal work has a damaging effect on children. The verdict, by and large, has been "not proven." However, this does not mean "no effect." The task now is to tease out specific effects associated with the dual-earner family as compared with other family structures.

Whereas much of the earlier research was based on examination of the conjecture that maternal work entailed damaging deprivation in the child's intimate environment, the next generation is likely to examine a number of specific variables, tying in with the larger fields of social structure and personality. This line of thinking is seen in some recent work in related fields (see, for example, Hiller and Philliber, 1982; Hoffman, 1982; Kohn et al., 1981).

We need more information on what kind of people are produced by different social structures, particularly family structures. But even more, we need to know more about how different structures actually work. Observational studies are needed of the child-rearing behavior of dual-worker parents. Concentration in the past has been on what arrangements they have for alternative child care. These patterns and their advantages and pitfalls are now fairly well understood, but little is known about how the various supplementary arrangements articulate with the parents' own values and behavior. The whole pattern is relevant for the personality formation of the developing child.

5. *Research is needed on the place of the dual-earner pattern in the family life cycle.*

Earlier generations of family research in the developmental framework assumed both a conventional family structure and a relatively standardized set of sequences—except where unusual or traumatic events interfered. Research on variations from the norm, as with mothers at work, tended to focus on the question of possible deleterious consequences to mental health or to family functioning. With a more pluralist conception of family norms and of the patterning of family formation and reconstitution, new conceptual models are needed. Joan Aldous has set the stage for this in her book *Family Careers* (1978). The need for further work along these lines is reinforced by Poloma and her colleagues in the present volume, and by Moen (1980) and Waite (1980).

We shall need to draw on the sophistication of the life-span developmental psychologists, while recognizing that we are considering family systems rather than individuals. Even more important, we shall have to put our theories to work to understand how families construct their cycles. Alice Rossi (1968) has analyzed some of the issues surrounding the joining of personal developmental cycles of family members in role-theory terms. Other theoretical perspectives will be required to understand the dynamics of negotiation and exchange, of communication, decision making, and conflict resolution. In short, we need to study the management of the family as a small social system.

Earlier analyses have pinpointed some of the elements in dual-earner career-family management that are disruptive, and some of those that are adaptive. More needs to be known about how the structure emerges and is sustained. Families, like individuals, have self-concepts and "identities." Under what conditions does the family self-concept as a dual-earner family get established, and what bearing does this have on the capacity of the family to handle stresses such as interruptions in the work pattern of one or the other spouse? What advantages or impediments do dual-earner families experience if they seek to redeploy their efforts in other life sectors? Implied in the dual-earner structure are linkages between the family cycle and the occupational cycle; but as we have argued elsewhere, it is useful to consider the *interaction* among the three life sectors—family, work, and leisure, the "triple helix" (Rapoport and Rapoport, 1975, 1980). We are now in a position to recognize that being a dual-earner family is itself a variable to consider diachronically.

6. *Research is needed on supports for dual-earner families.*

The importance of family support structures has always been recognized. A new emphasis on this element is likely to emerge in the next generation of research. Dual-earner families always a "case in need of social supports" are likely to find themselves in a new high-risk situation. The retrenchment of government spending is likely to hit hard at the provision of day-care facilities. Women's support groups could play an important role, perhaps different from when they were formed initially. Many such groups concentrated on arousing women's consciousness of sex-role inequities. A new emphasis on practical supports for working wives is needed.

It is widely assumed that employing organizations can and should carry a greater responsibility for facilitating employment. But one line of argument against this is that it would be inequitable to others to provide special support for married women. One variable will be the manpower situation. If it is necessary for the corporation to tap women-power, the corporation may respond differently, both with words and acts, than if there is an oversupply. But in addition to economic considerations, there are issues of human relations in industry. In current efforts to improve the quality of working life, an explicit focus is needed on how this new humanistic concern can be extended to families of employees.

Additional sources of support may be found in community groupings, voluntary caregivers such as "foster grandparents" or "big brothers." There may be a new efflorescence of self-help and mutual-aid organizations. These seem desirable, but little is known about how feasible it will be to form and sustain such groups in an atmosphere of sparse financial resources. It is paradoxical that many of the people in straitened circumstances are often very helpful to one another, as Carol Stack (1974) has shown. On the other hand, it does not follow that new poverty or new financial stringency always brings out a cooperative spirit. Some, accustomed to self-sufficiency or to government entitlements, may reject such moves. Nevertheless, networking, neighborhood community-building, and other purposeful construction of support systems are needed, and therefore this potential development will merit research.

There is also the idea of reawakening within the existing family structure many of the caring and nurturing elements that may have become dormant. In the sibling relationship, for example, we have become very familiar with the problems of sibling rivalry and even violence; we are much less familiar with the potential of children for mutual help and caring relationships. The capacity for cooperation and caring roles for siblings, long familiar in preindustrial families, needs to receive increasing attention in our own society. Similarly, a new emphasis on a greater availability of husbands who may be only partly employed or unemployed, and of grandparents who may have recently had careers but may now be retiring earlier because of cutbacks, may make possible something that was only recently felt to be infeasible. Research is needed on the functioning of informal as well as formal support structures (Bronfenbrenner, 1979).

7. *A needed research focus for the next generation is how to remove bottlenecks to gender-role equity.*

We earlier identified the equity issue as critical in a society valuing diversity (Rapoport and Rapoport, 1975). Two bottlenecks to achieving equity were identified: the occupational and the domestic. What movement has occurred seems to have been achieved by focusing attention on first one and then the other. Equal opportunities in education and occupation allowed the surge into work creating the high number of dual-earner families that we have witnessed. Little attention was given to the redistribution of domestic labor. Working wives were prevented, as a consequence, from taking on the level of commitment that many wanted. The prevailing assumption persists that the responsibility for domestic work, especially child care, is women's—even though their husbands might "help."

This bottleneck may be beginning to crack. Recent data indicate some increase in the willingness of men to become actively involved in the domestic economy, even in responsible fathering. This trend, as well as efforts to restructure the work-family relations from the workplace side, must continue. What we must do now is focus explicitly on the linkages between work and family, rather than focusing first on one set of bottlenecks, then on the other.

CONCLUSION

We have couched our seven research priority areas in terms of what research is "needed" in relation to the dual-earner family. What is "needed" is based partly on the evolutionary thrust of the field—from a precursor period, in which relevant research was oriented to diverse concerns in various disciplines, to a pivotal phase, in which a distinctive set of emergent family structures was identified, through a third phase of refinement and consolidation of concepts, method, and data.

As a result of the first three generations of work, we recognize both the distinction and commonalities between dual-earner and cognate family forms (dual-worker, dual-career, two-paycheck, two-wage, and so on). These and others form part of an emergent field of research on "work and the family." Research on dual-earner families will be affected by how the larger field develops. At this writing it is enjoying a vogue, and the interest in dual-earner families will inevitably provide a useful component.

Beyond this, there are forces that are not responsive to research data, such as those emerging in the evolution of this field. Minimally, we shall be able to study what is happening, and this will provide a scientific gain in the study of the present great and ramifying societal crisis.

In the long run, assuming a restoration of political and economic vigor and appreciation of the value of social reserach, a key task will be to restructure the whole pattern of relations among family, work, and community life. Dual-earner families will inevitably be key figures as this drama plays itself out.

REFERENCES

Aldous, J.
    1978   Family Careers: Developmental Change in Families. New York: John Wiley.
Bane, M. J.
    1976   Here to Stay. New York: Basic Books.
Bohen, H. H. and A. Viveros-Long
    1981   Balancing Jobs and Family Life. Philadelphia: Temple Univ. Press.
Bronfenbrenner, U.
    1979   The Ecology of Human Development. Cambridge, MA: Harvard Univ. Press.
Caplow, T., H. M. Bahr, B. A. Chadwick, R. Hill, and M. H. Williamson
    1982   Middletown Families: Fifty Years of Change and Continuity. Minneapolis: Univ. of Minnesota Press.
Elder, G. H.
    1974   Children of the Great Depression. Chicago: Univ. of Chicago Press.
Fogarty, M., A. J. Allen, I. Allen, and P. Walters
    1971   Women in Top Jobs. London: Allen & Unwin.

Fogarty, M., R. Rapoport, and R. N. Rapoport
   1971   Sex, Career and Family. London: Allen & Unwin.
Gowler, D. and K. Legge
   1982   "Dual-worker families," in R. N. Rapoport, M. P. Fogarty, and R. Rapo-
          port (eds.) Families in Britain. Boston: Routledge & Kegan Paul.
Hiller, D. V. and W. W. Philliber
   1982   "Predicting marital and career success among dual worker couples." J. of
          Marriage and the Family 44, 1: 53-62.
Hoffman, L. W.
   1982   "Methodological issues in follow-up and replication studies." J. of Social
          Issues 38, 1: 53-65.
   1963   "The decision to work," pp. 18-39 in F. I. Nye and L. W. Hoffman (eds.) The
          Employed Mother in America. Chicago: Rand McNally.
Kamerman, S. and C. Hayes (eds.)
   1982   Families That Work: Children in a Changing World. Washington, DC: Na-
          tional Academy Press.
Kamerman, S. and A. Kahn
   1981   Child Care, Family Benefits and Working Parents. New York: Columbia
          Univ. Press.
Kanter, R. M.
   1977   Work and Family in the United States: A Critical Review and Agenda for
          Research and Policy. New York: Russell Sage.
Kohn, M.
   1981   "Personality, occupation and social stratification," pp. 267-297 in D. G.
          Treiman and R. V. Robinson (eds.) Research in Social Stratification and
          Mobility, Volume 1. Greenwich, CT: Jai.
Laslett, P.
   1972   Family and Household in Past Times. London: Penguin.
Miller, D. R. and G. E. Swanson
   1958   The Changing American Parent. New York: John Wiley.
Moen, P.
   1980   "Developing family indicators: financial hardship, a case in point." J. of
          Family Issues 1, 1: 5-30.
Nelson, R. (ed.)
   1982   Families and the Economy. Washington, DC: National Academy Press.
Pahl, R. E.
   1980   "Employment, work and the domestic division of labour." Int. J. of Urban
          and Regional Research 4, 1: 1-19.
Papanek, H.
   1973   "Men, women and work: reflections on the two-person career." Amer. J. of
          Sociology 78, 4: 852-872.
Piotrkowski, C. S.
   1978   Work and the Family System. New York: Free Press.
Piotrkowski, C. S., R. N. Rapoport, and R. Rapoport
   forthcoming   "Families and work," in M. Sussman and S. Steinmetz (eds.) Hand-
          book of Marriage and the Family.
Poloma, M. M. and T. N. Garland
   1971   "The myth of the egalitarian family," in A. Theodore (ed.) The Professional
          Women. Cambridge, MA: Schenkman.

Rapoport, R. and R. N. Rapoport
  1980 "Three generations of dual-career family research," pp. 23-48 in F. Pepi-
        tone-Rockwell (ed.) Dual-Career Couples. Beverly Hills, CA: Sage.
  1975 "Men, women and equity." Family Coordinator 24, 4: 421-432.
  1965 "Work and family in contemporary society." Amer. Soc. Rev. 30, 3: 381-
        394.
Rapoport, R. and R. N. Rapoport with Z. Strelitz
  1975 Leisure and the Family Cycle. London: Routledge & Kegan Paul.
Redfield, R.
  1953 The Primitive World and Its Transformation. Ithaca, NY: Cornell Univ.
        Press.
Rossi, A.
  1968 "Transition to parenthood." J. of Marriage and the Family 30, 1: 26-39.
Stack, C.
  1974 All Our Kin. New York: Harper & Row.
Turner, C.
  1971 "Dual-work households and marital dissolution." Human Relations 24, 6:
        535-548.
Waite, L.
  1980 "Working wives and the family life-cycle." Amer. J. of Sociology 86, 2: 272-
        294.
Young, M. and P. Willmott
  1973 The Symmetrical Family. London: Routledge & Kegan Paul.

About the Authors

JOAN ALDOUS is William R. Kenan Professor of Sociology at the University of Notre Dame. Her coedited book with Wilfried Dumon, *The Politics and Programs of Family Policy: United States and European Perspectives*, was published in 1980 by the University of Notre Dame and the University of Leuven (Belgium). She has written *Family Careers: Developmental Change in Families* (John Wiley), using a life course perspective. Currently, she is doing research with David Klein concerning the effect of parent-child relations during the child-rearing years as well as of family size on intergenerational relations of preretirement couples.

HOWARD HAYGHE is a labor economist with the Bureau of Labor Statistics. He has written extensively in the fields of women's labor force participation and the work patterns of family members for the *Monthly Labor Review*.

JANET G. HUNT and LARRY L. HUNT are currently Associate Professors of Sociology at the University of Maryland, College Park. Janet teaches courses in sex roles and marriage and the family. Larry teaches courses in American society and sociology of personality. Their published research includes articles on black religion and mobility, father-absent families, gender socialization, and dual-career families.

JOSEPH H. PLECK, Ph.D., is a Program Director at the Wellesley College Center for Research on Women, following positions at the University of Massachusetts at Amherst and the University of Michigan. His research interests include work and family roles, and gender roles, especially the male role. He is the author of *The Myth of Masculinity* (MIT Press, 1981).

GRAHAM L. STAINES, Ph.D., was a Study Director at the Institute for Social Research, University of Michigan, before his current position as Assistant Professor in the Department of Psychology at Rutgers. His work focuses on employment and relationships between work and nonwork roles. He is the coauthor of *The 1977 Quality of Employment Survey* (Institute for Social Research, 1978).

LAWRENCE C. MARSH is currently Associate Professor of Economics and Economics Department Liaison with the Social Science Training and

Research Laboratory at the University of Notre Dame. He received his M.A. and Ph.D. from Michigan State University in economics. His work in econometric methods and applications has included modeling the socio-economic characteristics of schoolchildren in determining enrollments in parochial schools.

CHAYA S. PIOTRKOWSKI (Ph.D., University of Michigan) is Assistant Professor of Psychology at Yale University. She also is on the faculties of the Institute for Social and Policy Studies and the Bush Center on Child Development and Social Policy at Yale. She recently published a book on work and family life in working-class families. Currently, she is conducting research on the relationship of parental job stress to family dynamics and children's mental health.

PAUL CRITS-CHRISTOPH is a doctoral student in clinical psychology in the Psychology Department at Yale University.

BAM DEV SHARDA is Associate Professor of Sociology at the University of Utah. Professor Sharda is the author of a book entitled *Status Attainment in Rural India*, published by Ajanta Publications (India). Current research interests focus on the status attainment of working couples, especially the analysis of postmarriage status contingencies.

BARRY E. NANGLE is a statistician in the Vital Statistics Department of the State of Utah, and a doctoral candidate in sociology at the University of Utah. His interests include the effects of local labor segmentation on income inequality in the United States and sources of health lifestyle differentiation in Utah.

IDA HARPER SIMPSON is Professor of Sociology at Duke University. Her research focuses on occupations, work, and their interrelations with family and other institutions.

PAULA ENGLAND is Associate Professor of Sociology and Political Economy at the University of Texas at Dallas. She is currently engaged in research projects dealing with occupational sex segregation, portrayals of males and females in advertisements, and links among work, leisure, and psychological well-being.

MARGARET M. POLOMA is Associate Professor of Sociology at the University of Akron. She and T. Neal Garland worked together to collect the 1969 data and the 1977 followup data on two-career couples. The 1969 data were the base for her doctoral dissertation, in which she analyzed the interface between the woman's domestic and career roles. Her publications include articles on the dual-career family and on voluntary childlessness.

BRIAN F. PENDLETON is Assistant Professor of Sociology at the University of Akron. His published research is in demography, statistics, family, and community development. His current research projects include the statistics of ratio variable correlation, quantitative studies of the dual-career family, international development, and consequences of slowing population growth.

T. NEAL GARLAND is Associate Professor of Sociology at the University of Akron. His interest in the dual-career family stems from his doctoral dissertation, in which he analyzed the male responses from the 1969 data base. He has published a number of articles on the two-career family both as sole author and as coauthor with Poloma.

SUZANNE MODEL is Instructor of Sociology at Five Towns College in Merrick, Long Island, and a doctoral student in sociology and social work at the University of Michigan. Her current research interests center on both ethnic and sexual stratification, and she is currently investigating the role of minority associations in ethnic history.

BONNIE E. CARLSON is currently Assistant Professor of Social Welfare and Director, Undergraduate Social Welfare Program, State University of New York at Albany. She received her M.S.W. and Ph.D. from the University of Michigan in social work and developmental psychology. She has also done work in the areas of family and population planning and domestic violence.

RHONA RAPOPORT is a social scientist with training in psychoanalysis and field experience in Africa. She was Co-Founder and Director of the Institute of Family and Environmental Research, London, where she is at present Senior Consultant. She is coauthor of *Dual Career Families (Re-Examined), Fathers, Mothers and Society, Leisure and the Family Life Cycle,* and several other books and monographs. She is Consultant to the Ford Foundation and at the Bank Street College of Education.

ROBERT N. RAPOPORT is a social anthropologist and Founder and Co-Director of the Institute of Family and Environmental Research, London. He is now a Trustee of the Institute and Vice-President for Programs of the William T. Grant Foundation. Author of *Community as Doctor* and *Mid-Career Development,* he is also coauthor of *Dual-Career Families (Re-Examined), Fathers, Mothers and Society,* and *Leisure and the Family Life Cycle.*